Broadway Musicals

BROADWAY MUSICALS

A Hundred Year History

by DAVID H. LEWIS

McFarland & Company, Inc., Publishers
Jefferson, North Carolina, and London

The author is grateful to the following rights holders for permission to reprint lyrics:

James David: "I'll Never Fall in Love Again" by Hal David and Burt Bacharach © 1968 (renewed 1996) Casa David & New Hidden Valley Music. All rights reserved. Used by permission.

Tim Rice: "Circle of Life and "Chow Down" by Tim Rice. Used by permission.

Warner Bros. Publications U. S., Inc., Miami FL 33014:
    "Any Place I Hang My Hat Is Home" by Johnny Mercer and Harold Arlen © 1946 (renewed) Chappell & Co. (ASCAP). All rights reserved. Used by permission.
    "Call Me Mister" by Harold Rome © 1946 (renewed) Warner Bros. Inc. All rights reserved. Used by permission.
    "The Heather on the Hill" by Alan Jay Lerner and Frederick Loewe © 1947 (renewed) Alan Jay Lerner and Frederick Loewe. World rights assigned to and administered by EMI U Catalog Inc. All rights reserved. Used by permission.
    "New York, New York" by Betty Comden, Adolph Green, Leonard Bernstein © 1945 (renewed) Warner Bros. Inc. All rights reserved. Used by permission.
    "Night and Day" by Cole Porter © 1932 (renewed) Warner Bros. Inc. All rights reserved. Used by permission.
    "Old Devil Moon" by E. Y. Harburg and Burton Lane © 1946 The Players Music Group. © renewed, assigned to Chappell & Co. All rights reserved. Used by permission.
    "Speak Low" by Ogden Nash and Kurt Weill. TRO © 1943 (renewed) Hampshire House Publishing Corp. and Chappell & Co. All rights reserved. Used by permission.
    "When I'm Not Near the Girl I Love" by E. Y. Harburg and Burton Lane © 1946 The Players Music Group. © renewed, assigned to Chappell & Co. All rights reserved. Used by permission.

All photographs provided by Photofest.

Library of Congress Cataloguing-in-Publication Data

Lewis, David H., 1940–
       Broadway musicals : a hundred year history / by David H. Lewis.
          p.   cm.
       Includes bibliographical references, discography, and index.

       ISBN 0-7864-1269-0 (illustrated case binding : 50# alkaline paper) ∞

       1. Musicals—United States—History and criticism.   I. Title.
    ML2054 .L48 2002
    782.1'4'097471—dc21
                                                   2002009785

British Library cataloguing data are available

On the cover: Left to right: George M. Cohan with sister Josie and parents Jerry and Nellie on Broadway (Photofest). Background ©2002 Comstock.

Manufactured in the United States of America

McFarland & Company, Inc., Publishers
  Box 611, Jefferson, North Carolina 28640
  www.mcfarlandpub.com

To
Abel Green

Contents

Preface

If I could have but one wish granted from the world of higher entertainment, Richard Rodgers and Oscar Hammerstein II would be back working on a new musical. I was lucky to be alive and attentive during the creation of their last four works. Still vivid are my recollections of advance news reports announcing subject matter, song titles, and stars signed. Still vivid are the first out-of-town reviews in *Variety*—in particular the one which began "Sensational musical is on its way to Broadway" when *The Sound of Music* opened in New Haven. How fond are my memories of waiting anxiously to hear the songs for the first time, staying tuned to the radio for new releases that might bear their titles.

Then the ultimate thrill: listening to the recorded score, usually on a Sunday evening broadcast a week or so before the original cast album arrived at our local record store. There, I savored its newness in my hands. Once home, the album was the star of the house, morning, noon and night. And what a glorious note the masters would go out on! I would live to see my high estimation of *The Sound of Music*—their final opus—rousingly affirmed forty years later when audiences attended sing-along versions of the movie.

How did such an addiction begin? As far as I can recall, it was one evening in Santa Rosa, California, in front of the old console radio in the bedroom I shared with my older brother, Dick, when I heard Mary Martin singing "A Cockeyed Optimist" from the original cast album of *South Pacific*. Something quite extraordinary happened, for my young ears were riveted to the artfully constructed verse and the haunting music. Perhaps at that fateful moment the elevated world of Broadway songwriting claimed a part of my soul.

It might have proved only a passing infatuation had not my brother, Dick, gone to San Francisco a few years later and been unexpectedly swept away by a touring production of *Carousel*. As a result, he started bringing home show albums. In retrospect, his keen enthusiasms seem to have helped nurture the seed that

1

Mary, Dick and Oscar planted. What a time to fall in love with musical theatre. What a century. I am left with indelible memories of a greatness not guaranteed every age.

Those years of enchanted craftsmanship would not last forever. No "golden age" does. I had grown up during the last act, and it would take me many years to realize and appreciate that the first act had been even better. By that time, I had learned to endure something even more dispiriting than the arguable decline in a great American art form: a suicidal cynicism among insiders and hard-core fans against post–golden age developments. Many who lived through the halcyon days would turn intolerant and bitter as the faces and voices of singing shows changed, unable or unwilling to allow the occasional new musical with valid offerings into their closed hearts. Yet I can tell you this: If my most thrilling moment was watching Mary Martin sing "I'm in Love With a Wonderful Guy" when *South Pacific* played the Curran Theatre in San Francisco in 1957, probably the second greatest thrill was delivered from the same stage over forty years later when Petula Clark sang "As If We Never Said Goodbye" in a post–golden age show, *Sunset Boulevard*.

Perhaps the good new shows are fewer and farther between than they were in the 1940s and 1950s. Nonetheless, real musical theatre has not completely given way to mindless spectacle. Originality still struggles, now and then, to assert itself in fresh formats. And sometimes, still, the results can be compelling. If American writers lost their way the last quarter of the twentieth century, it was not for lack of a desire to experiment and extend or even—heaven, forbid—to entertain.

Creative forces from foreign shores would come at least to their temporary if unwelcome rescue. For a number of years the names Andrew Lloyd Webber and Steven Sondheim were considered the only two options on Broadway. How sadly limiting that was; it surely took some kind of toll on alternative voices striving to break free of cliché expectations. And truth be told, of late Broadway hasn't allowed in many new voices with strong visions of their own. When the producer assumes too much power over the act of creation itself, beware. Alan Jay Lerner was onto something when he wrote, "The theatre flourishes when it is a writer's theatre."

Once the final curtain falls and the lights and sets are struck, what remains are the cast albums—the tangible and permanent reminders of variable fortunes along 42nd Street. Cast albums live on to charm and exhilarate—and to annoy and irritate. We are confounded by the contradictory lessons they impart: How could such a marvelous set of songs have gone to bed with so dreadful a script? How could so legendary a success contain such mediocre words and music? We listen to magic and lament early closings. We endure banalities and are at a loss to understand why audiences rushed to embrace them in the first place. But those songs are only a fraction of what theatregoers experienced in the first place—a mere echo of a long-lost enterprise whose particular makeup in all its complexities can never be recaptured. Such is the fleeting beauty of the "living theatre."

And we are forced to deal with the elusive realities: A musical is an amalgam of many interchangeable components, including timing, luck, the production, and a producer's marketing savvy. A musical will rise or fall on the intricacies of collaboration—in collaboration with fate itself. Orchestra conductor turned educator Lehman Engle once argued naively for the libretto being perfect before rehearsals commenced as the only way of insuring regular success; that Mr. Engle was not subsequently engaged by the Shuberts to review incoming scripts suggests how far off the mark he was. Far smarter was Oscar Hammerstein, who acknowledged the irrationality of the outcome no matter how much thought had gone into it, and deferred humbly to "the intangibles," those elusive spiritual qualities that unexpectedly emerge between the lines of dialogue and verse. Having suffered his share of humiliating flops, Hammerstein would surely know. We read of celebrities who "saved" the run; of miscast stars who dogged the run; of directors blamed for turkeys; of directors acclaimed for "salvage jobs," as if anybody could have known for certain that the show would fail without an Abbott or a Prince at the helm. (They, too, directed turkeys.) We read of patchwork trivialities cheered by standing ovations; of trenchant, form-advancing work begging for patrons. The explanations advanced are about as sound as stock market predictions. Those maddening intangibles … yes, Mr. Hammerstein.

Through it all, that fetching infant, that child of irresistible charm who refuses to grow up—that is to say, the musical—invariably finds at the last moment a way back to the hearts of the public. A strut. A grin. A joke. A pratfall. A Mel Brooks. Even a great story. And the theatre stays a theatre instead of a super mall or an insurance building. And the crowds keep coming. And, too, tons of other shows the same season lose money and fade ingloriously into an early darkness. And *Variety* comes up with a promising new slant and headline for the next season ahead. These days the theatre owners who rent make predictable profits. Producers, many of whom seem to specialize in income tax write-off operations, keep alive at least the image of old Broadway as a booming place.

This is a book about old Broadway and new, image and reality, from the beginning of the twentieth century to the beginning of the twenty-first. Where does such a book come from? From a decade of listening to over three hundred cast albums, each graded song by song on at least two separate occasions. From the notes made, the story lines studied, the reviews examined and the themes compared. Then from a consideration of the scores in chronological order, out of which a landscape of American culture and the attendant changing patterns in musical theatre art began to take shape in my mind. These larger impressions shaped the narrative; that done, I immersed myself in Broadway histories and biographies, intent upon telling the story from a healthy range of viewpoints. Sources of those viewpoints include my own impressions of the 90 or so musicals I have seen in one form or another; first night reviews and box office records; revival history, if any; the creators themselves, whose quoted comments can offer rare first-hand insights; and selected authors and scholars who have been looking back thoughtfully ever since.

Vastly helpful were Steve Suskin's monumentally rich reference books, *Show Tunes* and *Broadway Opening Nights*—virtual libraries unto themselves. By serendipity, other valuable materials have come my way. Two Los Angeles friends were wonderfully generous: Rick Talcove gave me a wealth of TV-based specials on musical theatre, including Rodgers and Hammerstein's original *Cinderella*, and Michael Kohl supplied rare tapes of songs not included on cast albums and shared with me his copy of a little-known set of interviews with Richard Rodgers and Oscar Hammerstein. But interviewed when, where, and by whom? Thanks to Linda Watson, a reference librarian at the San Francisco Public Library, the identity of the interviewer, Tony Thomas, and his radio station were located one late Saturday afternoon. After a fruitless search on my part, from institution to institution and across miles of *New York Times* microfilm, Ms. Watson located the information on her pc within five efficient minutes.

About the lyrics quoted in this book: The omission of verse by some of the giants should not be construed as a conscious slight on my part. The task of securing permissions to quote from song lyrics is one of the most daunting obstacle courses known to an author, and for practical and economic reasons, one finds himself forced to make selections contingent largely upon ease of access, cost per verse, red tape involved, degrees of manuscript review required, and the reliability of negotiations with the respective copyright holders. Perhaps one day a pioneering attorney will persuade the United States Congress to amend vaguely defined "fair use" statutes, so that authors can safely and freely quote a fixed number of lines or a set percentage of words per song lyric without fear, justly shared by publishers, of unnecessary and unfounded litigation.

At any rate, I am happy to say that in my quest for permissions, a few friendly voices came out from behind telephone answering machines to offer welcome cooperation: Hal David and Jim David, Tim Rice, David Robinson of the Really Useful Group in London, and Rosemarie Gawelko of Warner Bros. Publications in Miami.

James Schlader of Oakland, who has produced and directed a multitude of musicals for over thirty years—after a career acting and singing on Broadway in many of them—kindly examined the manuscript for basic factual accuracy. Choreographer Harriet Schlader, wife of James and another Broadway veteran, helpfully answered all my telephone calls. At Photofest, Howard Mandelbaum and Eric Spilker were a breeze to work with on the fine illustrations that grace these pages.

Finally, my excursions across microfilm through back issues of *Variety* were especially enjoyable, for occasionally I would come upon a notice penned by Abel Green, the late editor of *Variety* and the man to whom this book is affectionately dedicated. Mr. Green was the first to publish me in his pages (under my then-used full name, David Lewis Hammarstrom). Less than a year after my first *Variety* byline, Mr. Green passed away. An amiable soul whose voice I never heard, whose face I never saw and hand I never shook, to me Abel Green will always be a giant— like the giants of his era who nearly spilled blood, laboring around the clock sometimes, to get a new musical out of town in working order for opening night. To create the songs that would enchant young ears attuned to scratchy old radios as far away as Santa Rosa.

David Lewis
January 2002

CHAPTER 1

Songs in Revolt

Out of the melting pot of the emerging American culture came the sounds of a new theatrical art form brimming with Yankee confidence and rhythmic ingenuity. From the streets of New York City—seething with the clashing tensions of immigrant dreamers determined to make for themselves a better life—a dissonant new tempo of both rebellion and individuality was rising up through the popular songs of Tin Pan Alley, and those songs were starting to land in stage shows.

Ragtime rhythms drove the finger-snapping melodies, composed by a newer breed of tunesmiths who now competed head-on with established, classically trained composers from abroad—composers whose staid operettas reflected that old world left behind. A steady succession of novice American songwriters knocked upon the doors of popular music publishers like Max Dreyfus, president of T. B. Harms and Co., who could send a promising talent into career orbit overnight. In publishing offices all around the district, theatrical producers came to listen to new tunes for possible insertion in their upcoming shows. Songs were needed for singers and specialty acts, as well as to "Americanize" imported British operettas to make them more appealing to local ears.

As the new American century dawned, no single figure better expressed this bold new songwriting dynamic than master showman George M. Cohan, father of the modern Broadway show tune. Born on the fourth of July in 1878 to an Irish family of traveling stage entertainers—the Four Cohans, "America's Favorite Family"—Cohan followed his destiny across the stages of vaudeville, where he acted, danced, strutted in blackface and sang, wrote, composed, directed and produced. At the age of 13, the plucky young egotist broke out on his own, landing a lead role *Peck's Bad Boy* (in which he was clearly a hit) and getting a taste of solo celebrity. Rapidly ascending the neon ladder to stardom, Cohan brought crowd-pleasing gusto to the fledgling art of American musical comedy.

Cohan launched his legendary contribution—a virtual new song template—

Raised on vaudeville: George M. Cohan (left) with (left to right) sister Josie and parents Jerry and Nellie in the family act.

in his third musical and first hit, *Little Johnny Jones*, a 1904 venture that lasted less than two months at the old Liberty Theatre, but which, after major revisions, played twenty more weeks in New York during two repeat engagements the following year. Cohan himself introduced the ground-breaking number in the role of the American jockey Johnny Jones, returning victoriously to his home town after being falsely accused of throwing a race at the London Derby.

> Give my regards to Broadway,
> Remember me to Herald Square;
> Tell all the gang at Forty-Second Street
> that I will soon be there!
> Whisper of how I'm yearning
> to mingle with the old time throng;
> Give my regards to old Broadway
> and say that I'll be there, e'er long.

The opening night house went wild with applause, refusing to stop until Cohan turned, bowed, and offered a few words of thanks. It was a turning point for Broadway and for its new star, who would go on belting out songs from his heart, songs characterized by Brooks Atkinson as "sublimations of the mood of their day. They said what millions of people would have said if they had Cohan's talent."[1]

On the serious side, Cohan expressed a humble philosophy of life that enamored him further with his working-class fans:

> Did you ever sit and ponder
> Sit and wonder,
> Sit and think
> Why we're here and what this life is all about?
> It's a problem that has driven many brainy men to drink
> It's the weirdest thing they've tried to figure out
>
> About a thousand different theories
> The scientists can show
> But never have yet proved a reason why
> With all we've thought and all we're taught
> Why, all we seem to know
> Is we're born, live a while then we die
>
> Life's a very funny proposition after all
> Imagination, jealousy, hypocrisy, gall
> Three meals a day
> A whole lot to say
> When you haven't got the coin,
> You're always in the way ...

And how fleeting were Cohan's gifts for connecting with the mood of the day: Within a mere four-year stretch, *all* of his songs destined for fame were introduced to Broadway. In his autobiography, he described the upbeat ditties as "ragtime marches,"[2] suggesting (rightly) that his inventions sprang from black music. Almost every composer who subsequently achieved success in musical theatre would pay tribute one time or another to Cohan's ragtime marches. Oscar Hammerstein would one day remark, "Never was a plant more indigenous to a particular part of the earth than was George M. Cohan to the United States of his day. The whole nation was confident of its superiority, its moral virtue, its happy isolation from the intrigues of the old country, from which many of our fathers and grandfathers had migrated."[3]

Dubbed by Gerald Bordman "America's first musical comedy genius,"[4] the multi-talented Cohan, who contributed to 21 musicals and 20 plays, pioneered the natural transformation of vaudeville into song-and-dance shows with scripted characters and story lines, however lightweight. His pulsing tunes and swaggering street-wise attitudes offered refreshing counterpoint to the more sedate operettas with their ponderous romantic tales played out by castle-dwelling characters of privilege. A strident non-elitist, George M. played as much to the lower classes up in the balconies as he did to the carriage trade down in the orchestra. His shameless flag waving shtick, though frowned upon by critics, was loved by the common man. In fact, the song-and-dance king found greater popularity on the road than he ever did in New York City.

Cohan would inspire a whole new generation of popular American stage composers. Among them was Jerome Kern, who came up through the pop trenches like most of his peers, starting off as the recipient of numerous rejections from music publishers. Then in 1902 came a note from Edward B. Marks's Lyceum Music Publishing Company with news that it was about to publish Kern's piano tune "At the Casino." The novice was only 17 when the name "Jerome D. Kern" first appeared on sheet music.

This led to his becoming a song plugger at Marks's company for $7 a week. Later he performed clerical duties for the smaller T.B. Harms publishing firm, run by Max Dreyfus. Dreyfus would work wonders for many young composers, hand-picking virtually every early-century tunesmith destined for musical theatre fame. For Kern, however, there was no such magic. Working for Dreyfus, he advanced only as far as sheet music salesman.

Impatient for songwriting opportunities, Kern threw his fate to the Brits. Shrewdly aware of the West End's dominance over New York, he journeyed to London and was soon composing throwaway songs for the humdrum first half-hour segments of stage shows, which were largely ignored by blasé late-arriving patrons.

In time, Kern's numbers were too good to ignore. And when finally his career took flight, Jerome Kern took a pioneering interest in the potential dramatic function of a song, longing to elevate its relevance in stage shows. Songwriters of the day, as remembered by Otto Harbach, "paid almost no attention to plot. They were indifferent to characters, even to the situations in which their songs were involved. They didn't care much about the kind of lyric that was being written for their melodies, just as long as the words could fit the tune."[5] Kern took a giant step in another direction when he joined forces with lyricists Schuyler Greene and Herbert Reynolds, and librettists Philip Bartholomae and Guy Bolton, to create for the 299-seat Princess Theatre the first of several small-scale musicals, the enthusiastically received *Very Good Eddie*. The buoyant little tuner contained a high-voltage set of razzmatazz, finger-snapping songs with none of the maudlin sentiment of the starchy operettas of old Vienna. The show's smart topical lyrics opened a door to the jazz age just ahead.

Eddie portrayed a chance encounter between a man and a woman, each embarking on a honeymoon voyage up the Hudson River, but by accident without their respective spouses. They come to find they are better suited to each other than to the loves they left behind. Insecure Eddie Kettle, thinking unhappily of his very tall, very domineering new wife back there on the dock, laments his embarrassing plight, courtesy of words by Schuyler Greene:

When you wear a nineteen collar
And a size eleven shoe
You can lead a pirate through
Smoke and drink and swear and chew
But you have to lock ambition up
And throw away the key
When your collar's number thirteen
And your shoes are number three!

Faithful to the production restraints of a Princess Theatre show, *Very Good Eddie* was confined to two sets; its locale was American; the theatrical muse it served was light comedy, and its cast did not exceed thirty in number. How to top its ebullient charms? Kern and Guy Bolton, along with P.G. Wodehouse, came back a couple of seasons later with the similarly styled *Leave It to Jane*, a college musical centered around a football game between two rival campuses. Jane snares her school's star football player in order to keep him from deserting to the other school. Kern's breezy score overflowed with more melodic delights. Wodehouse atypically wrote all the lyrics, supplying ample wit to such novelties as the worldly "Sir Galahad" and the clever "Cleopatterer." In the category of pure heart-raising charm, there was the show-stopping "The Sun Shines Brighter." Oddly, *Jane*, although in spirit a Princess Show, played the Longacre Theatre, possibly a bad move. Its run was half that of *Eddie*.

Kern and Wodehouse, numbered among the boldest innovators, daringly introduced ragtime, and they turned their backs on the sullen and somber operettas of Rudolf Friml, Victor Herbert and Sigmund Romberg, transplanted European-born composers who sold the stuffier images of a distant upscale culture to New York theatergoers. The younger generations naturally strove to shake things up, to bring a new sound into playhouses. Harry Tierney, another Tin Pan Alley pro, scored a huge 670-performance success in 1919 at the Vanderbilt with *Irene*; yet he mixed together a diversified score of older style refrains like "Alice Blue Gown" and modern work such as the jazzy "Sky Rocket" and the zesty "Hobbies." The *Times*' notice promised more than a silly surfeit of "girls and music and jokes and dancers and singers.... [*Irene*] has a lot of catchy music.... Also it has a plot."[6]

The new American songsmiths followed a commercial path by which virtually all show composers of the time honed and shaped their talents. Either they proved adept at reaching a mass public or they languished. Those who delivered the goods were invariably offered opportunities to have their most commercial numbers included in stage shows. Irving Berlin, another newcomer on the block, had been pitching his talents along Tin Pan Alley, too—first in the role, along New York streets, of a singing panhandler; next, as a singing waiter at a saloon in Chinatown; then as the lyric writer, in 1907, of his first published song, "Marie from Sunny Italy," with music by Nick Nicholson. In 1908, at the age of 20, Berlin started supplying his own music with "Best of Friends Must Part." He went to work for publisher and songwriter Ted Snyder, turning out mostly the words, as he would do for several years. Soon, Berlin became a partner in the firm, and he began getting his songs interpolated into musicals. Berlin's big break came when a lyric he wrote to a Ted Snyder tune, "She Was a Dear Little Girl," landed on Broadway in *The Boys and Betty*.

Within a couple of seasons, Berlin found producer support from Florence Ziegfeld, in whose lavish *Follies* his songs were famously received, and growing public favor in his lyric contributions to a steady succession of shows, some stateside, some abroad—among them *The Sun Dodgers, Hullo, Ragtime,* and *The Trained Nurses.* For the latter, a vaudeville act produced in 1913 by Jesse Lasky, Berlin composed and wrote "If You Don't Want Me (Why Do You Hang Around?)"

Watch Your Step, with Irene and Vernon Castle, which Charles Dillingham produced at the Globe Theatre in 1914, marked Berlin's first full score. Billed as a "syncopated musical," *Step* was considered a forerunner to the more pop-oriented musicals of the day which would follow. It held on for a handy 175 performances, and out of its 24 plus numbers, only one remains a standard: "Simple Melody."

Simple salty melodies. First pounded out on big old uprights in Manhattan. Pounded out to impress jaded Tin Pan Alley tycoons—characters like legendary Max Dreyfus, who spotted true talent as naturally as bees spot flowers and then goaded producers into taking chances on his untried finds and their unknown songs. King melody makers they became, selling the best to a demanding public. Theatergoers expected to whistle the refrains—not the scenery—on their way out of the New Amsterdam and the Winter Garden and the Globe.

Seven seasons later, Irving Berlin realized a fine stateside success with the first edition of *The Music Box Revue,* this one shipshaped into breezy perfection by director Hassard Short. Out of the show came another Berlin classic, "Say It with Music." And from the John Murray Anderson directed *Music Box Revue of 1924,* headlining Fanny Brice and Bobby Clark, came "All Alone," first sung earlier the same year at the Duke of York's Theatre in London in the rousing success *The Punch Bowl.*

Hundreds of memorable songs would first be introduced to America in hundreds of ultimately forgotten shows. During the 1920s, New York stages hosted over two hundred new legit productions *each* season.

Never to be forgotten was the syncopation-mad 1924 triumph *Lady Be Good,* a rousing culmination of Roaring Twenties sensibilities and the new American musical comedy show—all on the same stage at the same time. *Lady* also marked the coming of age of its young, restless composer, George Gershwin, who was now starting to dazzle the city's carriage trade with a rare kind of infectious, hyperactive music. Gershwin, a Max Dreyfus discovery, had displayed composing talent when he was an eleven-year-old lad who, away from a piano, rolled on fast wheels over some of New York's toughest streets, winning roller-skating speed contests. By fifteen he quit school to take a job plugging songs for music publisher Jerome H. Remick. Young George made money producing player piano rolls. His first song, "When You Want 'Em, You Can't Get 'Em," with words by Murray Roth, was published in 1916. The year before, at age 17, he had made his debut on Broadway at the Winter Garden Theatre with a single contribution: "The Making of a

Girl," which made it into *The Passing Show of 1916*—with a little help by an opportunistic young Sigmund Romberg. Romberg, then a lowly staff composer for the Shubert Organization, had taken a liking to Gershwin's compositions. He asked the book and lyrics man for *The Passing Show*, Harold Atteridge, to write words for one of Gershwin's melodies, after which Romberg took co-credit for the music.

Three years later, the adaptable George Gershwin found a more lucrative partnership with lyricist Irving Caesar when the two fashioned a song for the live pre-movie revue at the Capitol Theatre movie palace. In attendance one night was Al Jolson, who fell in love with the number and subsequently recorded it as Gershwin's first major hit, "Swanee."

Gershwin was now selling his songs to a number of theatrical producers and music publishers, most notably to several editions of *George White's Scandals*, whose 1922 version, with W. C. Fields in the cast and Paul Whiteman directing in the pit, featured Gershwin's second hit song, "I'll Build a Stairway to Paradise." His biggest break followed in 1924, when he suddenly acquired a talk-of-the-town reputation following the first performance of his groundbreaking symphonic jazz work composed for orchestra, "Rhapsody in Blue."

Later the same year George teamed up for the first time with brother Ira, a fine lyric writer, to create the solidly tuneful hit *Lady Be Good*. Ira's savvy words rode George's frenetic tunes with smart devotion.

Indeed, by 1924, in the district known as Times Square, the tunes of Tin Pan Alley were beginning to hold their own against the more conservative refrains of operettas (both imported and created afresh). *Lady* followed the recent openings of *Andre Charlot's Revue of 1924*—composed by, among others, Noël Coward, Eubie Blake and Noble Sissle ("Limehouse Blues")—and the Rudolf Friml, Oscar Hammerstein and Otto Harbach smash, *Rose Marie*. And it was followed, the very next night, by the opening of another old-time crowd pleaser, Sigmund Romberg's *Student Prince*. Unlike its stodgy formulaic competitors heavily laden with brooding love songs, *Lady Be Good* offered virtually no ballads. The George and Ira Gershwin romp danced on Jazz-age gusto—numbers like "Hang On to Me," "So Am I," and "Insufficient Sweetie." The kind of "excellent" tunes which, according to the *New York Times* reviewer, "the unmusical and serious-minded will find it hard to get rid of."[7]

The score's crowning centerpiece was "Fascinating Rhythm," the song which would forever symbolize the driving syncopation of the new American tuner. And it launched Gershwin's genius in the public's imagination. He and Ira would collaborate on fourteen shows over a brief eleven-year span. Music is mostly what they would be remembered for.

Lady Be Good was technically a "book" show—credit Guy Bolton and Fred Thompson for whatever narrative sense it conveyed, accidental or otherwise. The fragile story line told a then-typical rags-to-riches tale wherein true love overcomes class distinctions, Cinderella style. An evicted brother and sister living on the streets land a job entertaining at a rich estate. Each becomes romantically entangled through rather trite, implausible plot complications—the brother ending

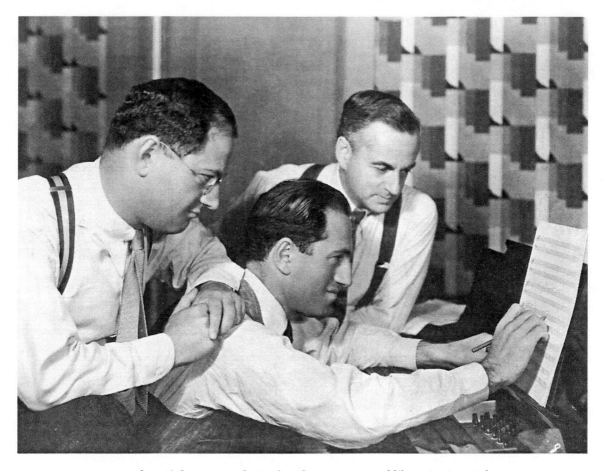

Left to right: Ira Gershwin, brother George, and librettist Guy Bolton.

up in marriage to a common girl, the sister, alas! to a millionaire—and the show serves up *four* happy weddings by final curtain. The brother and sister were played by a bright new song and dance team just returning from starring spots in a London hit, *For Goodness Sake*, and for whom the whole affair had been tailor-made—Fred and Adele Astaire.

Who could ask for anything more? The *New York Times* critic did, suggesting it needed more humor. Overall, however, the scribe was amply impressed, describing *Lady Be Good* as "a drama of outcasts, rents, social shinning, loving resolutions and well-ending marital fortunes," praising Adele as a new Beatrice Lillie, and favoring the paper-thin libretto because it favored Adele: "The book of the piece contains just enough story to call Miss Astaire on stage at frequent intervals, which thus makes it an excellent book."[8] Meanwhile, the beguiling beat of Gershwin's frenetic score rattled on like a Gotham subway train.

Gershwin the speed skater rarely slowed down at the piano. Why no slow numbers in *Lady*? Considering its preoccupation with pace, how easy it is to imagine director Felix Edwards fearing that a single moment of letup might reveal a certain lack of substance. And easy to imagine choreographer Sammy Lee holding out, in full accord, for nonstop Gershwin zip. Edwards and Lee may have waged an out-of-town campaign to nix any and all beautiful refrains. "The Man I Love"—yes, that lustrous Gershwin gem—was deemed not right for *Lady Be Good*. Dropped on the road. The flapper era had scarce patience or time for introspective ballads.

Instead, producers pushed for foot-stomping pizazz, the more the better. And across the Atlantic, when the show took a tour of London, George and Ira added a brand new number—yet another blast for dancing feet, "I'd Rather Charleston." The Gershwin brothers, perfectly in sync with the Roaring Twenties, had a bona fide smash at the Liberty Theatre, where *Lady Be Good* played for 330 performances. Ira's nimble verse added a sophisticated gloss to George's clattering refrains—though a noticeable dearth of comedy verse foreshadowed Ira's principal shortcoming. No ballads. No funny songs. Just heart-pounding melodies and nimble carefree words.

While the Gershwins were celebrating their first stage success, other newcomers who would eventually achieve similar status were still struggling for the Big Break. Cole Porter, for one. Another name not very well known—not yet—Mr. Porter was one of the many random, nearly faceless contributors to *Follies*. The native of Peru, Indiana, had only one hit tune to his credit, the quaintly sentimental "Old Fashioned Garden." He had written it for a 1919 flop, *Hitchy Koo*, built around the comic talents of Raymond Hitchcock—not funny enough to rally the crowds beyond a few weeks on the boards.

Porter had been struggling for success since 1915 when his first song to reach Broadway, "Esmerelda," went down with the inglorious *Hands Up*. Regrettably, that success had proved more elusive than the pleasures of the high life to which he had become gracefully addicted. The son of a well-heeled family, Porter served the briefest possible stint on Tin Pan Alley—long enough to sell a single number in 1910 entitled "Bridget." Ironically, two of the songs he composed for the famed *Greenwich Village Follies of 1924*, "I'm In Love Again" and "Two Little Babes in the Wood," were both destined to become popular several years after Porter's first stage success opened.

Mr. Porter, a Yale man who had specialized in composing songs for varsity revues and football games ("Bulldog, Bulldog! Bow! Wow! Wow!"), upon graduation in 1913 blithely skipped player piano plugging and instead advanced directly to New York City society. With wealthy family connections to sponsor him through a pampered apprenticeship of his own design away from the pop-tune sweatshops, still Porter had the instincts to give the public what they liked and at the same time urge them towards greater sophistication. And so he, elegant hedonist at heart, met his targeted audience with a decidedly worldly bent.

Porter pounded out a heap of unsalable melodies before he ever turned flush on annual royalties. His first known song, "Bobolink Waltz," was dashed off in 1902 when he was in his ninth precocious year. "Esmerelda" hit the sales racks in

1915, as reported above. Other numbers from *Hitchy*? "When I Had a Uniform On," "Bring Back My Butterfly," "My Cozy Little Corner in the Ritz" and "I've Got Somebody Waiting." He himself had to keep waiting for the next nine years, toiling through a number of ill-fated ventures.

In 1928 at the Music Box, when he was 37 years old, Porter finally arrived with a musical called *Paris*, which was produced by Gilbert Miller and E. Ray Goetz, directed by W. H. Gilmore, with a book by Martin Brown. It contained one of Porter's signature songs, the risqué "Let's Do It," so slyly in touch with the amorality of the era that audiences began to embrace the essential Cole Porter.

What other would-be tunesmiths destined for fame were still foundering in 1924 when *Lady* soared? Vincent Youmans could only deliver so-so trivialities to the *Lollipop* at the Knickerbocker theatre, while a still-struggling Richard Rodgers, like Cole Porter still far from a household name, worked with Larry Hart on the disappointing *Melody Man*, actually a play with songs (one being "I'd Like to Poison Ivy Because She Clings to Me") and a drama so pedestrian that the two managed to keep their names off it. Rodgers had labored with his partner through a frustrating string of failures. They had suffered rejection from famed Max Dreyfus, who dismissed some tunes Rodgers played for him, including "Manhattan," as "worthless."[9] *You'd Be Surprised* lasted all of one performance. *Fly with Me* stayed airborne for only four evenings. The composer, who in his impressionable youth had sat spellbound before a dozen or so performances of Jerome Kern's *Very Good Eddie* hearing the kind of music he longed to compose, now nearly walked away from Broadway, so distraught was he over a career choice going nowhere. For a deadly spell, Rodgers considered abandoning the music business to become retailing specialist in kids' underwear. Larry Hart, not quite so despondent, succeeded in etching out minor assignments applying his intricate baroque rhyming patterns to the melodies of other men.

Broadway would never be an easy place to conquer. Jerome Kern, the day's reigning melody king, was now experiencing mostly frustration, too. In 1924, while the Gershwin brothers exulted in their new-found glory, Kern's tepid *Dear Sir* was not politely answered by cheering ticket buyers. Nor was his more ambitious effort with P.G. Wodehouse, *Sitting Pretty*. Intended to resemble a Princes Street hit, it folded quietly without recapturing even a trace of his past glories associated with that theatre. Kern could only reminisce over the great days working at the Princess with tried and true collaborators Guy Bolton and Wodehouse and a jamboree of long-forgotten lyric writers.

Syncopated amusements were not an easy sell. The majority of ticket buyers flocked in even greater droves to the big successful operettas of the day. There was a reason: Not everybody found satisfaction in joke-filled revues strung together with flimsy story lines and salty player-piano tunes. The newer American shows routinely sacrificed plot development for a deference to song and dance. The typical operetta offered a durable libretto. And as easy as it is for critics of today to call them "silly" and "contrived," in many ways they were not far removed from the serious book shows that would dominate the theatre fifty years later—just not so sophisticated, and certainly not as local. Old-world operetta composer Victor Herbert had referred to his 1908 work, *Algeria*, as "a musical play,"[10] the same term used to describe a show that had opened eight years earlier, *Martin and Martine*. In the eyes of some, including author Ethan Mordden, Herbert was a bold innovator who sought "compositional unity,"[11] in contrast to the prevailing practice of interpolating popular songs that bore no relevance to the plot or theme.

Vaudeville versus narrative integrity. Herbert's *Babes in Toyland* had featured the villainous and miserly Uncle Barnaby, plotting to do away with his own niece and nephew in order to claim their inheritance. *The Red Mill*, another Herbert hit with book and lyrics by Henry Blossom, concerned a couple of tourists helping the young heroine secure her father's approval to marry her true love. How silly is that? The public naturally responded to dramatic situations set to music. Franz Lehar's *Merry Widow*, with a score rooted in traditional refrains, told the story of two ex-sweethearts eventually getting back together. Its universal appeal is evident in its touring schedule, which included cities in Africa, Asia and South America.

How much more substantial, really, is the story of a snobby English professor teaching a young cockney woman to speak proper English so she can impress a bunch of stiff necks (*My Fair Lady*) than is the tale of spouseless honeymooners discovering a superior match in one illicit embrace (*Very Good Eddie*)? It may reside in the execution. The operetta bore the imagery of substance and the semblance of storytelling. Some creators borrowed from epic historical tales, not unlike the work of Frenchmen Alain Boublil and Claude-Michel Schonberg sixty years hence. Rudolf Friml's 1925 hit *Vagabond King* dramatized the adventures and romantic intrigues of François Villon, a 15th century poet rebel at the time of King Louis XI. Broodingly romantic, the operettas of Herbert and colleagues found steady patronage.

Through the 1920s, the American-bred shows of the newer composers could not rival these old-world workhorses at the box office. *Lady Be Good*, a hit that closed in less than a year, paled commercially next to a couple of big operetta favorites: Rudolf Friml and Herbert Stothart's *Rose Marie*, which entertained almost twice as many patrons with a story about a singer who remains true to only one man despite the treacherous manipulations of a rival suitor; and the decade's longest-running musical, Sigmund Romberg's *The Student Prince*, a compelling melodrama about the bittersweet failure of the principals to rekindle an epic lost love. Both shows were marinated in an overabundance, by today's standards, of long-winded love songs—perhaps best illustrated by *Rose Marie's* contemplative "Indian Love Call." Oscar Hammerstein, who co-wrote the book and lyrics with Otto Harbach, would remark many times over that what playgoers primarily responded to were engaging stories they could follow.

Or to snappy songs they could hum on their way out. The younger tunesmiths, who stuck with uptempo music despite lingering audience loyalties to the European-style fare, found their natural medium in the then-thriving revue format, elastic enough to host an evening full of miscellaneous songs. Revues lived in the present. They poked fun at changing mores, satirized known figures in society and

Left to right: Adele Astaire, Leslie Hensen, and Fred Astaire in the West End production of *Funny Face*.

politics. They addressed the jaded sentiments of New Yorkers. Writers took big, bold chances on untoward subjects. From *The Charity Girl* came a subversive little verse thumbing its nose at Indian love calls—"I'd Rather Be a Chippie [street walker] Than a Charity Bum." In at least one city, police raided and closed down the charity girl.

Even some of the book shows courted a worldlier slant. Where to go for better source material? The Gershwin brothers certainly did not go anywhere far, not with *Lady Be Good*, nor with their 1926 sensation, *Oh, Kay*, which offered probably the most exciting score they would create together. It even contained a big ballad, "Someone to Watch Over Me," which was not dropped. The songs in toto brim with effervescence—"Fidgety Feet," "Clap Your Hands," "Don't Ask." Get the album and fly with it. Every single number rouses the heart. And what, bookwise, was *Oh, Kay* up to? The writers Guy Bolton and P.G. Wodehouse had bootlegging on their minds. They thought up a trite little yarn about a titled English bootlegger in America stashing away some hooch in the cellar of a Long Island home, while his sister, posing as a cook to keep an eye on the hidden spirits, falls in love with the homeowner just when he is about to wed somebody else. The romantic outcome should not be difficult to guess. Everyone sings the scores praises. Few talk much about its libretto.

It is a perplexing truth, long in the realization, that the libretto for the American musical would prove more problematic than perfectible during the *entire* twentieth century. Not all the so-called "frivolous" story lines associated with these early day tuners are as bad or unworkable as the residual ill-will of critics and historians would have us believe. Some contained heady doses of wit and amusing characters. Most of them were arguably no worse than the extensively revised scripts that would supersede them in "revival" productions. "Silly" and "contrived" are not confined to a particular era.

"When We Get Our Divorce," a song written by Hammerstein and Harbach for their and Jerome Kern's 1926 hit *Sunny*, took a dashing step away from the operetta attitudes they had grown up serving. And yet, only one month later, Hammerstein was back on the stodgier side of the street with his next successful opus, the stiff and stuffy *Desert Song*, whose strong score, "stirring male chorus" and "abundant plot ... floridly contrived" in *Variety's* opinion offered the public "full value" for its money.[12] Because he was by nature a playwright rather than a vaudevillian, because he longed to explore the human condition in greater depth, Hammerstein naturally gravitated to operetta. In fact, he would earnestly endeavor for the greater part of his life to link music and meaning more effectively. While younger composers of the day were chasing after Tin Pan Alley royalties, Hammerstein was lurching erratically towards a more advanced form of stage entertainment wherein libretto and songs were significantly integrated by virtue of absolute moment-to-moment relevance.

Came 1927. George and Ira Gershwin landed another big cake-walking charmer with *Funny Face*, a harmless little diversion about a young woman feuding with a guardian over a string of pearls belonging to her and having to engage her own boyfriend to steal them back. Less than a month later, however, a bold new American musical, with far more sobering issues on its mind, docked at the Ziegfeld Theatre. First nighters soon settled into their seats, silent and spellbound, toes rarely tapping, fingers rarely snapping. Losing themselves in the Mississippi River locale, they followed the story.

CHAPTER 2

Misery's Coming Around

The opening of *Show Boat* on December 27, 1927, doubtlessly stunned audiences with its atypical realism. Already that year, New Yorkers had attended a number of tuneful new openings, many involving chase scenes. Harry Tierney and Joseph McCarthy's *Rio Rita* followed the plight of a bank robber being hunted down through Texas. At the Belasco, the rousing *Hit the Deck* by Vincent Youmans, Clifford Grey and Leo Robin was built around a smitten female coffee shop owner, named Looloo, running after a sailor halfway around the globe. At the Alvin Theatre, the Gershwin brothers enjoyed second-time success with another Fred and Adele Astaire smash, *Funny Face*—which included a frantic chase through New Jersey to the Atlantic City Pier. B. G. DeSylva, Lew Brown and Ray Henderson brought a disarming football campus show, *Good News*, to the 4th Street Theatre, while Richard Rodgers, Larry Hart and Herbert Fields graced the Vanderbilt with their biggest Broadway success to date, *A Connecticut Yankee*, from which the public first heard "My Heart Stood Still" and "Thou Swell."

Then came the daring new musical about black folk all sweating it out on the Big River while the white folk lived it up in old plantation parlors and gardens. Although *Show Boat* marked a collaborative high point for its two creators, Jerome Kern and Oscar Hammerstein, it was Hammerstein's contribution in particular that made it a show for the ages. Many musicals with equally great scores do not succeed. It is usually the book that determines the ultimate reputation if not the lasting entertainment value of a work. And no single person in the history of musical theatre did more to advance its development and make of it a distinctly American art form than did Mr. Hammerstein. Simple, deep, compassionately poetic, without his family connections in the theatre world (his grandfather enjoyed a major producing career), he could just as easily have become a carpenter or railroad switchman, an accountant or history professor. Hammerstein's instinctive genius grew and blossomed out of two sources: European-rooted operettas in which he was trained, and his own basic humanity.

Those who knew him closely were amused by his rural mannerisms, so oddly out of place did they appear in the profession he chose to pursue. Indeed, Mr. Hammerstein could have lived the lives of his most fundamental protagonists—the riverboat Negroes who labored stoically from sunrise to sunset; the troubled social outcast and misfit of *Oklahoma*, Jud Fry; or the offbeat, self-taught marine biologist, Doc, of *Pipe Dream*, living humbly on the edge of life with ne'er-do-wells and cathouse madames. Hammerstein possessed a profound identification with the common man, which would essentially inspire the movement he led to make the characters in musical plays more like the down-to-earth neighbors of middle American cities and small towns.

Years later, when he was asked to comment on criticism that his work tended towards the corny, Hammerstein's ingenious reply was to answer that so was life. And six months before his death, he summed up his philosophy to Canadian radio interviewer Tony Thomas: "I think it's terribly important that some people like me must exist to keep affirming the beauties of life to offset others, even more eloquent, perhaps, who are decrying life and scoffing at it and telling you what's wrong with it. Surely there are things that are wrong, but then we must also admit that there are things that are right and beautiful and make it wonderful to be on earth. And this, if it isn't my mission, is at least one of my chief aims."[1]

Soft spoken and gentle by nature, on the awkward side socially, towering in height and lumbering in self-effacing humanity (at least in public), Hammerstein yet displayed a brilliant faculty for words both simple and complex, for understated rhyme schemes, and for direct and lucid philosophical content. In him the theatre realized its own poet laureate. Known for shunning parties or, when trapped in one, kindly retreating out the door well before it was over, and for solitary walks through the backwoods of his serene Pennsylvania farm while pondering plot lines and honing lyrics, Hammerstein had far more important things up his sleeve than run-of-the-mill tuners stocked with high flying dames and dandies.

Young Oscar started out as a stage manager, supervising his Uncle Arthur's operettas. Luckily he learned the tricky art of libretto construction through family connections, getting teamed up with veteran librettist-lyricist Otto Harbach, 24 years his senior. Considered by Alan Jay Lerner to be one of the most underrated figures who ever labored in musical theatre, Harbach, whose real name was Hauerbach, was born into a Mormon family of Danish descent in Salt Lake City in 1873.[2] He worked his way through college, taught at Whitman College in Washington State, then enrolled in graduate courses at Columbia University. Dazzled by a billboard ad touting a Weber and Fields show starring Fay Templeton in 1906, Harbach took an interest in musicals. He penned the words for "Cuddle Up a Little Closer" and landed script-writing jobs through the war years, eventually winding up in the office of Max Dreyfus. Referring to Harbach as "my dear friend and erstwhile tutor," Hammerstein credited him as being "the best play analyst I ever met.... He taught me to think a long time before actually writing."[3]

By the time he took up with Hammerstein, Harbach had written the book

Show Boat inspired five major revivals to play New York stages and three movie versions including, in 1929, one of the first part-talkies. Seen here in the 1946 revival are, from left, Ralph Dumke as Captain Andy, Carole Bruce as Julie La Verne, and Robert Allen as Steve Baker.

and lyrics for a handful of shows, from *Madame Sherry*, with music by Karl Hoschna (which gave us "Every Little Moment"), to Rudolf Friml's *Firefly*, produced by Arthur Hammerstein in 1912, to *Going Up*, a resilient 351-performance hit at the Liberty Theatre, for which Louis A. Hirsch composed most of the tunes, Irving Berlin the rest. Harbach turned out the hugely successful *Wildflower* in 1923 at the Casino Theatre, with his young collaborator Oscar Hammerstein assisting on both book and lyrics, Vincent Youmans and Herbert Stothart composing the music. In 1924, Harbach and Hammerstein provided similar services for Rudolf Friml's *Rose Marie*, for which, again, the relatively unknown Stothart supplied additional music.

Destined to suffer, just the same, the crushing vicissitudes of life in the theatre, Oscar would flounder mightily along the way to success. Still, he harbored a burning belief in the controlling importance of the libretto as the vehicle most able to sustain an audience's attention span over the course of three hours.

Actually, no musical is a play alone. It is the infinitely complex amalgamation of three major elements: book, score and production, the latter comprising not only the direction, cast, sets, costumes, orchestrations, etc., but the image-building power of the producer's promotional and advertising campaign. While many shows might succeed on the strength of two of these three crucial components, few would ever survive on only one. A fine set of songs alone will rarely carry the evening. Neither will a good book, nor, with rare exceptions, a production. Ideally, all need each other. Rarely are they of equal strength.

Showmanship. Songs. Stories. These remained the ever-elusive elements with which a century of gifted creators would wrestle. If there is a key, a magic formula, to guarantee success, no one has yet discovered it. In *Show Boat*, perhaps the greatest of all American musicals, Hammerstein demonstrated how a serious topic can be made appealing if it is conveyed in hummable songs and by likable characters caught up in dramatic situations. Others will contend that Jerome Kern's music is what really made the show so indestructibly enduring. By the most blessed stroke of luck, Hammerstein, only 31 years old, joined forces with the theatre's most advanced composer. Hammerstein and Kern had begun their association only two years earlier with the immensely popular *Sunny*. Kern's flexibility and eclecticism (his repertoire included cakewalks, stentorian ballads, blues, jazz dances, and Viennese waltzes) would well serve the narrative's shifting tones and tensions as it expanded forward in time over a forty year period in American history.

It was Jerome Kern who, only halfway through reading the new novel *Show Boat* by Edna Ferber in the fall of 1926, called up Oscar and said, "I think it would be great for us to make a show of this."[4] Oscar, who would end up in life feeling boundless affection for his collaborator, once stating that Jerry Kern "had a greater grip on my whole being than anyone else I have known," went out and bought a copy of the book, and accepted the invitation in a timely fashion.[5] They lavished unusual attention on the project, nurturing it through a difficult editing journey out of town. With the show one hour and forty-five minutes too long in D.C., cuts were furiously implemented. In Philadelphia, three scenes and eight songs were deleted. In Pittsburgh, believing that Magnolia and Gaylord Ravenal needed a second act duet, Jerry and Oscar penned "Why Do I Love You?"

Steeped in the most fundamental ongoing American conflict—the story's central theme of miscegenation haunts the sprawling narrative—so realistic were *Show Boat's* characters and dramatic situations that Abel Green, covering opening night for *Variety*, wondered if music and lyrics were even necessary: "Meaty and gripping, rich with plot and character, it's almost a pity the Edna Ferber novel wasn't dramatized 'straight,' sans the musical setting." Granting the inevitable, Green spotted history in the making: "But, musicalized and Ziegfeldized, it's worthy, sturdy entertainment. It has everything, and tops everything ever done by Ziegfeld. It has story, music, production, casting and consistent entertainment from 8:30 to 11:30 curtains, and in a show which defies fidgeting as the conventional zero hour of theatre curtain time approaches. One forgets the clock."[6]

Show Boat had not just a great story and score. It had a great production, too. Its unlikely presenter, the flamboyant Florenz Ziegfeld, had routinely confined his efforts to lavish revues laden with popular songs, beautiful dancing girls, and leading comics of the day. In a rare act of theatrical courage, Ziegfeld took a fancy to the Kern and Hammerstein work and invested it with his showmanly flair. Historian Gerald Bordman points out the importance of the Ziegfeld touch to the show's initial success. In addition to the principal and supporting players, the 1927 production boasted "a chorus of ninety six, and surrounding the cast were Joseph Urban's eye-filling sets."[7] The verities of the stage abound: To think that Ziegfeld himself, the man who started out working on carnival midways and for the Buffalo Bill Wild West Show, would end up producing the musical theatre's most revered work!

Show Boat advanced in broad strokes a movement already in motion towards the musical play whose songs were an integral part of the action. In the calm estimation of Ethan Mordden, *The Desert Song*, presented the previous season, with a book by Frank Mandel, Oscar Hammerstein and Otto Harbach, was "all of a piece, as neatly composed as a pane of glass, a libretto that extends so fully into the action that most of the numbers are a mixture of underscored dialogue and song."[8] At least as far back as *Very Good Eddie*, songs were written to help advance the story. Hammerstein would one day reflect, "There are a few things in life of which I am certain, but I'm sure of this one thing, that the song is the servant of the play, that it is wrong to write first what you think is an attractive song and then try to wedge it into the story."[9] In fact, integration of song and story was then, as it still is now, more a concept denoting depth of character and story development, a guideline.

And what was the show's impact on this emerging movement in musical theatre? It caused a tremor through show circles—but not an earthquake. Two years following *Show Boat's* historic premiere, the stock market took its catastrophic tumble, and the prolonged depression that ensued did not favor a string of Show Boats. Box office records reveal that during the 1930s, people who could afford pricey theatre tickets generally did not enjoy stories of social injustice; rather, they preferred patronizing light satirical revues and trite book shows. In 1930, *thirty-four* new musicals opened on Broadway, only five fewer than the year before. The entertainers ruled. Little wonder why the Gershwin boys and DuBose Heyward flopped out in 1935 with their monumental work of life along catfish row in Charleston, South Carolina, the oh-so-serious *Porgy and Bess*, which lasted a paltry 124 performances. Gershwin's exalted musicalization of Heyward's novel—more soaring but less universal than *Show Boat*—would eventually be awarded due acclaim. Its book, all sung-through on opening night, would benefit by future revisions, in particular by the replacement of excessive recitative with dialogue. *Porgy*, however, would forever be relegated in the popular imagination to a narrow if mesmerizing view of black ghetto life, whereas *Show Boat* encompassed in its sweeping, time-traversing vision practically the whole of the American experience. *Porgy* sulked and sizzled in an urban ghetto. *Show Boat* sailed the broad waters of America.

Porgy marked the end of the line for the Gershwin brothers, who had enjoyed an enviable record of six sparkling hits over a mere seven-year period—*Lady Be Good, Oh, Kay!, Funny Face, Strike Up the Band, Girl Crazy, Of Thee I Sing. Girl Crazy* unleashed onto the legit stage the high-voltage Ethel Merman, blowing forth a gust of new classics—"I Got Rhythm," "Biding My Time," "But Not for Me," "Embraceable You." *Of Thee I Sing*, by today's sensibilities a tad more silly than significant, garnered the Pulitzer Prize in 1931. Not for George. Not for Ira. For librettists George Kaufman and Morrie Ryskind. Yet more remembered than the award-winning libretto, about a fickle presidential candidate reneging on a campaign promise to wed a Miss America contest winner, are the songs—among them "Love Is Sweeping the Country," "Who Cares?" "Wintergreen for President" and "Of Thee I Sing."

One composer ill-suited to please Depression-era audiences was German-born Kurt Weill, whose austere upbringing was irreversibly shaped by his association with fellow traveler, playwright Bertolt Brecht, of the self-anointed didactic school of drama. In essence, Brecht insisted on minimizing as much as possible the emotional impact of theatre. He wanted to reach the minds rather than the hearts of the audience. He and Weill struck out on America soil with their first offering, the grizzly across-the-tracks *Threepenny Opera*, which lasted all of 12 performances at the Empire Theatre. Full of cynicism and despair, its hard-edged songs were cold and downbeat, its low-life scenes of usury and betrayal among whores and outlaws on the parasitic edges of society an affront to Depression-era audiences. Years later, led by the enthusiasm of Marc Blitzstein, and then with Leonard Bernstein lending his support, in 1954 *Threepenny* played a limited ten-week engagement off–Broadway. It earned such a firestorm of approval from theatergoers and critics like Brook Atkinson that it was brought back. Six years later, *Threepenny* finally closed out a phenomenal return, and "Mack the Knife" was now Kurt Weill's most popular song. Thereafter, it would prove a difficult sell. It did not so much follow *Show Boat* as circumvent it.

Socially conscious writers, in fact, all tended to circumvent musical theatre

Lotte Lenya plays Jenny the street walker and Scott Merrill is Mack-the-Knife in *The Threepenny Opera.*

traditions out of disdain for commercialism, even though they signed contracts and presumably hoped to earn royalties. Marc Blitzstein, of the Weill and Brecht school, was an innovator too daring for his own good. He came in, late thirties, with a blistering diatribe against corporate greed and worker exploitation called *The Cradle Will Rock*. It won him instant admiration from the literati—hardly the force of a box office stampede. Blitzstein's one-sided polemic, commissioned by the WPA and presented after venue cancellations in a bare recital format, earned early notoriety, all from the fragile legacy of a 14-performance run. When revived in 1947, *Cradle*, described by Stanley Green as "little more than an animated left wing political cartoon," again failed to attract an audience.[10] Restagings in 1964 and 1983 proved similarly futile.

The Blitzstein libretto may have been the very first in musical theatre not to revolve around a standard romance. The stark, experimentally unsentimental score to this day impresses. The composer's hyperactive "Let's Do Something!"—a shrieking send-up to the madness of inflated consumer-driven activity for activity's sake—opened the orchestra pit to a dissonance that would brilliantly influence a very young Leonard Bernstein. *West Side Story*, then still years away, owes something to *Cradle*.

Through the 1930s, a decade when 175 new musicals opened on Broadway, the songwriters who profited nicely were the ones who avoided taking themselves too seriously. Newcomer Harold Rome fared famously well with his long-running union-sympathetic revue, *Pins and Needles*, which depicted the organizing efforts of a likable group of garment workers—played by real-life garment workers—while Rome poked good-natured fun at two-faced politicians, foreign dictators (always a safe target) and some not-so-pretty croon-spoon aspects of American life. Pop king Irving Berlin found a middle ground for his songs in topical revues and book musicals produced by Sam H. Harris. His 1932 offering *Face the Music*, with a book by Moss Hart and direction by Hassard Short and George Kaufman, satirized a host of quirky New York socialites down on their luck singing "Let's Have Another Cup of Coffee," and the show stayed around for a respectable 162 performances.

When Berlin returned the following season, with the same collaborators minus Kaufman, he mined real box office gold in *As Thousands Cheer*. Cheer, they did. The show was scenically structured in the form of a newspaper, with succeeding headlines spelling out the issues underpinning songs and skits, a few of which rose above the predictably light weight. Among these was the chilling "Unknown Negro Lynched by Frenzied Mob," a number deemed by *Variety* "completely out of line with the spirit of the show,"[11] to which Ethel Waters, making her first appearance in a "white" Broadway show, responded with a triumphant rendition of Berlin's tragically affecting "Suppertime." Out of this big walloping hit came "Heat Wave," "Harlem On My Mind" and the immortal "Easter Parade." And it marked Marilyn Miller's twelfth and final Broadway show.

During most of the 1930s the revue remained gloriously in vogue. *Bandwagon*, a 1931 hit at the New Amsterdam starring Fred and Adele Astaire (in their last

Broadway appearance), is considered by many to be the finest revue of all time. It had songs by Arthur Schwartz and Howard Dietz—"New Sun in the Sky," "Dancing in the Dark," "I Love Louise"—sketches by Dietz and Kaufman, and direction by Hassard Short, whose deft staging work *Variety*, evidently not hearing the score others heard and not finding the humor much more than "crude," termed "the biggest thing connected with this pleasant evening."[12]

Schwartz and Dietz were back in 1935 with the less successful *At Home Abroad*. Vincent Minnelli directed a star-laden cast of present and future celebrities including Beatrice Lillie, Ethel Waters, Eddie Foy, Jr., Vera Allen and Eleanor Powell. The revue toured a world of locales, and its songs offered plenty to praise: "Get Yourself a Geisha" and "That's Not Cricket," the latter coming with an equally top-notch tune, were two hilarious highlights. "Got a Brand New Suit" whirled itself into a rhythmic Gershwinesque fever, while "What a Wonderful World" simply cheered the heart. Schwartz and Dietz had actually profited the most working on earlier revues: *The Little Show* at the Music Box in 1929, featuring Clifton Webb, Fred Allen and Libby Holman, and *Three's a Crowd* at the Selwyn Theatre in 1930, with the same headliners, and for which Burton Lane and Vernon Duke contributed additional songs. By the end of the Depression, the revue format was fading fast.

How infinitely easier it was to compose a batch of good songs than to devise a libretto in which they could be logically fitted. The looser revue structure helped some marvelous songwriters excel outside the maddening constraints of the new book show. Cole Porter tried to make it with credible librettists. Mostly they succeeded *with* him, and he despite them. Porter's unrivaled capacity for sophistication naturally favored paper-thin librettos wrapped around the giddy, gilded environs of New York society night life. "Love for Sale" may stand as Porter's signature piece. First introduced in *The New Yorkers* in 1930, it was ordered off the airwaves for a time by radio executives. In night clubs and dance halls, though, the number soon enjoyed wide appeal and became an almost instant standard.

In a sense, most of the transient love about which Porter so sensually composed was likely informed by his own active though closeted homosexuality.[13] Even those who end up together in a Cole Porter musical seem bound to break apart— the lure of another illicit party up the street being too strong to resist. Interviewed by *American* magazine in 1935, Porter quipped, "I'm a hard working boy from Indiana, and I'm engaged in the business of entertaining myself, which enables me to entertain, as much as I can, the world."[14]

Anything Goes, Porter's finest work, is so rich in sky-crashing choruses ("Blow, Gabriel, Blow!"), in witty love anthems ("I Get a Kick Out of You," "You're the Top"), in lovely emotion ("All Through the Night"), that it stands almost alone in its triumphal completion. *Variety* termed it "a festival of lyrics, an engrossing

Opposite: Ziegfeld Follies star Fanny Brice, appearing in her last edition ('36), with Bob Hope in the skit "Baby Snooks Goes to Hollywood."

exhibition of poetic sleight of hand that looks very well indeed, but listens even better ... a funny book, smart dialogue, and a production that's worthy of all these things.... Miss Merman is 100% right ... a delicious poke at the gangster theme."[15] In Cole Porter, the American musical had found its most gifted one-person collaboration—that rare soul who creates both words and music.

Porter's 1939 offering, *DuBarry Was a Lady*, nearly matched the 400-plus performance run of *Anything Goes*. *Panama Hattie*, which opened at the 46th Street Theatre in 1940, topped it by 80 shows, and a Danny Kaye vehicle in 1941, *Let's Face It*, did even better. In between, there were the lackluster *Jubilee* and *Red, Hot & Blue*, followed by a solid hit, *Leave It to Me*, in which Mary Martin, making her Broadway debut, sang another Porter classic, "My Heart Belongs to Daddy."

And what of Richard Rodgers? In 1925, shortly following his contemplated career change to underwear salesman, he and Mr. Hart caught the elusive Broadway express at last. They did it by writing *Dearest Enemy*, followed by *The Girl Friend*, *Peggy Ann*, and *A Connecticut Yankee*. Then came a reason, or nine reasons, to reconsider the retail apparel market—*nine* flops in a row. And stints out in Tinseltown working on mostly forgettable movies after delivering up, in 1932, one flat-out classic, *Love Me Tonight*, which starred Jeannette MacDonald and Maurice Chevalier and gave the world "Isn't It Romantic" and "Mimi."

Then came 1935 and a Rodgers and Hart rebirth in the perilous form of *Jumbo*, a huge spectacular at the moribund Hippodrome that had been dark for five years, now rebuilt to resemble a circus arena. Produced by Billy Rose and directed by George Abbott and John Murray Anderson (who would one day direct the actual Ringling Bros. and Barnum & Bailey Circus), *Jumbo* spent more time in rehearsal— six months—than it did entertaining the public. It was so costly to operate that Rose shut it down after 233 showings. Still, *Jumbo* had the look and certainly the sound of a winner, and Rodgers and Hart were back in favor. For a spell, the invincible giants walked on water, as *On Your Toes* followed in 1936; *Babes in Arms* and *I'd Rather Be Right* in 1937; *I Married an Angel* and *The Boys from Syracuse* in 1938. *Too Many Girls*, which opened in 1939 with Eddie Bracken, Van Johnson and Desi Arnaz in its cast, surprised with a Latin-flavored score rather atypical, though not unexpected, for Rodgers and Hart.

They wrote to the popular tastes of the day, and they wrote so many songs so easily (and to such wildly vacillating standards), and were so adaptable to composing their way through constant script changes, that Rodgers once estimated their total output to be over one thousand songs, a few hundred of which, he surmised, had been discarded and lost forever.[16]

Rodgers and Hart delivered romantic books filled with agreeable everyday-type characters, and they preferred fast-paced productions, as did George Abbott, who sometimes co-wrote the book with Rodgers and Hart or Kaufman, other times stuck to the direction alone. Most of the shows remain barely revivable. Of the lot, *Jumbo's* score is the most hit-laden. *On Your Toes* utilized ballet for the first time to help tell the story, and Shakespeare got his start in singing and dancing shows, thanks to *The Boys from Syracuse*, a Rodgers and Hart musical, with a book by George Abbott, based on the bard's *A Comedy of Errors*. *Pal Joey* broke major new ground in musical theatre realism.

In that most prolific and magical period between 1936 and 1939, each of their six hits in a row easily topped 200 performances. Only four other new musicals (among them, *Hellzapoppin!* and *The Show Is On*) also exceeded the 200 mark during that time. The secret to their success? "Don't have a formula, and don't repeat it," they are said to have once remarked.[17]

The personal story behind Rodgers and Hart is more dramatic than anything they ever brought to the stage. Poor Larry, short of stature and with a head too large for his frame, all along suffered his own bitter loneliness, consecutively rejected in his romantic longings by women—or men, or even Richard Rodgers— depending on whose account you may wish to believe. He drove himself farther away from the people who should have mattered the most to him, drinking himself through lonely nights, cruising up bars and back alleys. Near the end, Rodgers would have to go out on rescue missions, tracking and pinning down his erratic drunken collaborator. Some of the lyrics were completed, if not entirely written, by Rodgers himself. Larry Hart "was about as varied a personality as you can possibly imagine," said Rodgers. "He was difficult in many ways, but never meant to be difficult. He was a sweet man. He was a very good man. He was a very kind man."[18]

Hart's attitude towards his craft grew ever more flippant. At work on *I Married an Angel*, he flabbergasted director Josh Logan by coming up with the irrelevant comedy show-stopper "At the Roxy Music Hall." Logan confronted Hart head on, protesting that the number would not fit the story's Budapest setting.

Explained Larry, "Oh, we'll just bring up the subject of New York and she'll start singing it."

"It has nothing to do with anything," argued Logan.

Shot back the cocky, confident Hart: "We've got to do something different, that's all, and give people a little fun. They'll forgive anything that's good!"[19]

Relevance to the libretto notwithstanding, is there a love song more perfectly realized, more truthful than Rodgers and Hart's "My Funny Valentine"? Anything funnier than their "To Keep My Love Alive"? The crippled team managed to produce some of their finest material towards the end of their prolific partnership, delivering, in 1940, one of the century's greatest musicals, *Pal Joey*. In a sense, Larry *had* finally found a property very close to his own non-romantic existence in bars and other sundry dives. "He had spent thousands of hours in exactly the kind of atmosphere depicted in the stories," wrote Rodgers in his book *Musical Stage*, "and was thoroughly familiar with the pal Joeys of this world."[20] Based on a series of short stories in the *New Yorker* by John O'Hara, *Pal Joey* tells the tale of a would-be club owner, Vera Simpson, who falls for a self-professed gigolo and pays for his companionship until it bores her. Hart never wrote more insightful lyrics.

By that time, Oscar Hammerstein—remember him?—was a flop-ridden loser.

After *Show Boat*, he had worked with Otto Harbach and Henry Myers on the book for the fairly successful *Good Boy*, which had music by Harry Ruby, Herbert Stothart, and Arthur Schwartz, lyrics by Bert Kalmar. The show's claim to fame was "I Wanna Be Loved By You," sung by Helen Kane, quickly dubbed the "Boop-Boop-A-Doop" girl. Three more money-making ventures followed: Hammerstein contributed the lyrics and co-wrote the book for Sigmund Romberg's *The New Moon*, which contained a very fine score ("Softly, As in a Morning Sunrise"). And with Jerome Kern he did both book and lyrics for *Sweet Adeline* in 1929, and, three years later, for *Music in the Air*, from which the world first heard "I've Told Every Little Star" and the rhapsodic "The Song Is You."

Throughout the rest of the thirties, Hammerstein stumbled through a humiliating series of box office blunders. Included among these was another worthy effort with Kern, the marginally pleasing *Very Warm for May*, which delivered a number deemed by jazz musicians and cabaret singers to be about the best song ever composed: "All The Things You Are." Hammerstein and Kern's most ambitious post–*Show Boat* effort was a Civil War musical, in collaboration with Otto Harbach on book and lyrics, *Gentlemen Unafraid*. It died after six tryout performances in St. Louis in 1938.

The once invincible duo could only lick their wounds while a rather thematically inconsequential spectacle of crowd-pandering vulgarity, *Hellzapoppin!*, starring the musical theatre's new reigning champs, Olsen & Johnson, racked up box office records in the late 1930s without any help from the critics. Its belligerently non-integrated score featured such soul-searching ditties as "Fuddle De Duddle" and "Boomps-A-Daisy."

From their newly humbled perspective, the former giants could watch George M. Cohan, now a living legend, return to the stage for the first time in ten years, cast reluctantly as Franklin Roosevelt in Rodgers and Hart's *I'd Rather Be Right*, the first show in which he appeared that he did not also write. Or they could marvel—or shake their heads in disbelief—over the sight of an anti-hero holding center stage in *Pal Joey*. Watching the success of others with more commercial properties or sexier productions while struggling to regain their own mastery, they sank deeper into the abyss of has-beens. Collaborating with Arthur Schwartz who composed the music, Oscar wrote the book and penned the words for *American Jubilee*, a patriotic pageant with a cast of 350 at the New York World's Fair of 1940. Following the dismal fold of *Very Warm for May*, Kern did not compose another score. Six years later, while in New York City attending auditions for a 1945 revival of *Show Boat*, Jerome Kern suffered a cerebral hemorrhage, fell to the street without any i.d. on his person, was driven to a derelict's facility on Welfare Island, and died alone among destitute strangers.

Oscar's World's Fair assignment gave us four anonymous numbers—"How Can I Ever Be Alone?", "My Bicycle Girl," "We Like It Over There" and "Tennessee Fish Fry." Washed up, out of touch, old-fashioned and clearly over the hill—so cried members of the cynical New Haven crowd. Three years later, however, he got back on his feet once again and sent the musical spinning off into uncharted territory. He would yet conquer the eternal infant with a mastery of libretto and lyric writing that to this day remains unsurpassed and with a showmanship that astonished possibly even himself. And this time, the whole world would follow.

CHAPTER 3

Lyrical Courage

Stars in the night
Blazing their light
Can't hold a candle
To your razzle-dazzle
— *E. Y. Harburg*

The New Haven Crowd—New Yorkers who would take the train up to Connecticut to see new musicals on their way to Broadway, jealously hoping to find turkeys-in-the-making to gloat over—must have found the 1940s an especially stressful decade, for during the war years most of the finest writers were at work. Innovation flourished. From fantasy to drama, from exotica to backwoods America, the decade produced a canon of musicals not before or since equaled. Call it the *golden* golden age.

At the forefront of excellence stood Richard Rodgers and his two successive collaborators, Lorenz Hart and Oscar Hammerstein II. First, Hart: Nearing the end of his troubled life, Hart found the inspiration to capture in musical theatre language the seedy world of night clubs and rented liaisons in a work of astonishing realism, *Pal Joey*. "Nothing was softened for the sake of making the characters more appealing," wrote Richard Rodgers. "Joey was a heel at the beginning and he never reformed. At the end the young lovers did not embrace…in fact, they walked off in opposite directions."[1] This was the score that gave the world such gems as "I Could Write a Book," "Zip," "Den of Iniquity" and "Bewitched, Bothered and Bewildered."

And here was the project that totally absorbed the otherwise erratic Hart. He did not stand Rodgers up at any of the work sessions. Most of the songs were completed in *three* weeks. And what a formidable accomplishment it was, so consistently fine in every category. In "What Do I Care for a Dame?" Rodgers and Hart experimented with the extended soliloquy, a refreshing departure from the stan-

32

Harold Lang and Vivienne Segal in the 1951 revival of *Pal Joey*.

dard AABA song structure. The song segued excitingly into a ballet, with the music erupting into a jumbled cacophony of big city street noises during rush-hour— the sort of sound tapestry that Leonard Bernstein would employ years later in two musicals set in New York city.

Pal Joey's bleak anti-hero theme, judged by Abel Green of *Variety* "perhaps the major negative aspect to what otherwise is an otherwise amusing musical comedy,"[2] did not find instant favor with everyone, even though a majority of critics endorsed it and it ran for 374 performances at the Ethel Barrymore Theatre. Cecil Wilson of the *London Daily Mail* found "a slyness and sophistication rarely encountered in a musical comedy."[3] Brooks Atkinson, who would later recant, is rumored to have caused Hart particular anguish by his terse dismissal: "Although *Pal Joey* is expertly done, can you draw sweet water from a foul well?"[4] It would take ten more years of like-minded efforts to earn *Joey* the complete and widespread acclaim it deserved. Jule Styne brought it back to Broadway in 1952, where it handily topped its original run. Now, the reviews were unanimously favorable. "I am happy to report," wrote Richard Watts, Jr., "that the famous musical comedy is every bit as brilliant, fresh, and delightful as it seemed when it set new standards for its field over ten years ago." Now, others, at last, concurred. Now Brooks Atkinson saw the unsparing frankness of it all with belated praise: "It tells an integrated story with a knowing point of view…. Brimming over with good music and fast on its toes, *Pal Joey* renews confidence in the professionalism of the theatre."[5]

Three seasons later came a new rural realism through the resurrected Oscar Hammerstein, who transformed his talent and fate by teaming up with Richard Rodgers to write the legendary *Oklahoma!* Just what drove the new collaborators to believe they could conquer the box office with the tale of a farm girl agonizing over competing invitations from two men for a box social may never be known. Was it sheer inspiration from the play by Lynn Riggs upon which it was based, *Green Grow the Lilacs?* When first presented by the prestigious Theatre Guild in 1931, that play ran a paltry 64 performances. Or was it the driving foresight of the Guild's Theresa "Terry" Helburn, who, after attending the opening night performance of the 1940 revival of *Lilacs*, shared with cast members backstage a sudden desire to turn it into a musical? Or perhaps the burning determination of has-been Hammerstein to resurrect himself? With Richard Rodgers, whose current resume was far more impressive, Hammerstein approached the farmyard story with calm fidelity. Instead of raising the curtain on the usual stage full of dancing girls, the new collaborators arrived at "an extraordinary decision," in the words of Hammerstein. "We agreed to start our story in the real and natural way in which it seemed to want to be told."[6] That meant the curtain would go up on the seated lone figure of old Aunt Eller, pumping away at a butter churn, while Curly, offstage at first, sang about a glorious haze rising over the meadow in "Oh, What a Beautiful Morning!"

On the wings of Hammerstein's new-found poetry, the entire play soared. On the road to New York, where it first played under the title *Away We Go*, the show's disregard for conventions—the oddly quiet opening scene, for example—tickled the New Haven crowd who, despite noticeable audience pleasure up in Connecticut, smugly reported back to their smart friends with smirking it's-a-flop glee, "No girls, no gags, no good."[7] How wrong the cynics were. *Oklahoma!* established beyond resistance the template for the integrated musical. Overnight, Oscar Hammerstein's lyric writing skills went from b+ to a+. The Riggs play gave him the kind of middle–America characters with whom he identified, realizing a kind of rural rapture in such perfect refrains as "The Surrey with the Fringe on the Top," "People Will Say We're in Love," and "Out of My Dreams."

And hounded, some said, by likely comparisons to Larry Hart, Hammerstein delivered humorous verse in such surprises as "I Can't Say No" and "Poor Jud Is Dead," the latter a tongue-in-cheek lament for a corpse fast fouling the air.

Virtually all the words came *first*, another drastic departure from the way such collaborations were usually run. Rodgers felt that working from this direction gave his music a more serious quality. What it gave Hammerstein was greater control over his own creative instincts, since he no longer answered to the set structure of already-composed music. Typically in the new R&H arrangement, a lyric that would take Hammerstein two or three weeks to write, once placed in typed form on Rodgers' piano, would have a tune within minutes. Together they created a new standard of excellence for musical theatre, imbuing the form with two attributes that would characterize almost everything they did: craftsmanship and magic.

Only a few hours before the show's New York opening at the St. James Theatre on March 31, 1943, Oscar took a walk with his wife Dorothy on a country road in Dolyestown. Haunted by the memory of the five previous musical shows upon which he had worked, all failures, he confessed, "I don't know what to do if they don't like this. I don't know what to do because this is the only kind of a show I can write."[8]

Oklahoma raised its inaugural curtain on a more hospitable era for Mr. Hammerstein. "Within ten minutes" of its opening, wrote Brooks Atkinson in his book *Broadway*, "a Broadway audience was transported out of the ugly realities of wartime into a warm, languorous, shining time and place where the only problems were simple and wholesome, and the people uncomplicated and joyous. The opening song seemed like a distillation of something that had been hovering in the air since life began on earth."[9]

"It has, as a rough estimate, practically everything," reported John Anderson. "*Oklahoma* really is different—beautifully different," declared Burns Mantle. "With songs that Richard Rodgers has fitted to a collection of unusually atmospheric and intelligible lyrics by Oscar Hammerstein II, *Oklahoma* seems to me the most thoroughly and attractively American musical comedy since Edna Ferber's *Show Boat*."

Still, *Oklahoma* did not completely escape the ill will of the New Haven crowd in at least one of the reviews, this one by Wilella Waldorf for the *Post*, who was not bowled over by its "old fashioned charm," and went on to elaborate, "For a while last night, it all seemed just a trifle too cute.... A flock of Mr. Rodgers's songs that are pleasant enough but still manage to sound quite a bit alike, are warbled in front of Laurey's farmhouse, one after another, without much variety in presentation. It was all very picturesque in a studied fashion, reminding us that life on a farm is apt to become a little tiresome."[10]

This "tiresome" picture was actually a triumph, whose old fashioned charm kept it on the boards for the unprecedented record of 2,248 shows. More importantly, *Oklahoma* signaled a tectonic shift in musical theatre plates; it pushed the integrated book show into maturity. Many people now viewed operetta as old hat, failing to credit its logical evolution into the book musical (unlike the *Variety* reviewer, who in a positive notice fittingly declared *Oklahoma* "further proof that the operetta form of musical show is still, and probably will continue to be, part of Broadway's fare").[11] Even Brooks Atkinson displayed an irrational disdain for the earlier form whenever he crossed its path in a new work, walking out on the opening in 1948 of Sigmund Romberg's roundly panned *My Romance*.

Oklahoma was anything but simplified operetta. Mr. Hammerstein presented two divergent worlds moving ahead on parallel tracks—the romantic one of Laurey

and Curly, blessed by good looks and promising futures; the other, the barren existence of a clumsy loner and menacing misfit, Jud Fry, who can only dream of amorous embraces. Laurey agrees to attend a box social with Fry only because she has had a momentary tiff with Curly, whom she really loves. In the end, Fry's anguish is multiplied by the realization of it all. In "Lonely Room," Hammerstein paints a chilling portrait of Fry's harrowing social isolation, trapped in a creaky old shack full of field mice scuttling about for crumbs, and feeling as inconsequential as a cobweb.

Jud Fry's plight invests the show with a sobering realism which many still overlook; indeed, from Fry's harrowing vantage point we see how precarious are the time-bound illusions of the young lovers. People might say they are in love, and they might be. They might also end up in their own lonely rooms. In a frightening sense, most of us live in personal fear of Jud Fry's fate. In the end, the vengeful Fry crashes Curly and Laurey's wedding, gets into a fight with his rival, and is accidentally killed with the knife he pulls on Curly.

Death stalks the most memorable Rodgers and Hammerstein shows, almost like a saving grace sparing each from terminal sweetness. In *Carousel*, their next work, Dick and Oscar pursued a similar social dichotomy, and once again they excelled with a love story between unequals. Julie Jordan succumbs to the crude charms of a carousel barker, Billy Bigelow, whose meager livelihood is supplemented by his gigolo association with the carousel owner. A triangle keeps the three in a tango between true and kept love. All the complex questions that arise over the ill-fated choice of mates form the fascinating bedrock of this masterwork, based on Ferenc Molnár's play *Liliom*, which had originally been produced in Budapest in 1909, then by the Theatre Guild in 1921. Rodgers would call *Carousel* his personal favorite.

Hammerstein's extended "Soliloquy," a work of profound stature, charts the transformation of Bigelow from an out-of-work drifter growing restless in marriage, to a new man of conscience as he faces the prospects of fatherhood. At first Billy proudly anticipates raising a son. Then he wonders, in a state of shock, what he will do if the child is a girl.

So overwhelmed does Bigelow become with the contemplated responsibility, that he is murdered during an attempted robbery to raise money for his expected daughter. In the original play Billy returns to earth as a beggar, granted the brief visit by Providence for the purpose of performing a good deed. He only causes more mischief and harm—hardly the way to end a musical, in the opinion of Dick and Oscar. This lead them to interpolate the graduation scene, a device of their own making wherein Billy's daughter, Louise, realizes self-worth through the inspiring "You'll Never Walk Alone."

Among the ringing endorsements *Carousel* received, possibly none was more perceptive or eloquent than that of John Chapman, who wrote, "One of the finest

Opposite: "The Farmer and the Cowman" in *Oklahoma* featured dancers Marc Platt and Rhoda Hoffman.

musical plays I have seen and I shall remember it always. It has everything the professional theatre can give it—and something besides: heart, integrity, an inner glow—I don't know just what to call it…. *Carousel* is tender, rueful, almost tragic, and does not fit the pattern of musical comedy, operetta, opera bouffe, or even opera. Those looking for a happy and foolish evening had better go elsewhere…. The zip, the pace, the timing of the ordinary musical are not in it, but if offers stirring rewards for the listener who will adapt himself to the slower progression and let it tell and sing its story in its own way."[12]

Other composers and lyric writers were inspired by the bold achievements of both Hart and Hammerstein to forge their own more deeply felt theatrical visions, and together they made the 1940s a particularly enchanting era.

German-born Kurt Weill put his political leanings on hold in the early forties to create a couple of commercially accessible pieces. First stop: the analyst's couch. Weill tackled the jaded ambivalence of a wealthy neurotic who spends more time with her head shrink than she does with a trio of suitors among whom she is having a devil of a time choosing. The lyrics were by Ira Gershwin, the libretto by a real-life survivor of the couch, Moss Hart. *Lady in the Dark*, the result, managed to pull some effective theatre songs from Weill and Gershwin at a time when Freud was in vogue and when perhaps half of the audience was in psychoanalysis. The show's then-fascinating premise kept it at the Alvin Theatre for a fine stay.

Another profitable collaboration for Mr. Weill was the light-hearted fantasy *One Touch of Venus*, about a statue of Venus coming alive when an admiring barber places a ring on its finger. Poet Ogden Nash wrote the lyrics and worked on the book with S. J. Perelman. It opened in 1943, six months after *Oklahoma's* premiere, at the Imperial Theatre. In the cast was Mary Martin, making her first starring role in a Broadway show and introducing to the world, from a score rich in rueful sophistication and enchanting melody, one of the most haunting ballads ever written:

> Speak low when you speak love
> Our summer day withers away
> Too soon, too soon
> Speak low when you speak love
> Our moment is swift
> Like ships adrift
> We're swept apart too soon
>
> Speak low, darling, speak low
> Love is a spark
> Lost in the dark
> Too soon, too soon
> I fear wherever I go
> That tomorrow is near
> Tomorrow is here
> And always too soon

Time is so old
And love so brief
Love is pure gold
And time a thief

We're late, darling, we're late
The curtain descends
Everything ends
Too soon, too soon
I wait, darling, I wait
Will you speak low to me
Speak love to me
And soon

One Touch drew strong critical favor, with *Variety's* Abel Green calling it a "musical smash," its score "brilliant," and predicting that "Speak Low" would become Weill's "most durable ditty."[13] Louis Kronenberger, typically in step with his colleagues, wrote, "Whatever is wrong with it, *One Touch of Venus* is an unhackneyed and imaginative musical that spurns the easy formulas of Broadway, that has personality and wit and genuinely high moments of music and dancing."[14]

During the war years, Americans preferred uplifting entertainment, and a number of New York–centered writers reached out beyond their normal milieu in an effort to connect with the population at large. While Irving Berlin had turned out a workable revue, *This Is the Army*, Cole Porter composed two second-drawer offerings of timely appeal based on the lives of ordinary soldiers and their spouses or girlfriends. The first was *Let's Face It*, which gave Danny Kaye, its undisputed star, his first big starring role, and which he kept on the boards for 547 performances. The second was a schmaltzy Ethel Merman package without a hit song to its name, *Something for the Boys*, which at least proved that Mr. Porter might be able to function a few miles away from Gotham glitz and decay.

All rather pedestrian stuff, cheerfully executed by big name entertainers. Fortunately, there were younger writers with fresh ambitions who found ample drama and comedy in the plight of servicemen and the lives of those they touched. Leonard Bernstein, Adolph Green and Betty Comden launched their careers in musical theatre with a work of rare exuberance and sass, *On the Town*, the story of three sailors about to ship out and wishing for one last evening of romance, American style. Bernstein borrowed on themes from his symphonic work *Fancy Free*, weaving some into individual songs. Stand-up comics Comden and Green supplied taut attractive lyrics, by turns gutsy, sensitive and hilarious.

We've got one day here and not another minute
To see the famous sights!
We'll find the romance and danger waiting in it
Beneath the Broadway lights
And we've hair on our chest
So what we like the best are the nights
Sights! Lights! Nights!

New York, New York—a helluva town
The Bronx is up—and the Battery's down
The people ride in a hole in the groun'
New York—New York—it's a helluva town!

Manhattan women are dressed in silk and satin
Or so the fellas say
There's just one thing that's important in Manhattan
When you have just one day
Gotta pick up a date
Maybe seven—
Or eight—
On your way—
In just one day.

"I Get Carried Away" was a laugh-fest. And if "New York, New York!" made
the city seem like the most exciting place on the face of the earth, "A Lonely Town"
turned it into a skyscraper canyon of haunting isolation. And in the end, when
the sailors went off to war and their one-night girlfriends were left to ponder a
night of temporary romance just ended, there was the painfully pensive "Some
Other Time."

Oh, what an inspiring war it was. And after it was over, the very talented and
sensitive Harold Rome found the words to evoke the mixed emotions that people
faced in its aftermath—after the boys came home and everyone had to adjust. Rome
cast his *Call Me Mister* with many ex–G.I.s and U.S.O. entertainers. He wrote:

It's a beautiful day, ain't it?
So exciting and gay, ain't it?
There's a beautiful hue in the beautiful blue
CALL ME MISTER!

Lovely weather we've got, ain't it?
Not too cold or too hot, ain't it?
There's a beautiful breeze in the beautiful trees
CALL ME MISTER!

There's a lift in the air;
There's a song ev'ry where;
There's a tang in,
A bang in just living
Da-di-ah-da-da

It's a beautiful time, ain't it?
All the world is in rhyme, ain't it?
It's a beautiful shore
From New Jersey to Oregon
Just call me Mister
Be so kindly, call me Mister
Just CALL ME MISTER FROM NOW ON!

"Take It Away" was Latin all the way. "The Red Ball Express" referenced the forgotten plight of returning African-American servicemen. "Vitality and finesse are blended happily in *Call Me Mister*," wrote Howard Barnes in the *Herald Tribune*. "This G.I. show about G.I. Joes is something of a boisterous romp as it takes satirical cognizance of military life, problems of reconversion, Park Avenue, the deep South, and even South American dances.... The Rome music and lyrics are as excellent as they are varied."[15]

Other writers found their music in the new post-war euphoria and emerging prosperity. In the last of seven revues they wrote together, Arthur Schwartz and Howard Dietz celebrated down-home America, all of it outside the city limits of New York, New York, in their lively if limited *Inside the U.S.A.* Light satirical touches seasoned the upbeat festivities, one being a stop in Pittsburgh, site of industrial pollution being challenged by a choral society. The title song captures the innocent patriotism of those celebratory days—the rights of free and equal people to speak their minds, to worship freely and to join the political parties of their choices.

Another new team of Rodgers & Hammerstein–style romantics were Alan Jay Lerner and Frederick Loewe who after two flops finally took Broadway, with *Brigadoon*, the recipient of seven unqualified raves when it opened on March 13, 1947 at the Ziegfeld Theatre. Lerner and Loewe had helped raise the $150,000 needed to finance it by performing the score at *fifty-eight* backer's auditions, the final one pitched during the show's third day in rehearsal. *Brigadoon* took its patrons on a walk up a winding path into a world that has sadly all but vanished.

> Can't we two go walkin' together,
> Out beyond the valley of trees,
> Out where there's a hillside of heather
> Curtseyin' gently in the breeze?
> That's what I'd like to do:
> See the heather—but with you.
>
> The mist of May is in the gloamin',
> And all the clouds are holding still.
> So take my hand and let's go roamin'
> Through the heather on the hill.
>
> The mornin' dew is blinkin' yonder;
> There's lazy music in the rill;
> And all I want to do is wander
> Through the heather on the hill.
>
> There may be other days as rich and rare;
> There may be other springs as full and fair;
> But they won't be the same—they'll come and go;
> For this I know:

Left to right: George Keane, David Brooks, and William Hansen in *Brigadoon.*

That when the mist is in the gloamin',
And all the clouds are holdin' still,
If you're not there I won't go roamin'
Through the heather on the hill,
The heather on the hill.

Less misty-eyed was Irving Berlin's 1946 triumph *Annie Get Your Gun*. It was produced by none other than Richard Rodgers and Oscar Hammerstein II, whose looming presence seems to have inspired Berlin to new heights. He created a set of songs amounting to almost one standard after another: "I Got the Sun in the Morning," "Doin' What Comes Natur'lly," "The Girl That I Marry," "They Say It's Wonderful" "You Can't Get a Man with a Gun," "There's No Business Like Show Business," "I Got Lost in His Arms," "Anything You Can Do" and "I'm an Indian, Too." (Contrary to myth, however, only two—not nine—of the songs made it into Hit Parade territory: "Doin' What Comes Natur'lly" and "They Say It's Wonderful."[16]) With a book expertly crafted by Dorothy and Herbert Fields, *Annie Get Your Gun* held court at the Imperial Theatre for over one thousand performances.

When Mr. Berlin returned to the Imperial a few years later, hoping to duplicate his Annie Oakley success with a new show starring the Statue of Liberty, patriotic sentiment got the better of him and *Miss Liberty* proved only moderately diverting. It did contain the moving "Give Me Your Tired, Your Poor" and the exhilarating waltz "Let's Take an Old Fashioned Walk." But theatergoers in 1949 were not too moved by a contrived story about two rival newspapers caught up in a competitive search for the model who posed for the Statue of Liberty. Among a slate of wildly mixed notices from raves to pans, Richard Watts, Jr., wrote, "It is pleasant, good looking, tuneful, and surprisingly commonplace."[17] *Miss Liberty* generated one Tony Award, for a stage technician, Joe Lynn.

Unless they could make 'em laugh, could lift them with song and dance, they couldn't much expect to move the audience with messages. When the war was over, Kurt Weill returned to his lecture podium and faltered, if nobly, through a series of morosely dramatic works. *Street Scene*, a 1947 entry, sounds all too similar in setting and tone to *Porgy and Bess*. A tale of ghettoland adultery replete with murder, it is honestly conveyed in songs very good but very depressing, with an added layer of suffocation supplied by the darkly brooding lyrics of American poet Langston Hughes. Surely the lyrics did not help Mr. Weill to compose any particularly memorable melodies for the average theatre patron. The show was doted on by critics ("his masterpiece," exuded Brooks Atkinson;[18] "Taut, tuneful and moving," raved *Variety*), avoided by the public.[19]

One year later, Mr. Weill took on Alan Jay Lerner, and they moved ahead with the problematic *Love Life*, a vehicle both praised and scorned by the reviews. Several of its songs, available on vinyl, are consistently bad. Weill's next offering, *Lost in the Stars*, with mediocre lyrics by Maxwell Anderson, proved to be yet another naggingly uneven venture that split the critics and attracted hardly a soul. Set in racially divided

Ethel Merman plays Annie Oakley in *Annie Get Your Gun.*

South Africa, as with so many of Weill's works the heavy-handed polemics evidently left theatre patrons feeling more like parishioners facing a stern pastor. The "profitable box office success"[20] projected by *Variety* amounted to 28 performances.

Weill wasn't the only artist sympathetic to social injustice. Another venture featuring the downtrodden was *St. Louis Woman*, a notable flop with excellent songs. *Carousel* director Rouben Mamoulian could not save the downbeat affair, the labor of co-writers Arna Bontemps and Countee Cullen adapting Bontemps's novel, *God Sends Sunday*. Not at the Martin Beck Theatre, he didn't, where *St. Louis Woman* drew generally unfavorable notices and lasted only a few months. "Too much drama and not enough laughs,"[21] wrote a skeptical *Variety* critic. "The story is obvious and commonplace, with a certain folk-operatic flavor," wrote Louis Kronenberger, "but without the proper operatic sell and excitement.... The show rations its fun very skimpily."[22] Served without rations, however, were the wonderful contributions of lyricist Johnny Mercer and composer Harold Arlen—illustrating once again how remarkably unsuccessful a great score can be when straddled to an abysmally uninviting libretto. Among the gems, there was this:

> Free an' easy—that's my style
> Howdy do me, watch me smile
> Fare thee well me after while
> 'Cause I gotta roam
> An' any place I hang my hat is home
>
> Sweetnin' water; cherry wine
> Thank you kindly, suits me fine
> Kansas City, Caroline
> That's my honey comb
> 'Cause any place I hang my hat is home
>
> Birds roostin' in the trees
> Pick up an' go
> And the goin' proves
> That's how it ought to be
> I pick up, too
> When the spirit moves me
>
> Cross the river; round the bend
> Howdy, stranger; so long, friend
> There's a voice in the lonesome win'
> That keeps a whisperin' roam
> I'm goin' where the welcome mat is
> No matter where that is
> Cause any place I hang my hat is home

Lena Horne withdrew during out-of-town tryouts, complaining openly to the press, "It sets the negro back one hundred years ... is full of gamblers, no goods, etc., and I'll never play a part like that."[23] Sorrowfully, Cullen, a promising Harlem poet, died two days before rehearsals began.

A decade of giants—some of them old pros finding fresh inspiration, others just breaking in. E. Y. Harburg, who grew up on the East Side next to the East River—"with all the derelicts, docks, lots of sailors and gangs"[24]—shared Kurt Weill's compassion for society's oppressed classes. Luckily for Harburg, he possessed a flair for crowd-pleasing satire and rhyme. With Harold Arlen, he crafted in 1944 *Bloomer Girl*, based on an unpublished play by Lilith and Dan James about the design of the hoop skirt by radical feminist Evelina Applegate at the time of the Civil War. The lovely atmospheric score produced by Arlen and Harburg—containing such delights as "The Eagle and Me," "When the Boys Come Home," and "Right As the Rain"—strangely did not reflect the show's two most dramatic conflicts, the freeing of a family slave in the Deep South and the outbreak of the Civil War.

For the movies Harburg had written the classic "Brother Can You Spare a Dime" and had penned all the marvelous lyrics for *The Wizard of Oz*. So, following *Bloomer Girl*, back to Hollywood in the forties he traveled in search of more sunshine, palm trees and movie work. Instead, the proud life-long defender of progressive causes landed on the blacklist, a sobering experience that hastened his early return to New York City. Hollywood's loss was Broadway's gain. Harburg teamed up with Burton Lane in 1947 to create one of the finest scores ever, the heaven-sent *Finian's Rainbow*. Harburg based the meandering libretto, which he wrote with Fred Saidy, on an idea of his own about a group of sharecroppers struggling to retain possession of their land and turning to a leprechaun for magical help.

One thing remains certain: The Lane and Harburg numbers—among them "How Are Things in Glocca Morra?" and "Look to the Rainbow"—overflow with wonder, wit and scrumptious melody.

> I look at you and suddenly
> Something in your eyes I see
> Soon begins bewitching me
> It's that old devil moon
> That you stole from the skies
> It's that old devil moon
> In your eyes
>
> You and your glance
> Make this romance
> Too hot to handle
> Stars in the night
> Blazing their light
> Can't hold a candle
> To your razzle dazzle
>
> You've got me flying high and wide
> On a magic carpet ride
> Full of butterflies inside

Wanna cry, wanna croon
Wanna laugh like a loon
It's that old devil moon
In your eyes

Just when I think I'm
Free as a dove
Old devil moon
Deep in your eyes
Blinds me with love.

Harburg's singular genius for playful rhyming—technically an extension of a similar though less developed Ira Gershwin bent—took wry liberties with word spellings:

Ev'ry femme that flutters by me
Is a flame that must be fanned
When I can't fondle the hand that I'm fond of
I fondle the hand at hand

My heart's in a pickle
It's constantly fickle
And not too partickle, I fear
When I'm not near the girl I love
I love the girl I'm near

What if they're tall or tender
What if they're small or slender
Long as they've got that gender
I s'rrender

Always I can't refuse 'em
Always my feet pursues 'em
Long as they've got a "boo-som"
I woos 'em

"Excuse my rave review," wrote Robert Garland, one of five enchanted first-night reviewers, "but—this is it. The brand new musical has everything a grand new musical should have.... *Finian's Rainbow* is something about which to rave, an answer to a theatergoer's prayers. It has the genius which is the result of the taking of infinite plans. The story has fact and fancy. The lyrics are racy and romantic. The music is melodious and modern. And the production—direction, scenery, costumes, choreography—is fresh and effective."[25]

So many fine new shows drew inspiration directly from the war years or from their positive impact on American culture. Even jaded Cole Porter, who had spun most of his magic through an almost endless cycle of glib revues and silly book contrivances, surprised everyone by rising to the challenge of the new integrated book show when he composed the score for *Kiss Me Kate*, based on Shakespeare's *The Taming of the Shrew*. Silly and fun and theatrical, yes. Also a literate work of the newer musical theatre pattern that would enjoy numerous revivals in the years ahead. It has a very good script, and its songs are knockouts: "Another Opening," "Why Can't You Behave?" "Always True to You," "Too Darn Hot," "So in Love," "Wunderbar." The critics all fell glowingly in line. Stated Brooks Atkinson, "Occasionally by some baffling miracle, everything seems to drop gracefully into its appointed place in the composition of a song show, and that is the case here."[26]

At a time late in the glorious forties when new songwriters were beginning to make their own marks—Frank Loesser with *Where's Charley?*, Jule Styne and Leo Robin with *Gentlemen Prefer Blondes*—old pros Oscar Hammerstein and Dick Rodgers looked back over the war years as depicted in a best-selling novella from first-time author James Michener, and they delivered yet a third full-blooded masterpiece, *South Pacific*. It was their only show ever to earn a perfect set of raves. Never was musical theatre more down-to-earth or up in the clouds, more challenging or corny or exhilarating or political all at the same magnificent moment, than when Mary Martin, playing a young American nurse courted by an older Frenchman, sang exuberantly of her love for a wonderful guy.

CHAPTER 4

On to the Hit Parade

Out of sleek new high fidelity sets in the chrome-plated 1950s blasted a big-band fanfare. Then came the swinging voice of authority crooning:

> Night and day you are the one,
> Only you beneath the moon and under the sun.
> Whether near to me or far,
> It's no matter, darling, where you are,
> I think of you night and day.
>
> Day and night why is it so
> That this longing for you follows wherever I go?
> In the roaring traffic's boom,
> In the silence of my lonely room,
> I think of you night and day.

Frank Sinatra was reinventing a Cole Porter classic on his long-playing album *A Swinging Affair*, masterfully arranged and conducted by Nelson Riddle. Sinatra's sizzling journey through 15 numbers from the great American songbook featured many from stage shows: "Night and Day," originally composed for Fred Astaire, was from Porter's *Gay Divorcée*; two other Porter gems, "At Long Last Love" and "From This Moment On," from two Porter flops, *You Never Know* and *Out Of This World*. "I Wish I Were in Love Again" hailed from Rodgers and Hart's *Babes in Arms*; "I Won't Dance" from Kern's *Roberta*, "I Got Plenty of Nothing" from Gershwin's *Porgy and Bess*.

Typical for a singer of the day, Sinatra, who had grown up during the war years in that most melodic of musical theatre decades, turned show songs into Hit Parade favorites.

Through the golden age of musicals when composers regularly aimed a good portion of their work at radio markets, hundreds of songs destined for popularity

49

would come from shows that lost money. Hummable tunes would always be easier for writers to produce than the scripts capable of joining them in narrative wedlock. This still-perplexing paradox goes back at least to the turn of the century when producers, with their eyes on the audience, assembled shows like candy merchants offering samplers. Script continuity was often nonexistent.

To illustrate: The contract for Ukulele Ike (Cliff Edwards) to appear in Jerome Kern's 1925 hit *Sunny* stipulated that Edwards would perform his specialty act between 10 and 10:15 P.M., so the script had to be tailored to facilitate the eccentric agreement.[1] Numerous composers were randomly engaged to provide song interpolations. That is how they, not offended in the least, made their living.

Things changed by the 1950s, when a composer who would not or could not function in both spheres—theatre scoring and popular music—was likely doomed to failure. No wonder the stage show eluded the grasp of more than a few talented pop songwriters, who lost their footing in the tricky zone where story and song must intersect with persuasive force. None seems to have been more vexed in his desire to master it than the prodigiously unsuccessful Vernon Duke, a superb melodist justly revered by many, and most famously remembered for "Autumn in New York." That song came out of a 1934 disappointment, *Thumbs Up*, that went thumbs down quickly, even with the comedy team of Bobby Clark and Paul McCullough in the cast. The words, written by Duke as well, are as eloquent as the melody itself, evoking so unapologetically the urban poetry of the huge metropolis.

Of the fourteen complete show scores that Vernon Duke composed, only three were attached to successful ventures. His known refusal to compromise personal standards for commercial considerations did not help. Only a precious few of Duke's songs—among them "Taking a Chance on Love," "Irresistible You," and "April in Paris"—became standards. His only full score available for near-complete perusal is 1940's *Cabin in the Sky*, full of generously endowed compositions from early soul to blues to swing, all given a fine boost by John Latouche's splendid lyrics. And without the fine songs Duke wrote with lyric writer Ogden Nash for the 1955 off-Broadway fizzle *The Littlest Revue*, on which a number of other songwriters labored, the score would not have amounted to much at all.

Very little of Vernon Duke's music, unfortunately, made it onto vinyl, so we are left to ponder the enthusiasms of his professional admirers, one being the late revue and record producer Ben Bagley, who called Duke flat-out the finest theatre composer ever,[2] but whose "Revisited" album of some unknown Duke songs unintentionally conveys otherwise. Only a few of the numbers rise above the pleasantly mediocre to match the Bagley ballyhoo. The star discovery is surely "Words Without Music," written with an Ira Gershwin lyric for *Ziegfeld Follies of 1936*.

Even then, a talent for reaching the Hit Parade was rarely enough. There were numerous songsmiths who also found musical theatre a journey fraught with heartache and failure. Blame it, as they usually did, on ill-conceived librettos hastily mashed together, sometimes to showcase a cache of undiscovered gems from some composer's trunk.

Pop king Leroy Anderson struck out in his two attempts at stage fame. *Wonderful Town* was originally to have been composed by Anderson, with lyrics by Arnold Horwitt—until the composer ran into creative disharmony with the authors, one of them Joseph Fields (also the director), the other Jerome Chodorov. The assignment ended up on the piano of Leonard Bernstein, where trusted cohorts Comden and Green gathered to apply their amusing verse.

Anderson's only Broadway outing to reach opening night, where it clung to the boards of the Lunt Fontanne Theatre like an unwanted house guest for five months, was the much anticipated *Goldilocks*. A leading drama critic, Walter Kerr, was one of its writers. On balance, Anderson composed, in the Anderson vein, a few very appealing numbers, on which, unfortunately, rode the amateurish words it took not one, not even two, but three writers to produce—John Ford, Walter and Jean Kerr. Notwithstanding the hackneyed verse, Anderson's "Lazy Moon" was a toe-tapping charmer in the older Kern style. So were "Give the Little Lady" and "The Pussy Foot." Anderson's delightful tunes would never grace another Broadway stage. A pity.

Another popular songwriter not lucky on 42nd Street was lyric genius Johnny Mercer, whose finest work ("Laura," "Skylark," "Something's Gotta Give" among countless treasures) was written for film or records. On stage projects, his talents tended to dissipate under the demands of narrative and character. His only Broadway success was *Li'l Abner*, written with composer Gene De Paul. He had earlier contributed both music and lyrics for the Phil Silvers 1951 almost-hit, *Top Banana*. With five raves on the marquee, it was a profit maker with a future—until Silvers took a much needed summer vacation and audiences decided to boycott his replacement, Jack Carter. Producers Paula Stone and Mike Sloan lost so much money while Silvers was out relaxing that they had to close down *Banana* before he could return.

Mercer courted anonymity with composer Robert Emmett Dolan on two varied offerings. The first, *Texas Li'l Darling*, was a work full of engaging songs not only forgotten but ignored by most tuner tomes. Perhaps it simply got lost in the late 1940s shuffle when shows like *South Pacific* were opening. According to *Variety*, which spotted strong commercial prospects out of town but which deemed the show on opening night not yet ready for Broadway, "deplorable" direction and production doomed an "amusing" book, "standout lyrics" and "several sure fire hit hummers"[3]—all greeted acrimoniously by six pans, one favorable notice and one no-opinion. And still, it lasted for 300 performances.

With the same obscure composer, Mercer embarked fourteen years later on another musical, *Foxy*, adapted loosely from Ben Johnson's 1616 play *Volpone* and conceived as a vehicle for Bert Lahr, who quibbled endlessly with the writers over his constant improvisations. Despite moments of hilarity, promising reviews, and a Tony for the aging clown star, the Bert Lahr show depended too much on Lahr, whose popularity with the public by then was well on the wane. Producer David Merrick closed down after 72 underattended performances.

Mercer's best work by far was with composer Harold Arlen. Their rich contributions to the 1946 box office yawner *St. Louis Woman*, a work fraught with book problems and a gloomy similarity to *Porgy and Bess*, included the aforequoted "Any Place I Hang My Hat Is Home," as well as "Leavin' Time," "Riding on the Moon," "Come Rain or Come Shine," and, before it was dropped, the pensive "I Wonder What Became of Me," later recorded by Lena Horne. In 1959, Mercer returned to Broadway with a fine set of tunes for *Saratoga*, a new musical plagued with too many settings, revengeful characters and leaden pacing, according to flop show coroner Ken Mandelbaum.[4]

For Johnny Mercer, the big Broadway hit remained forever out of reach. Once during an interview while praising shows like *West Side Story* and *The King and I*, he remarked, "Wouldn't it be wonderful, to come in with a show like that? But it's tough as hell to come by one, I can tell you ... so I'll just keep looking."[5]

Bright attractive tunes—even great scores—are no guarantee against inept materials or confusingly wrought stagings. Contained in the Vincent Youmans 1929 effort *Great Day* (dubbed "great delay" owing to prolonged out-of-town rewrites and personnel changes) are three of the composer's finest creations, the title number, "More Than You Know" and "Without a Song." All of which caused Alan Jay Lerner to lament, "No failure in the history of Broadway ever produced so many great songs."[6]

One thing that *Jamaica*, another Harold Arlen musical with plenty to sing about, could not be accused of was stilted pacing or confusing locales. For this modestly profitable 1957 David Merrick contrivance, Arlen turned back to E.Y. Harburg, with whom he had worked in the past on *Bloomer Girl* and the film classic *The Wizard of Oz*. They devised an offering full of poetry, sensuality, and typical Harburg anti-consumerism satire. They may, in fact, have been headed up a better runway before Harry Belafonte, for whom the work was conceived, fell ill and withdrew. Drastic revisions were made to facilitate Belafonte's replacement, *Lena Horne*—yes, that's the kind of a show this was—against the grudging cooperation of two flabbergasted writers, co-librettists Harburg and Fred Saidy. Ms. Horne, three raves, a book that stayed out of Horne's way and some strong musical payoffs kept *Jamaica* on the Imperial Theatre marquee for well into the next season. As they sometimes say, *that's* entertainment.

What might have passed in earlier times—miscellaneous jokes, leggy high-kicking dames, interpolated songs—came upon increasingly less forgiving audiences and critics into the "golden age." The "integrated book" came to represent the expected standard. Songwriters faced a more daunting task: how to make their material both textually relevant and commercially viable. Patrons came to demand logical plot development, and they also desired melodically accessible scores. Because a new Broadway musical typically landed a tune or two on radio music programs, the public subconsciously equated hit-producing scores with a hit show, even though such was not always the case.

During the '50s and beyond, when a new musical opened in New York, a major incentive for show composers to fashion popular songs was the *The Ed Sullivan Show*, televised on Sunday evenings, which regularly showcased numbers from just-opened musicals. Sullivan, who offered tremendous coast-to-coast exposure and who favored songs of popular appeal, might invite a cast back to appear a second time. Thus was the entire nation continually confronted with Broadway entertainment. When members of the original cast of Frank Loesser's serious folk opera *The Most Happy Fella* sang for Sullivan, the upbeat rendition of the atypically bright "Standing on the Corner" no doubt helped propel the number onto the radio airwaves and stimulate more ticket sales for the musical itself. Even Oscar Hammerstein proudly acknowledged trying to stay always in step with the times by monitoring Hit Parade trends of the day. He allowed them their necessary influence over his work.

Two of the shrewdest songwriters of 1950s musicals were Richard Adler and Jerry Ross, who bridged the growing chasm between stage and popular music with two back-to-back hits, *Pajama Game* and *Damn Yankees*. Both scores, especially the rousing *Pajama Game*, played well in both mediums. Three big *Pajama Game* originals—Rosemary Clooney's number one hit single, "Hey, There," "Steam Heat" and "Hernando's Hideaway" (lasting for 117 weeks on the charts)—gave America plenty to sing about. From *Yankees* came "Whatever Lola Wants," which Sarah Vaughan carried to the 12th position. Adler and Ross duplicated in spirit the wide-ranging appeal of *Show Boat* in its own day. Their accomplished partnership was tragically short-lived; Ross died of a bronchial ailment only six months after the premiere of *Damn Yankees*.

Not all writers with the same commercial instincts enjoyed success. Another score much in the winning Adler-Ross mold, *Happy Hunting*, with Ethel Merman behind it, did not bring similar fame and royalties to its neophyte composer, Harold Karr, moonlighting away from his day job as dentist, or lyricist Matt Dubey, day job unknown. Merman, who claimed to have "discovered"[7] Karr and Dubey, did her cracking best at the Majestic Theatre to put over their zany send-up of the wedding of Grace Kelly to Prince Rainier. In the spoof, which was co-authored by Howard Lindsay and Russel Crouse, a Philly matron barred from attending the Monaco nuptials sets out in spoilsport fashion to stage a rival wedding ceremony for her own daughter.

A majority of the critics were just as amused as Robert Coleman, who called the show "tuneful, sassy, and satiric ... it's a smasher, old bean, a smasher!"[8] Not quite. At a respectable Merman-sustained run of 412 performances, still short of a profit, *Happy Hunting* did manage to send a pair of high-octane novelty numbers—"A New Fangled Tango" and "Mutual Admiration Society"—onto radio play lists for a spell. And the roof-raising anthem that Merman belted out upon first hitting the stage, "Gee, But It's Good to Be Here!" was so effective that she would use it to open her touring concert act in later years.

Musical theatre is full of cruel contradictions. Rarely in the modern era would the presence of a popular song in a show spell the difference between profit or loss. Consider, Exhibit Number One, that *West Side Story*—probably the most dynamic and exciting Broadway score ever composed—did not generate a single song that reached into top 100 territory. Not, in fact, until the movie version came out did the score find a tiny opening into popular favor, when Roger Williams's version of "Maria" squeaked through to the number 48 slot on the *Billboard* charts. Consider, also, Exhibit Number Two: Both *Pipe Dream* and *Me and Juliet*, neither show considered by any means a Rodgers and Hammerstein success, produced hit and near-hit tunes.

Composers on occasion have to cut pop-oriented numbers when they glaringly fail to fit in anywhere. Deadbeat look-at-me songs can actually hinder the action and frustrate audience patience. Then there are, rarely, the irrelevant songs with obvious commercial appeal that pull audiences *into* mediocre shows. Experts speculate that Harold Rome's thoroughly mediocre *Wish You Were Here* achieved its unexpected solvency by having a wonderful title song that captured the hearts of radio listeners everywhere (as well as by offering, built into the set, a real swimming pool complete with water). Rome redeemed an otherwise abysmal score by the several fine numbers that end it, from the joyful "Summer Afternoon" to the oh-so-elevating "Wish You Were Here." Better to save the best for last. By then, however, the critics were not the least fooled, and most of them registered disfavor. *Wish You Were Here* has not been heard from since.

How good does the score have to be? Not very, although rarely does a successful show come with the persistently lackluster songs of a *Once Upon a Mattress*. Conversely, many good to outstanding scores have gone down in utter ruin under the hulk of troubled librettos or fatally unlucky productions—or politics. *Flahooley*, a 1951 flop obscure to all but the most fastidious cast album collectors, is an utterly charming songfest, created under crisp inspiration by Sammy Fain and E. Y. Harburg. Their high-flying choruses put to shame many pedestrian scores that have enjoyed long life on the stage by virtue of the crowd-pleasing shows they were lucky to serve.

The Harburg satire, written in collaboration with Fred Saidy, poked hilarious fun at senseless merchandising. Some felt *Flahooley* to be dangerously subversive for the times, rubbing uneasily up against virtuous 1950s patriotism and a booming consumer-driven economy. In the post-mortem analysis of Ken Mandelbaum, Harburg got accused of anti–Americanism. The self-assured socialist evidently could not break the habit. Critic John Chapman loved what he saw and heard—"tuneful, extraordinary, beautiful and definitely imaginative." Mr. Atkinson did not, dubbing its plot "one of the most complicated, verbose and humorless of the season."[9] Fine score plus unwanted politics equaled gloomy reviews and 40 performances.

Now, of countless so-so scores attached to money-making properties, surely the cobbled together patchwork for *Peter Pan* must head the list. Irritatingly disjointed at the seams and with a slightly stale air of exuberant blandness, it resurfaces on the touring circuit more frequently than NASA can land photo equipment on distant planets. And for all its allusion to human flight, *Peter Pan* feels remarkably stagebound. Credit the show's original producer, Los Angeles Civic Light Opera impresario Edwin Lester, who in the beginning sensed a deficiency in the original numbers provided by Moose Charlap and Carolyn Lee, dumped about

half of them and called in Jule Styne, Betty Comden and Adolph Green to provide better replacement parts. That they did, though not without a resulting schism
in styles. The manufactured result is decently workable.

Jule Styne, who composed most of the best numbers for *Peter Pan* (among
them "Never Land," "Wendy," "Ugg-A-Wugg," "Hook's Waltz") demonstrated
then, as he ordinarily did during the course of his checkered career, the knack for
moving things along. The last of the older-era pop composers to stay productively
engaged on Broadway stages well after his peers had faded from the scene, Styne's
prolific career predated Sinatra's and lasted nearly as long. He came into the theatre during the '40s from popular music, which is a big reason why he enjoyed his
fair share of success as opposed to the fate that befell the Vernon Dukes of the
world. It helps to have the beat of the public in your heart. London born, Styne
grew up in Chicago, on the south side. He organized a swing band, and in *1926* he
composed his first hit, "Sunday," to a lyric by Ned Miller. Eight years later, he transferred to New York City, where he worked as a vocal coach. In 1938, just when
Frank Sinatra was getting noticed, Styne went out west to Tinseltown to be a vocal
coach for Fox Pictures at $900.00 a week. Shirley Temple was one of his charges.

What Styne really longed to do was compose, so he took a drastic pay cut—
down to $165.00—for the opportunity to write cowboy songs at Republic Pictures
for Roy Rogers, Gene Autry, and their respective horses. In 1941, Styne set a Frank
Loesser lyric to music and had another hit, "I Don't Want to Walk Without You,
Baby." That same year, he sold a tune to *Ice Capades*.

Styne teamed up with Sammy Cahn to compose a string of hits for the radio
and movies. They answered the call of Broadway in 1944, creating words and music
for *Glad to See You*, a sentiment not mutually shared by audiences in Philadelphia, where it closed. Three years later, however, the same team set the cash reg-
isters a-jingle with *High Button Shoes*, half of whose songs, even with insipid words,
are mighty good, indeed. Styne got hooked on stage shows, said goodbye to Hollywood prosperity, and America is the luckier for it. Cahn returned to Southern
California to work in film, and again we are the luckier. Styne's next tuner, another
big hit, *Gentlemen Prefer Blondes*, had much better words by veteran Leo Robin.

Jule Styne ended up a lifelong slave to musical theatre, where his keen talents
often were compromised in the service of practical, sometimes hastily assembled
properties. He is most famously known for his and Stephen Sondheim's masterwork, *Gypsy*; for *Bells Are Ringing*, a collaboration with Comden and Green; and,
finally, for *Funny Girl*, which he wrote with Bob Merrill. At various times in
between, he would dash off tunes for the movies; his lushly romantic "Three Coins
in a Fountain" is arguably the finest melody he ever turned out.

Of twenty shows composed completely by Styne, seven of them were money
makers and an impressive number of the rest enjoyed respectable though profitless
runs. Although he had only two hits with Comden and Green—*Bells* and an earlier effort, *Two on the Aisle*—yet Styne went back to Betty and Adolph time and
time again, and the results were naggingly uneven at best. There was one notable
exception in the money-losing *Hallelujah, Baby!* their stylish and sensual black

musical which surveyed a sixty-year period of race relations between whites and blacks and which starred Leslie Uggams instead of Lena Horne as originally planned. With a book by Arthur Laurents that some of the critics found trite and liberally condescending, the show received wildly mixed notices, but won Tonys for Styne, Comden and Green. It held on for nearly three hundred performances at the Martin Beck Theatre.

The Styne, Comden and Green musicals can sound carelessly created, as if motivated only by firm revenue-generating deadlines. *Do Re Mi*, which logged an impressive though profitless 400 performance run, was one of their best efforts after *Bells Are Ringing*. It too suffers, though, from glaring inconsistencies. The same score that gave us "Make Someone Happy" also gave us too many substandard moments, like the wordy and vacuous "Adventure," or the sprawling "All of My Life," a potentially moving soliloquy that fritters away its impact on extraneous wordiness. *Fade Out, Fade In* begins with such promise—"Oh, Those Thirties," "It's Good to Be Back Home," and the uproariously funny "Fear"—and then goes down hill with second rate numbers. *Say, Darling* doesn't say nearly enough beyond the superficial recreation of a few square dance and big band numbers. The peculiar billing which gave the three collaborators credit for both music and lyrics suggested that they wished to avoid taking credit for specific violations of craft.

During the same period, Styne had better luck at the box office working with Bob Merrill, whose *Funny Girl* lyrics inspired some of his best music, even if it all seemed so pervasively sad—true to the story of Fanny Brice and her depressing short-lived affairs. Walter Kerr wrote that "inspiration wanes, and craft must make do in its place."[10] That craft gave the world one of the most honest love songs ever written, "People." And it gave the Winter Garden theatre a three-year hit. Barbara Streisand, who starred, repeated her role in the 1968 film version.

Following his muse to the last dying day, Styne composed a full nine more musicals after *Funny Girl*. Included during this drive was the composer's first and only opus with lyric great E.Y. Harburg, the 32-performance blowout *Darling of the Day*, a work, in its opening segments, of unexpected charm and grace in the *My Fair Lady* mode—if only Styne and Harburg could have sustained themselves beyond the first seven ingratiating numbers. Of Styne's eight other shows, only one of them, another collaboration with Bob Merrill called *Sugar*, made money. And then came a domino succession of near hits and, in the end, all-out folds. *Red Shoes*, composed when he was nearly ninety, marked Mr. Styne's final Broadway show. Less than a year following its disastrous opening, Styne died in New York City, on September 20, 1994.

One year before *Red Shoes* premiered, Frank Sinatra went back into the recording studio for the first time in a decade to lay down the tracks for his parts on *Duets*. Sinatra invited a number of contemporary singers to join him. Through advanced studio technology and dubbing techniques, Barbara Streisand, Luther Vandross, Carly Simon, Anita Baker, and others of the platinum class were invited to record their tracks separately. The tracks were meticulously merged, and the world heard Sinatra singing "The Lady Is a Tramp" with Vandross, "Come Rain or Come Shine" with Gloria Estefan, "They Can't Take That Away from Me" with Natalie Cole, and so on. Within weeks of its release as a CD, *Duets* sold one million copies, and soon it topped the *Billboard* charts.

While Jule Styne's *Red Shoes* could only offer the world the sadly diminished talents of a once fine pop-turned-show composer, Frank Sinatra's *Duets* offered that same world the songs of a bygone era in musical theatre when all America sang the tunes of Times Square. Most of *Duets'* songs had been around for over thirty years, and a new generation would now experience them, thanks to Sinatra's ingenious marketing. The surprising success of *Duets* was followed, one year later, by *Duets II*. Came more excellent tunes, in 1994, from the Broadway canon of yesteryear. Sinatra and Chrissie Hynde sang "Luck Be a Lady." Patti LaBelle lent her voice to "Bewitched, Bothered and Bewildered," Sonny Bono to "I've Got You Under My Skin," Jimmy Buffett to "Mack the Knife." While Frank sang "My Funny Valentine," Lorrie Morgan sang in counter melody, "How Do You Keep the Music Going," a fitting tribute to a singer who had spent most of his life finding ways to keep classic show tunes alive in the popular imagination.

In the end, Sinatra's Broadway may have passed into history. Not so its music. Not the lingering magic that the Voice still seemed able to mine from the songs of Arlen and Duke and Rodgers and Hart. A good song will nearly sell itself. And so, at the age of nearly 80, Frank Sinatra was still Number One, Top of the Heap, King of the Hill, when he sang ...

> Night and day under the hide of me
> There's an oh, such a hungry yearning
> Burning inside of me.
> And it's torment won't be through
> 'Til you let me spend my life making love to you,
> Day and night,
> Night and day.

CHAPTER 5

Cockeyed Optimists

His one abiding love being musical theatre, Richard Rodgers was not known for sustaining close friendships. When asked during an extended Canadian radio interview with Tony Thomas shortly after the opening of *The Sound of Music* if he was not "impervious to the feeling" that success gave him, he answered without a single nod to the social pleasures: "Never, Never. There are certain elemental things that are always gratifying—eating, a warm bath, making love, and having a successful show."[1] As fondly recalled by his daughter, Mary, "He loved staying up till two in the morning trying to figure out what to do with a show. He loved going to see his shows over and over, standing anonymously at the back of the theatre. He bought the whole package."[2]

Rodgers spoke of Oscar Hammerstein as "a dear friend,"[3] and just as warmly about Lorenz Hart. "Each, during our association, was the closest friend I had."[4] Yet about fifteen years following Hammerstein's death, Rodgers confessed, "I was very fond of him—very fond of him—and I never did find out whether he liked me or not. To this day I don't know."[5] Oscar was equally insecure about where he stood with Dick, once spilling out his insecurities to protege Stephen Sondheim: "What do you think of Dick? Because I don't know him at all. We've worked together all these years and I don't really know him…. Dick's life is the office or the box office of the theatre…. I just don't understand."[6]

There were few individuals willing to express any affection for Rodgers. He reportedly disliked a number of people himself. Away from the media, he showed a tactless side, once lambasting the late Gertrude Lawrence, who introduced Anna in *The King and I*, for her off-key singing. And those who served him well were not always accorded reciprocal respect. So obsessed did he become with his success and reputation, that during an extended bout of depression and drinking in the late 1950s, Rodgers voluntarily submitted himself to the Payne Whitney Clinic after auditions for *Flower Drum Song* were complete. He stayed under psychiatric surveillance for 12 weeks. From all reports, he fretted over his status with each passing show, as if he lived in perpetual fear of losing his talent.

Insecurities are not confined to underachievers. Only three days after the smash opening of *South Pacific*, Rodgers found himself socially in the company of Kurt Weill and Lotte Lenya at Hammerstein's Upper East Side home, where he was driven to a near panic, up on his feet and pacing while Weill played for the guests a sampling of the music from his new show in the works, *Lost in the Stars*. America's most successful show composer struck Weill as suffering "a terrible case of inferiority complex which he tries desperately to hide behind arrogance.... I almost began feeling sorry for him."[7] Unable evidently to endure the compositions of a perceived rival—and hardly a rival of note in the commercial sphere— it is easy to trust Mr. Rodgers telling his interviewer, Tony Thomas, that for him, happiness was having a new show to work on.

Having narrowly escaped the alternative fate of infant's underwear salesman during the bleak break-in years with Larry Hart, Rodgers then spent the rest of his life acting as if at any moment that fate could still befall him—as if the precarious world to which he clung show by show might suddenly come crashing down. He had no doubt witnessed the early demise of other show composers. His professional focus was fiercely possessive. No time for friendships.

No time for friendly talk about politics or world affairs, or anything outside the next show at hand when he and Oscar Hammerstein got together for weekly brainstorming sessions. Insiders have surmised that the two partners, by silent mutual understanding, steered tactfully clear of personal disagreements that might infringe on their collaboration. Who was more aloof? One thing was certain: Richard Rodgers seized the reins of corporate control. He struck many as being cold-hearted in his impersonalized manner of overseeing the operation of Rodgers & Hammerstein. In reply to Tony Thomas's question, "You're a businessman?" the belligerent tone of Rodgers' answer sounds laughably disingenuous. "No," he flatly replied, "I'm not a businessman in any sense. I'm a very bad businessman and I don't do any business. I have people who do it for me. I don't hire anybody. I don't let anybody go. I don't talk money with anybody.... At this moment, I can't tell you the salary of anybody who works for me."[8]

Tales of Dick's chilly behavior as de facto head of the R&H empire are legion. When Joshua Logan came to Hammerstein's rescue during work on the script for *South Pacific*, volunteering to supply dialogue about military life that Oscar was unable to write, Logan rightfully felt that he should receive credit as co-librettist. Hammerstein agreed, telling him, "I'm sorry I didn't offer it to you myself. Of course you can have it. We'll work out the exact details later."[9] The case that Hammerstein tried making for Logan's input did not succeed at first with Rodgers, who is unkindly remembered for having tersely opposed the idea. He eventually relented, four days before rehearsals commenced. It left Logan so embittered that when Rodgers and Hammerstein offered him participation on *The King and I*, including full co-authorship, he declined.

Dick Rodgers was first and foremost a composer, and composers need a kind of existential flexibility to survive. After all, it is they who must accept the words given them by their collaborators, they who must agree to go along with the images and messages conveyed by others. Rodgers certainly navigated his way through marked changes not only in the content and style of his own profession, but in the ever-evolving landscape of American society. He was bound to have scored shows whose thematic grist did not jibe with his own personal beliefs or assorted grudges. He had faithfully stuck it out for twenty-five years with Larry Hart, dutifully compensating for his partner's unreliable, sometimes infuriating ways. In that collaboration, Rodgers played the role of devoted long-suffering spouse with admirable fidelity. In fact, he stuck with Larry Hart long after most teams would have split. Loyalty or desperation? Considering the precarious, short-lived nature of such affiliations and the ability of Rodgers to attract any number of other lyric writers, he displayed remarkable loyalty. After joining forces with Hammerstein, Rodgers told director George Abbott, "I never want to have another collaborator as long as I live."[10]

If on the surface Rodgers revealed scarce compassion, yet what a flood of wonderful music came rolling forth from the man's soul. The sheer speed of his composing talent boggles the mind. Tunes were born in five, ten, easily fifteen or twenty minutes. No wonder Mr. Rodgers hung out so often at the office—even if he didn't know how much money anybody in his employ was making. He came close on one occasion to bearing a degree of guilt over his effortless creativity. "It's been said about you," asked Tony Thomas, "that you can write melodies as easily as if it were in the same league as eating, drinking and breathing. Now, is it really that easy for you?"

Answered Rodgers, "You could say that it was as easy as eating, for instance, if you started with the beginning of eating, which would be raising the cattle which provide the meat, or growing the vegetables or the fruit, and then the actual process of eating is quite simple, provided you have some teeth, which I'm happy to tell you I have. The easy approach is to say, 'Oh, look, Oscar handed him a lyric...and out came the tune in five minutes.' Well, the tune didn't come out in five minutes. We had gone through months of discussion about the play. We knew a great deal about the situation in which the particular song occurred. We had reached a mutual decision as to the time signature, so that it would fit in with the song before and the song after. All these things condition the actual composing. And you carry it around with you subconsciously, and consciously very often, for a great length of time, and finally you reach the moment of composition. And it comes in a rush."[11]

He was not the first or only tunesmith to deliver the goods in a rush. And with Hammerstein supplying the words first, Rodgers found the job even easier. "Having the lyric in addition to the situation in the play is very helpful to me," he said. "It gives me an extra push into the solution to the problem of finding the tune." He spoke glowingly of his partner's craft: "Oscar is one of the few writers in the entire world who has a tremendous sense of construction. And, without a tune, his lyrics are beautifully built."[12]

In private, all that "construction" was still far too time-consuming for the restless Richard Rodgers, who could never quite fathom why it took Oscar so long just to come up with a few new verses. And comparisons to his previous partner—the one who scribbled out finished couplets as fast as a pencil could form them on paper against the edge of a piano—were bound to provoke impatience and suspicion. Rodgers confided, years later, to Alan Jay Lerner before blowing off their fruitless attempt at collaborating on *On a Clear Day You Can See Forever*: "He would go down there to his farm in Bucks County and sometimes it would be three weeks before he appeared with a lyric. I never knew what he was doing down there. You know a lyric couldn't possibly take three weeks."[13]

Lerner knew it *could*. Another perfectionist, he slugged through ninety versions of the title lyric for *Clear Day* before he had what he wanted. What Oscar did do down there on the farm was to agonize over every single word. After laboring for five wrenching weeks on "Hello, Young Lovers," which finally crystallized in the last 48 hours, Oscar proudly sent over the finished lyric to Dick via courier. Then he anxiously awaited a phone call from Dick acknowledging receipt and maybe offering some praise. The expected call never came. Oscar, feeling painfully slighted, kept it to himself. A week or so later when the two were conversing about something else, Dick casually mentioned "Hello, Young Lovers" in passing, indicating only that it fit the melody he had composed for it.

Before his unparalleled successes with Hammerstein, Rodgers had presided over some notable innovations, as heretofore noted, principally the knuckle-bare realism of *Pal Joey*. He did not shy away from controversial subjects, so he was prepared to hold his own with Hammerstein or anyone else. The partners courted popular tastes, careful to infuse each new show with songs that could serve both theatre and radio markets. For instance, *South Pacific* generated a trio of Hit Parade favorites, with Perry Como's "Some Enchanted Evening" commanding the number one position on the charts for many weeks, "Bali Ha'i" reaching the number 5 slot, and "A Wonderful Guy" number 12.

To the 1948 movie *State Fair*, for which Oscar wrote the screenplay, they contributed six top-notch numbers, including another big hit—the sublimely wistful "It Might As Well Be Spring"; a rousing waltz, "It's a Grand Night for Singing"; and two uptempo, atypical R&H numbers that bounced to the prevailing beat of the day, "That's for Me" and "Isn't It Kind of Fun."

In the late 1940s, the unique Rodgers and Hammerstein magic seemed perfectly in step with the positive postwar mood of America. A little jewel dropped from *Oklahoma!* and subsequently recorded as a single by Judy Garland, "Boys and Girls," evoked a small-town innocence that enveloped the nation. "My Girl Back Home," a number deleted from *South Pacific* (and later used in the movie version), was sung by Lt. Cable, a Philadelphia native serving duty in the South Seas, reminiscing over the distant dreams of a simpler time and place.

It would have been politically easier to remove from *South Pacific* another song, quite daring for its day, which dealt with racial intolerance. The dissenters warned that the lyric might offend audiences and endanger the show's commercial prospects. Hammerstein took his concerns to James Michener, author of the novel from which *South Pacific* was adapted. Michener is well known for having replied that if they dropped the number they would be pulling out the show's thematic foundation. To their everlasting credit, Dick and Oscar held firm against pressure from trusted friends and associates during out-of-town tryouts in New Haven, and Cable sang, all the way to opening night and beyond in New York City, an eloquent protest against culturally conditioned bigotry, "You've Got to Be Carefully Taught."

The musical was awarded the Pulitzer Prize, along with countless other awards, including multiple Tonys. "I wept," confessed Kenneth Tynan in his *New Yorker* notice. "And there is nothing in criticism harder to convey one's gratitude for that…. This is the first musical romance I have ever seen which has seriously involved an adult subject."[14]

Into the 1950s, the theatre's reigning musical giants had one more major coup up their sleeves. It was *The King and I*, adapted from Margaret Landon's novel *Anna and the King of Siam* with superior skill by Hammerstein, who would receive just acclaim. "A libretto that stands on its own merits," sang Otis L. Guernsey, Jr. "The most important part," agreed John Chapman, "is the work of Mr. Hammerstein as librettist and lyricist. It is an intricate and expert piece of showmanship in which the story comes first."[15] *The King and I* is surely one of the two or three best integrated musicals ever mounted on a New York stage. And its music courts an Eastern air with haunting relevance. Mr. Rodgers's soaring refrains sent such tautly expressive lyrics as "My Lord and Master" and "I Have Dreamed" into melodic ecstasy. His stirring "March of the Siamese Children" is quite possibly the finest piece of theatre music he ever wrote. Jerome Robbins directed the entire affair into brilliant completion.

The universality of Hammerstein's compassion was never better expressed than in the hopeful "We Kiss in a Shadow." Here was a lyric that would come to stand for the lonely aspirations of so many ostracized lovers longing for ultimate acceptance from an intolerant society. Hammerstein pursued his clear line of reasoning to its triumphant conclusion—when, at last, the couple no longer have to hide from the world but can express their love in the sunlight.

The King and I builds its conflict steadily to a harrowing climax. The king discovers his concubine Tuptim trying to escape to run off with her lover, Lun Tha, and prepares to punish her with a whip lashing. He suffers humiliation at the hands of Anna, who argues him away from such brutality. The next scene finds the demoralized king on his death bed, turning over the reins of power to his son, whose youthful ideas for progress and change he heroically encourages, and who, as a result, begins right there setting into motion a more humane way of life for his subjects. The musical's resolution, a rarity in musical theatre, comprises a terrific drama all in itself. Few shows are so tautly developed from start to finish.

On their own, away from established source material, R&H fell short of the magic. Original ventures were not their forte, although the flawed *Allegro*, the show that came between *Carousel* and *South Pacific*, showed promise in its

South Pacific original co-stars Mary Martin and Ezio Pinza.

Whistling a happy tune on *The Ed Sullivan Show* in 1951: Richard Rodgers (at the piano), Oscar Hammerstein and Gertrude Lawrence, star of *The King and I.*

enthralling first act. But after intermission, Hammerstein railed tritely against the pursuit of material success at the expense of losing one's soul and connection to community. In one of his cleverest pieces, "Money Isn't Everything," he chided upper class consumerism.

   Allegro was originally intended to depict the entire life of Joseph Taylor, Jr., who grows up to be a prosperous doctor in a large city. Alas, the librettist didn't quite make it to the end; the final curtain was lowered instead on Taylor's returning home to the small town where he was raised, amidst an outpouring of touchy-feely love from folks all designed to appear more noble than heartless city dwellers. Hammerstein scarcely grappled with the more perplexing issues inherent in his play, such as the value and practice of medicine in a large city as opposed to a small town. He did not confront this central theme in any of the songs. Rodgers and Hammerstein beat around the bush, only alluding to greed and immorality in a big city by showing how disillusioned it made their hero, and then by struggling to make his hometown, in comparison, seem less shallow and therefore more worthy of a doctor's true devotion. It is a tuner told in black and white. Some critics looked past the melodrama to impressive innovations. "The season's most unusual attraction," noted Jack Pulaski of *Variety*, "... creates a virtually new theatre form."[16] The other half were left totally irritated. "A shocking disappointment," wrote Wolcott Gibbs in *The New Yorker*. "An elaborate sermon," complained John Chapman.[17]

And yet the first act is vigorously full of Joseph's infancy, adolescence and young adulthood, and it brims with sentimental realism. The music sets it all gloriously a-sail. It is the skeletal second act that falters, standing there in a shell like a kind of construction zone full of interesting parts yet to be fully assembled and merged. A pair of fine songs, "Money Isn't Everything" and "The Gentleman Is a Dope," whose minor strains foreshadowed a developing musical language of Rodgers's that would blossom in *South Pacific*, keep the diminished proceedings alive.

Allegro's first act blossomed in full when the Glendale, California, Civic Light Opera mounted the show in 1983, with a full orchestra. The savvy assessment of Brooks Atkinson thirty-five years earlier applied just as persuasively to the new performance as it had then: "Before the mood breaks after the first act it is full of a kind of unexpected glory.... Mr. Rodgers and Mr. Hammerstein have just missed the final splendor of a perfect work of art."[18] Looking back many years later over his vast body of work, Mr. Rodgers called this show the one "most worthy of a second chance."[19]

Allegro is thought of by many to be an early "concept" musical. Some claim it to be the first. By presenting its themes through a Greek chorus which served as the author's alter ego, it moved away from the primal force of character-driven revelation into the more cerebral artifact of lecture. This intellectual format would come into dubious vogue twenty-five years later. However, if it worked for the first act of *Allegro*, why not the second act too? Because by the time Hammerstein got there, he relied too much upon his Greek chorus for ballast, failing to flesh out dramatically Joseph's actual involvement with his patients and with the boards of directors to whom he reported with increasing skepticism. The show collapses into a saccharine one-note "Come Home, Joe!" resolution, intended to convey the evil of the Big City compared to the virtue of Small Town life. Rather than feeling inspired over Joe's answering the call to return to his birthplace and take up with real people again, we are bludgeoned by a ponderously self-righteous pitch, "Come Home, Joe," for everything pure and constant that awaits him there, for honest friends and men with strong hands and hearts.

They left us in limbo. After *South Pacific* and *The King and I*, Rodgers and Hammerstein concocted a sprawling, at times turgid, valentine to the theatre, *Me and Juliet*—if we are to believe everything we have heard and read about this failed, forgotten work. No wonder it was the only R&H show on which George Abbott would ever work; he tried to direct some life into the contrivance, and he succeeded to a degree, for amazingly it managed to turn a tidy profit on its one-year residency at the Majestic Theatre.

It is not so difficult to understand why the show did as well as it did, for the libretto is more dramatically interesting (at least to read) than the dreary impression of it left by many downbeat accounts. Briefly, Hammerstein's linear story is driven by Joe, a variation on the clumsy Jud Fry character with membership in the stage electrician's union. Joe turns into the Phantom of the *Me and Juliet* company when he threatens to beat up if not murder any man who dares go near his girlfriend, Jeanie, about whom he refuses to get serious but to whom he claims exclusive rights. When Jeanie shows some romantic interest in the director, Larry, the pressure builds, and in one of the most eerie and threatening first act closers ever, Joe discovers Jeanie and Larry in a kiss during a rehearsal from the bridge of the stage where he is working, and angrily redirects a spotlight onto them. But the "Phantom" threat is not carried through in the slumping second act. Joe comes to accept Jeanie's intention to marry Larry, and he redeems his violent nature in a mushy-eyed turnaround.

The electrician's anger did not evidently make for a very engaging evening. Of all the Rodgers and Hammerstein shows, this one received by far the worst set of reviews. "We kept saying over and over to ourselves," wrote Robert Coleman, "'Dick Rodgers and Oc Hammerstein didn't do it. They couldn't have done it. They'd have taken this one off in Boston for revamping.'" There was only one favorable rating in the bunch. Book problems vexed their every move, made even worse by the heavy-handedness of Hammerstein's more earnest moments in verse. In the estimation of Brooks Atkinson, *Me and Juliet* added down to "a book that has no velocity ... looks a little like a rehearsal."[20]

Dick and Oscar did manage to create five quite excellent numbers, some in the older Rodgers and Hart vein. To a haunting tango which Rodgers had composed the previous year for his acclaimed 26-part television series, *Victory at Sea*, Hammerstein added words and it became the instant popular hit, "No Other Love," recorded by Perry Como, who also scored additional airplay with his zippy rendition of the clever "Keep It Gay." Joe Stafford turned "I'm Your Girl" into a moody LP standard. The tongue-in-cheek "Marriage Type Love" bounced with a 1930s charm, while "We Deserve Each Other" revealed with painterly precision two quirky offbeat characters (not from *Allegro* land) who find much in common, including non-intellectual bents.

A handful of bright stellar songs could not redeem all the unwelcome dialogue and blurry plot lines—and this after gigantically talented George Abbott was given permission by the boys to cut the script to smithereens for clarity and pacing. Plodding it remained. Plodding surely describes "The Big Black Giant," an epic embarrassment of which Oscar was delusionally proud, about the changing faces of the audience as seen by the cast.

That was 1953. What the two foundering partners did with their follow up attempt to recapture the old magic was theoretically good. On paper, the adaptation of John Steinbeck's novel *Sweet Thursday*, about a sub-community of good-natured across-the-tracks characters on Monterey's Cannery Row, presented a colorful locale and different view of life. The story, however, hardly contained a major dramatic conflict save for the fuzzy plight of Suzy, a homeless drifter ("Everybody's Got a Home But Me") who takes up work at a house of ill repute, Bear Flag Cafe, operated by Fauna, a role not much enlivened by opera star Helen Traubel, and Doc, a self-made marine biologist. *Pipe Dream* caused some wonderful music to be written, and Hammerstein responded to the subject matter with sensitive originality. From "It Takes All Kind of People," Doc draws deft comparisons to the animal kingdom, where various creatures, not so attractive to the eyes of humans, can be quite desirable to each other. Another oddball delight is "Tide Pool," set to turbulent music, which surveys the survivalist games below water.

Several of *Pipe Dream's* songs landed in hit parade territory long enough to validate the still-populist instincts of Dick and Oscar. The plaintive "Everybody's Got a Home But Me" was recorded by Eddie Fisher. Carmen McRae's brisk rendition of the contemporary "The Next Time It Happens" flirted in the upper reaches of the top 100, while Perry Como's soft crooning of the slow beguine, "All At Once You Love Her," took it to the number 24 position on the charts.

Beyond a fairly fascinating score which has never received due credit, *Pipe Dream* (ironically billed "a musical comedy") lost its potential punch in a sugar-coated vagueness not so different from *Allegro's.* The main problem was Suzy's identity. Skittish about prostitution, Hammerstein failed to confront the heroine's red-light district involvement at the Bear Flag and make it dramatically engrossing. Tiptoeing around the issue, his subtly humorous "The Happiest House on the Block" alluded to the world's oldest profession as practiced on Cannery Row with safe innuendos.

Worse still, it was not even clear if Suzy actually serviced a single client under Fauna's aegis. Outside that happy little house, Suzy falls in love with Doc, and they meander passively-aggressively through a standoffish flirtation, goaded on primarily by local denizens who feel the two belong together. *Pipe Dream* contained the seeds of a dramatic tour-de-force, if only its creators could have faced the darker music—as Rodgers with Hart did in *Pal Joey.* During rehearsals the initial force of the piece was watered down. Suzy, the intended prostitute, came off looking, in John Steinbeck's opinion, more "like an off-duty visiting nurse."[21] The author sent notes of concern, then of mild protest to O.H, in one of them addressing Suzy's position in the Bear Flag: "It's either a whore house, or it isn't. Suzy either took a job there, or she didn't.... My position is that she took the job all right but wasn't any good at it."[22] The question was never decisively answered in dialogue or action, so Hammerstein's quirky comedic touches, of which this show had many, and Rodgers's adventurous free-flowing music were destined to carry *Pipe Dream.* The authors could only allude to a philosophical tolerance for life's unconventional free souls. They could only think the best of their misguided heroine, acknowledging, in "Suzy Is a Good Thing," that like everybody else Suzie was bound to make mistakes now and then.

So did *Pipe Dream.* Directed by newcomer Harold Clurman, it did not strike the New York critics as a very good thing. It did no better than *Me and Juliet,* gain-ing only one favorable notice. Among the dissenters, Robert Chapman observed, "Rodgers and Hammerstein ... are too gentlemanly to be dealing with John Steinbeck's sleazy and raffish denizens of Cannery Row." John McClain's bleak dismissal—"This is a far cry from the exalted talents of the team that produced *South Pacific*. They must be human after all"[23]—surely gave Dick and Oscar pause.

In the words of Rodgers looking back years later, "We had simply gone too far away from what was expected.... It had to be compared to other works and that identifiable thing called the Rodgers and Hammerstein image."[24] *Pipe Dream* closed in the red after 246 performances at the Shubert Theatre, and within a year its promising new stars, Bill Johnson and Judy Tyler, both died, he of a heart attack, she from an automobile accident. Helen Traubel, blamed by many for the show's lackluster center, would never sing in another Broadway show.

Judging by their work that followed, *Pipe Dream* marked a turning point for Rodgers and Hammerstein—a turning away from any further experimentation of the sort that had made them so interesting to anticipate and watch. They now settled artistically downward into a pattern of offering the public their high standards of craft in commercially risk-free properties. For the fledgling medium of television they were given the rare opportunity to adapt *Cinderella*, and they brought off the assignment in high style, with a bright score containing some of Rodgers's most exhilarating waltzes. Hammerstein's verse, while rarely measuring up to his best work, was more than suitable and contained some gems. His witty "What's the Matter with the Man," in which Cinderella's homely stepsisters bemoan her appeal to the prince, was the sharpest of the lot. "Do I Love You Because You're Beautiful" was an intriguing twist on the standard love song, wherein the Prince and Cinderella thoughtfully engage in a dialogue on the nature of physical attraction.

It is thrilling to remember that *Cinderella* was filmed before *live* cameras in a relatively small space when television was still in its infancy. The meticulously rehearsed production cavorted, skipped and soared before a succession of artful camera angles. "Waltz for a Ball" was particularly memorable for its quick yet magisterial movements, deftly designed to fill out every area of the limited space. Staged with inspiration by choreographer Jonathan Lucas, it remains one of the most uplifting dance numbers ever seen in a musical.

Transmitted across 245 stations on March 31, 1957, *Cinderella* was seen by 107,000,000 viewers, and the original cast album sold well. Rodgers and Hammerstein were once again on top—and soon back on Broadway, with *Flower Drum Song*, actually a more engaging show than today's critics believe it to have been. Consistently amusing, light hearted, freshly melodic, it breezed across the boards, gleaming with a sparkling professionalism that was a joy to behold. The atmospheric score evokes the jumbled clash of occidental and oriental cultures in San Francisco's bustling Chinatown. Only one of the fine songs—"You Are Beautiful," recorded by both Johnny Mathis and the Stylistics—entered the top 100 charts. Best remembered today is the now culturally despised "I Enjoy Being a Girl," introduced with belting force and pizazz by Pat Suzuki, the Asian Merman.

In their haste to make *Flower Drum Song* fool-proof at the box office, Dick and Oscar turned the dramatic novel on which it was based into musical comedy. Joseph Fields was engaged to co-script the libretto, and he inserted topical jokes. Gene Kelly was brought in to direct, and he provided buoyant pacing throughout. Further to insure against uncommercial seriousness, Oscar undercut the novel's dramatic climax, the suicide of Helen Chao, by removing it altogether. For her grief as the woman used in a one-night stand, Chao was given the show's most powerful ballad to sing, "Love Look Away." So Rodgers and Hammerstein deprived themselves of another chance to accomplish something more dramatic on the level of *Carousel* or *The King and I*. Did they never pause to note the key role that death had played in all four of their major works?

Nevertheless, with this safer road to the box office they pulled off a modest success, and they could add two raves and four positive write-ups to their scrapbook. Some reviewers spotted the old magic, if a tad more manufactured. "There is a formalized air about *Flower Drum Song*," reported Frank Aston, "but there can be no doubt about it—here is a walloping hit."[25] Aside from reservations for "uninspired jokes," *Variety's* Hobe Morrison reported, "Rodgers and Hammerstein are back in business…. The master collaborators practically never miss … a supple and, with few exceptions, convincingly motivated book…. *Flower Drum Song* has what it takes for average audiences and hefty box office…. It'll do."[26] Not so for Kenneth Tynan, one of the doubters nauseated by excessive cuteness and good will: "Simply a stale Broadway confection wrapped in spurious Chinese trimmings … a world of woozy song."[27]

From Grant Avenue, San Francisco, California U.S.A., to the Swiss Alps. For their next safe venture, Dick and Oscar turned to the saga of the Von Trapps, an Austrian family of singers who escaped the Nazi takeover of their country. Who could have guessed that the R&H collaboration would end in such a blaze of glory? With Oscar facing his own death sentence—having been the year before diagnosed with terminal cancer—it would seem blasphemous to fault him for having erred excessively in the affirmative. After all, hope and mercy were his enduring mantras.

The stricken Mr. Hammerstein in those last months did, remarkably, muster the will to pen some of his better lyrics. In the deceptively simple "Do Re Mi," his gifts are on full display. Somehow, Hammerstein found a way to turn each of the notes of the scale into an image, and to fit them all perfectly into a tight, delightful little puzzle. What, for instance, to do with the impossible "la"? According to O.H., "la" is a note to *follow* "sew." One would be hard pressed to find a more cleverly wrought lyric.

Anchored to a durable old fashioned libretto, the work of aging veterans Howard Lindsay and Russel Crouse, Dick and Oscar delivered a first rate set of original songs, overall their best work since *The King and I*. Rodgers told Tony Thomas what a joy his work at the piano had been: "I had the time of my life. The stuff just rolled off."[28] And much of it would roll famously on, achieving long-lasting favor with the public. Tony Bennett's "Climb Every Mountain" and Patti Page's "The Sound of Music" made it onto the pop 100 charts, as did "My Favorite

Things," recorded by none other than Herb Alpert and destined to become the darling of jazz musicians and cabaret singers.

Two unusual numbers give the stage musical version cynical relief. (And, as Walter Kerr sensed on opening night, certain patrons to the exceedingly cheery *The Sound of Music* might ache for a little cynical relief.) Despite the fact that by this time they usually seemed unable or unwilling to convey anything but optimism, Dick and Oscar broke the pattern with the blasé "How Can Love Survive" and a gem about amoral political compromising, "No Way to Stop It." Calling to mind a Kingston Trio-style song of the day, "No Way" amounted to perhaps the first rock song ever introduced in a Broadway musical. Oddly enough, it is an *anti-protest* song.

On its way to Broadway, the show won *Variety*'s approval as a flat-out "sensational musical."[29] And when *The Sound of Music* opened at the Lunt-Fontanne Theatre on November 16, 1959, contrary to a lingering myth advanced by even Richard Rodgers himself about it getting mixed reviews, the critical enthusiasm (three raves and three favorable notices) was decisive. In fact, there was only one unfavorable opening night review. Brooks Atkinson, who found it occasionally "glorious," was quick to note a superior achievement from the masters: "The best of *The Sound of Music* is Rodgers and Hammerstein in good form ... but the scenario ... has the hackneyed look of the musical theatre [they] replaced with *Oklahoma*."[30] Beyond the feared and revered jury of those seven newspaper critics, dissenters on the sidelines included Kenneth Tynan, of the *New Yorker*, calling it "Rodgers and Hammerstein's great leap backward."

What happened a few years later may be a testament more to the commercial avarice of Mr. Rodgers, self-professed non-businessman, than to the talented humanity of Mr. Hammerstein: When the film version was made, several years after Mr. Hammerstein's passing, Mr. Rodgers wrote two new songs for it himself, for which he also supplied the lyrics, and he allowed the movie *not* to include "How Can Love Survive?" "No Way to Stop It," and "An Ordinary Couple." By then, there was no way to stop *him*. For a time, the three deleted songs were even left out of at least one national road company of the stage show; the Rodgers and Hammerstein office likely figured they could sell more tickets by duplicating the movie score. This resulted in the unprecedented act of gauchely inserting into a Rodgers and Hammerstein stage musical songs with lyrics not written by Mr. Hammerstein, but by someone else—Mr. Rodgers. Worst of all, the two numbers (which seem to caricature the worst of Rodgers and Hammerstein) are noxiously saccharine, adding that much more nauseating wonderfulness to an already sugar-intense work. For the record, they go by the names "Something Good" and "I Have Confidence In Me." Maybe we should not be surprised—only mildly infuriated—to note that in the end the team of Rodgers and Rodgers was not up to the sound of music.

CHAPTER 6

Fie On Goodness!

Tired old Ozzie and Harriet cracks aside, not all 1950s musicals were reality-deficient Rodgers and Hammerstein sound-alikes. Consider, for example, Leonard Sillman's sophisticated revue which John Murray Anderson directed, *New Faces of '52*. In *Variety*'s estimation, "brilliantly conceived," the material "skillfully edited,"[1] the show surveyed the gamut of love from adolescent infatuation to clumsy adult infidelities.

Comedienne Alice Ghostley confessed in "Boston Beguine" of having fallen for the wrong guy, now variously suspected of expedient behavior including petty theft but, worst of all, falling asleep between the sheets. Virginia de Luce played a businessman's mistress with smug ennui, confessing that for him she was a tax write-off. June Carroll, delivering with wistful regret Murray Grand and Elisse Boyd's stinging "Guess Who I Saw Today," recounted for her husband having observed two happy lovers while dining out that afternoon—one of them being him.

French charmer Robert Clary played, one moment, a school boy pining over his teacher, Miss Logan; the next, in "It's Raining Memories," a grown up wallowing in self-pity over another failed affair. World traveled sex kitten Eartha Kitt yawned her way through "Monotonous." Ronny Graham sang "Take Off That Mask!" to Alice Ghostley at a masquerade—until the wish was granted, at which moment the repulsed Graham reversed course, exhorting Miss Ghostley to put that mask back on. Even the initially lyrical "Love Is a Simple Thing" got turned on its romantic head when sung "through the eyes" of a Charles Adams character.

Contrary to legions of apologists, the 1950s were rife with enlightened culture—think Tennessee Williams in theatre, Leonard Bernstein's young people's concerts on TV. Nevertheless, Broadway remained mostly in step with the Eisenhower era, making certain that the image of heterosexual happiness occupied center stage in virtually every musical. If not everyone truly believed that love was

New Faces of '52: Robert Clary (left), Eartha Kitt and Paul Lynde.

just somewhere around the corner or up over the crest of a purple hill, most the-atergoers still appreciated being moved by the notion.

While this aesthetic satisfied mainstream audiences, it dogged more poten-tially realistic shows, forcing artistic compromises that proved fatal. Rodgers and Hammerstein's *Pipe Dream* is a perfect example, with its sad little quasi-prosti-tute—if that's what Suzy really was—appearing to find good wholesome love iron-ically in the arms of a bohemian self-taught marine biologist who toils outside academia, preferring the company of uncouth bums and cannery workers. Victor Young and Stella Unger achieved much the same feel of romantic redemption through their melodically fertile *Seventh Heaven*. It is about a street walker, Diane, who becomes involved with Chino, receiving from him a promise of marriage that must be postponed by his going off to fight a war. Years later, Chico, now blinded, returns and the two are happily reconciled. The infectiously warm score, so typical of 1950s tuners, contains as buoyantly wonderful a song as you are likely ever to hear in a theatre, "Sun At My Window, Love At My Door." It is full of Mary Martin and Dick and Oscar.

Patrons paid good money to be so inspired, and resented it when inspiration waned. Between the cheerful numbers in *Seventh Heaven*, there were others not so uplifting, and the show expired after only five weeks in 1955 at the ANTA Theatre. Its watered-down portrait of prostitution failed to impressed the critics. Reported Walter Kerr, "The one thing that *Seventh Heaven* had all the years in memory, anyway—is a fond, schmaltzy innocence, an honest and wistful and appealing grade of corn. This is the quality that librettists Victor Young and Stella Unger have apparently been afraid of, and they have pared it away to make room for a commodity often referred to as 'sex.' For all its determination to seem new-hat and reasonably red hot, *Seventh Heaven* does not really capture the sort of sizzle that has been known to drive good family men to fatal distraction."[2]

Selling so ambiguous a vision was near-impossible in the fifties. Most Americans felt far more corny than callous towards life and love, still basking in the euphoric post–World War II days of wine and barbecue gratitude. Leonard Sillman navigated the tricky terrain with limited success. Of the only two editions of *New Faces* which he could raise the money to produce during the 1950s, the '52 opus turned a respectably modest profit on a 365 performance run. Sillman's 1956 bash, not nearly as well received—plenty enjoyable to experience from a record player—lasted only six months though it supplied basically the same smart blend of exemplary behavior and mischief.

Romance in the key of Rodgers and Hammerstein, and how to sell it—or, how to sell the getting around it? *Guys and Dolls* in development started out on a lovely note, something in the vein of what Dick and Oscar might have plotted. After *eleven* writers came up with unsatisfactory individual librettos, producers Cy Feuer and Ernest Martin engaged radio and TV comedy writer Abe Burrows to supply something aimed more for laughs that would fit the songs already composed by Frank Loesser.

In truth, American musical theatre had rarely been a purveyor of high moral values. During the '50s, however, the McCarthy Senate hearings turned the American landscape into a place of fearful conformity and outwardly virtuous conduct—another reason for song and dance shows to soft-pedal controversial subject matter and lower their final curtains on morally uplifting outcomes. One can only speculate to what extent Oscar Hammerstein's tepid approach to adapting John Steinbeck's raffish cannery row novel into *Pipe Dream* may have been driven by his own fear of being summoned to Washington to testify about possible ties to un–American activities.

Unlike the more daring work turned out by Rodgers and Hammerstein, the collaborations of their leading colleagues in sentiment, Alan Jay Lerner and Frederick ("Fritz") Loewe, altogether avoided dealing with contemporary stateside

Miss Adelaide (Vivian Blaine) and Nathan Detroit (Sam Levene) in a scene from *Guys and Dolls*.

Frederick Loewe and Alan J. Lerner.

topics. Lerner & Loewe set their musicals in historically or geographically distant locales or exotically imagined places. About the closest they came to passing any comment on the American experience were the brief New York scenes in their fantasy classic, *Brigadoon*—put there to dramatize, in comparison to a quaint Scottish village, just how numbingly superficial a corporate-driven society can become. By the show's end, American tourist Tommy Albright renounces the business world and returns to Brigadoon, there to claim his true love and to enjoy everlasting marital happiness in the surreal sleepless void of a village that wakes up for only one day every one hundred years.

On their way to *Brigadoon's* lucky opening night in 1947 at the Ziegfeld Theatre, Lerner and Loewe had already written two shows together, neither of which clicked: *What's Up*, a 1943 wartime musical directed by George Balanchine, and the promising *The Day Before Spring*, a 1948 venture that did not survive split notices. After *Brigadoon*, they returned to Broadway with another troubled original,

Paint Your Wagon, which lasted nine months, was eventually made into a troubled movie and left behind some wonderful songs that captured vividly the drama and color of the Gold Rush days in which the story was set. "I Talk to the Trees," a soft Latin-intoned beguine, foreshadowed how flexible Lerner and Loewe would be in dealing with a wide array of times and places.

Nonetheless, *Paint Your Wagon* struck most of the reviewers as leaden and humorless, a slight that seems to have instigated in Mr. Lerner a rapid transformation into one of the theatre's most witty lyricists. His and Mr. Lowe's next undertaking and the team's second show to earn unanimous raves, *My Fair Lady*, was about as perfectly wrought a musical as ever there was. "It does not bully us with noise," remarked Kenneth Tynan. "The tone throughout is intimate, light and lyrical.... The authors have trusted Shaw, and we, accordingly, trust them."[3] The show's comedy entries are brilliantly steeped in the idiosyncrasies of the characters. In "A Hymn to Him," for example, Henry Higgins shares his exasperation about women with his friend, Col. Pickering, wishing that they could behave more like his amiable male friends—who, he assumes, would never throw a fit were he to take out another man. Yet the show does not lack for romance: The joyous "On the Street Where You Live," which got radio airplay galore and helped advertise *Lady*'s superior score, was atypically lush among otherwise sardonic songs.

At the center of this very offbeat musical was the cantankerous relationship between Henry Higgins, a jaded linguist, and Eliza Doolittle, a common flower girl hauled out of the gutter by Higgins on a dare to make her a proper-speaking English lady. Along the gilded way, the rumblings of a growing platonic attachment between the two feed the narrative with chemistry and conflict. "I've grown accustomed to her face," Henry Higgins acknowledges to himself in the end, shortly before mustering up the humility and courage to invite Eliza Doolittle to stay on. She accepts, and, true to the fifties (though not to the ending of George Bernard Shaw's play, *Pygmalion*, upon which the musical is based), romance at least shines promisingly ahead by last curtain.

What, might we ponder, could Lerner and Loewe have ever done to equal or surpass *My Fair Lady*? Give Mr. Lerner credit for trying. And trying. And trying. He threw himself into T.H. White's *The Once and Future King*, a novel full of romance and intrigue and loftily fought principles of honor in times of war. And in his overly fervent adaptation called *Camelot*, Mr Lerner managed to render it as piously solemn as a Lutheran church service. On higher ground, it came with heavily melodic ballads and some very funny songs. Trapped in a libretto overloaded with Mr. Lerner's heart-entrenched yearnings, the songs come piercing through like imprisoned birds gasping, upon release, for fresh air. Still, *Camelot* had two big things in its favor: 1950s audiences and the names Lerner and Loewe.

Other composers and writers, as well, took their cues from the Rodgers and Hammerstein–Lerner and Loewe syndrome. Tunesmith Albert Hague realized his longest-running success in 1955 at the Mark Hellinger Theatre, when he, in concert

Opposite: Julie Andrews as Eliza Doolittle in *My Fair Lady*.

with lyricist Arnold B. Horwitt and book writers Joseph Stein and Will Glickman, delivered up the lovely, entrancing *Plain and Fancy*. With Barbara Cook in the cast—a big reason the reviews were so sunny—the musical bore a spiritual similarity to *Brigadoon* in the way it thrust two jaded New Yorkers into a far off world—in this instance, to Bird-in-Hand, Pennsylvania, land of the Amish. Though now considered hopelessly dated for revival prospects, *Plain and Fancy* offered gracefully crafted songs, including a radio favorite, "Young and Foolish."

Harold Rome's weakest score was fashioned for his most romantic book show and his biggest box office success, *Fanny*. Not without a few tuneful highlights, it is nevertheless largely mediocre, on the stuffy side and a distant cry from the lilting charm of Rome's *Call Me Mister* or the blitzing brilliance of his later work, *Destry Rides Again*. Accepting the *Fanny* assignment, Rome did the show that David Merrick, producing the first of some 27 musicals that he would bring to the stage, had originally wanted Dick and Oscar to do. And had Dick and Oscar said "yes," maybe the result would have had more bounce. Maybe the reviews would not have been so dismally mixed. "Sad to report," reported John McClain, "*Fanny* is a serious disappointment.... It is big and beautiful, but it is also hollow."[4]

Frank Loesser also turned to matters of the heart in his operatically expansive *Most Happy Fella*, a dramatic departure for the composer of such lighthearted comedies as *Guys and Dolls* and *How to Succeed in Business Without Really Trying*. Remarkably rich in atmosphere, the *Fella* score contained thirty separate numbers, and from it just one pop hit, "Standing on the Corner," emerged. The older man–younger woman tale marked a turn off the beaten path for Loesser. Into the world of Rodgers and Hammerstein he went, and the lyrical if slightly stilted result, while a moderate success, did not capture the same large crowds of Loesser's better attended works. Wrote Brooks Atkinson, "Mr. Loesser has caught the anguish and the love in some exalting music. Broadway is used to the heart. It is not accustomed to evocations of the soul." Walter Kerr sensed a degree of contrivance, finding the musical "heavy with its own inventiveness."[5]

Meredith Willson made it aboard the Rodgers and Hammerstein bandwagon with his rousing *The Music Man*, an ode to small-town life in middle America. And also in the upbeat category, Sandy Wilson's triumphantly melodic *The Boy Friend*, reminiscent in its buoyancy to Kern's *Very Good Eddie* and the first successful West End import since the 1920s, stayed around long enough to turn a perky profit in 1954, and to remind Yankee audiences that the British could still stir up a corking good evening's fun. The reviewers loved it, and when *The Boy Friend* was revived two years later off–Broadway where it more naturally belonged, it racked up a run nearly twice the length of its original stay.

Not by historical accident did *The Boy Friend* outlast *The Most Happy Fella* at the box office. In a musical show, levity was easier to sell than pathos. *She Loves Me*, the widely revered Bock and Harnick classic that has enjoyed post–Broadway life in regional and community playhouses around the country, did not succeed when first it tried, nor did it when it tried and tried and tried again. *She Loves Me* offers an intimate love story set in a cosmetics shop and a generously endowed score. Why have mainstream crowds never responded in force? "Too romantic," according to Steven Suskin, "too good for the average man."[6] Walter Kerr, there on opening night in 1963 at the Eugene O'Neill Theatre, complained of plotting top-heavy in exposition and of a libretto too narrowly focused. And on larger stages, this rich little confection has been observed to get lost and wither away— like a quartet of puppeteers thrown to the mercy of a huge concert hall without amplification.

Another contributor to fifties lore was composer-lyricist Bob Merrill. On Sunday night radio broadcasts of original cast albums, his shows usually came off sounding almost passive in their artificial straining to achieve just the right degree of sentimentality. *New Girl in Town,* with the best score of the lot; *Take Me Along,* a Jackie Gleason vehicle based on Eugene O'Neill's *Ah, Wilderness;* and *Carnival* all enjoyed decent investor-pleasing runs and drew generally respectable write-ups. Revivable? *Carnival* has been heard from now and then in the hinterlands. On Broadway, *Take Me Along* made a pitiful comeback attempt in 1985, failing to take anyone beyond a one-night ride. David Merrick, who produced both *Take Me Along* and *Carnival,* did not manifest in his choice of shows any particular edge or passion beyond a preference for slick, fail-safe work. Brooks Atkinson, who reviewed the opening of *Take Me Along* in 1958, wrote, "The music blares, the dancers prance, and Broadway goes through its regular routine—substituting energy for gaiety. Everything is in motion, but nothing moves inside the libretto."[7]

Merrill did better when he concentrated on writing the lyrics to Jule Styne's music for *Funny Girl* and *Sugar.* Once back on his own, however, supplying both words and music, Merrill endured a trio of failures, from the closed-during-previews disaster *Breakfast at Tiffany's* to *Henry, Sweet Henry* and *The Prince of Grand Street,* not so grand on a Philadelphia street at the Forrest Theatre, beyond which it failed to advance.

Writing book shows about love was not a simple thing. Not for composer Arthur Schwartz, who found no success at all in the sentimental 1950s or any time thereafter. Working with lyricist Dorothy Fields, Schwartz worked his way through two romantic disappointments, the highly distinguished *A Tree Grows in Brooklyn,* which Mr. Atkinson predicted would enjoy "a long and affectionate career"[8] at the Alvin Theatre and didn't; and its successor, *By the Beautiful Sea,* another undertaking with Dorothy Fields who, this time out, did not support one of the theatre's finest tunesmiths with deserving lyrics.

In 1961, Schwartz next turned to a promising reunion with his original partner, Howard Dietz. *The Gay Life,* their third book show, amounted to a barely passable, fairly tuneless affair, hailed by the critics yet off the boards within fourteen weeks. A second comeback attempt by the same team, two years later at the Majestic, was the rambling and disjointed *Jennie,* not so charitably received. The show starred Mary Martin, who portrayed an actress with her husband touring in melodramas. The fractured story, besides offering up a romantic triangle involving a playwright, also allowed Miss Martin to sing upside down while tied to a torture wheel, and to hang from a tree while struggling heroically to rescue her infant from the falls of a mountainside, all the while being pursued by a bear and a sinister man named Chang Lu. From this bundle of miscellaneous adventures, nothing other than the star was well received. "The songs can sing about the sun and the stars as much as they wish without really making a dent in the overcast," wrote Walter Kerr, summing up impatiently. "Miss Martin forever, but not as Jennie."[9] The actress was out of work within a few miserable months, and Boston critic Kevin Kelly's comments that the songs sounded derivative of Rodgers and Hammerstein and others resulted in Kelly's being sued by Schwartz and Dietz.[10]

Brighter, glibber fare had lit up stages in the twenties and thirties, and many writers who tried matching the magic of Rodgers and Hammerstein during the golden era were either better suited to musical comedy or too simple-minded in their earnest imitations. Frank Loesser tried his hand at another serious work with the exceedingly pleasant *Greenwillow*, a vaguely wistful hybrid of infinite good will and down-home love that nearly drowned in its own artificial tears. The songs were poetically affecting; there were just too many of them, and so they became cloying. A bigger problem seems to have been the story—that is, if there actually was one. Frank Aston was dumbfounded to observe, "Frank Loesser's musical can't make up its mind what it is." Walter Kerr had an idea, he thought: "Do it yourself folklore.... *Greenwillow* is nowhere ... spun right out of somebody's head instead of out of somebody's past."[11] From Kenneth Tynan: "After Rodgers and Hammerstein's nuns, we now have Frank Loesser's curates.... He has reached the end of the line, and we must all wish him a rapid recovery, followed by a speedy return to the asphalt jungle."[12] Corpse inspector general Ken Mandelbaum, surveying the 95-performance derailment and noting the ironic praise showered on it by none other than Brooks Atkinson, termed Loesser's curiously abstract creation "too quaint and precious for its own good."[13] The score, though not without a few rays of melodic redemption, certainly supports Mandelbaum's assessment.

Lofty ideals alone will not a musical make. Meredith Willson tried adapting the movie *Miracle on Thirty Fourth Street* for the stage. He called his labor *Here's Love*, and for it he composed several quite charming numbers. Willson's sunny valentine to Santa Claus struck Harold Taubman as "machine tooled," while Richard Watts, Jr., conceded, "It would be virtually un American to suggest that the sweetness and light tended to become a little oppressive. The danger of the cheery *Here's Love* is that its concentration on benevolence could bring out the beast in you."[14] Willson's good-will-towards-men showmanship elicited raves from four of the reviewers, and the show lasted nearly long enough to please its benevolent backers. Santa Claus is better left to sing inside chimney tops one night per year.

Next—and maybe last of all—to follow the path of Rodgers and Hammerstein were Harvey Schmidt and Tom Jones. While students at the University of Texas, they began working on a musical that would end up being performed in dozens of countries around the world (through a staggering ten thousand productions). It opened at the off–Broadway Sullivan Street Playhouse, on May 3, 1960, and closed nearly 42 years later, on January 13, 2002. It is, of course, *The Fantasticks*, which fledgling producer Lore Note saw in an early version at a summer program at Barnard College in New York and, following more revisions which he requested, took to New York. It tells a heartfelt little tale of a boy and a girl who fall in and out of love through infatuation, hardship, disillusionment, and (perhaps above all) the meddling of their fathers—and end up together. The show's enduring standard, "Try to Remember," helped sustain it in the early years—so say those in the know. So did another hit, "Soon It's Gonna Rain."

And soon it would rain on Schmidt and Jones, who enjoyed commercial success over a brief three-show, six-year span, with each effort bringing down the curtain on a happily-ever-after stage picture. After *The Fantasticks*, they wrote the powerful *110 in the Shade*, based on the play *The Rainmaker*, about a woman who fears encroaching spinsterhood and finally finds love; and *I Do! I Do!*, the Mary Martin and Robert Preston tour-de-force about married life, filled with thoughtful verse and entrancing tunes. Thereafter, Schmidt and Jones wandered without any luck through a daunting series of troubled ventures, writing and rewriting for regional stages. *Celebration* is their most notable failure, for the exhilarating score is deftly carved out of modern jazz phrasing. As for its reportedly smug libretto about the young and beautiful prevailing over old age and corruption, Richard Watts, Jr., dubbed it "one of those pseudo morality plays."[15] In search of invention and release from the tried and the true, Schmidt and Jones lost their romantic compass.

As the 1950s faded away, so too did the dominance of the romantic musical. Ironically, the form's most successful proponents helped spell its doom. By the time they opened their last show, *The Sound of Music*, Rodgers and Hammerstein were facing yet another team of imitators who could only mimic their optimistic side: Rodgers and Hammerstein. Remember that Dick and Oscar had in better days shaded their sunny stories with characters and situations not so idealized—with loneliness and suicide, with sexual opportunism and death and imperial allusions to misogyny. Walter Kerr grew uneasy opening night on the Swiss Alps when confronted with a gaggle of giggling moppets and nuns. "Before *The Sound of Music* is halfway thorough its promising chores it becomes not only two sweet for words but almost too sweet for music.... The cascade of sugar is not confined to the youngsters. Miss Martin, too, must fall to her knees and fold her hands in prayer, while the breezes blow the kiddies through the windows.... the people on stage have all melted long before our hearts do."[16]

Over to Lerner and Loewe: Their long-winded *Camelot*, which began cranking forth its knights-of-the-round-table platitudes only one year after the lonely goatherd hit town, fooled few of the critics but did deliver an attractive score and plenty of spectacle. President John F. Kennedy was said to have loved the title song, resulting, it was also said, in box office salvation. *Variety* called *Camelot* "beautiful and not very bright," finding the score "excellent" but the "heavy, humorless book ... overlong to the point of tedium."[17] Observed Howard Taubman, "*Camelot* is weighed down by the burden of its book.... It shifts uneasily between light-hearted fancy and uninflected reality."[18]

Cupid's eternal warrior, Alan Jay Lerner, returned five years hence with an even more improbable audience assignment, *On a Clear Day You Can See Forever*, about a psychiatrist hypnotizing a patient and falling in love with the person she reveals herself to have been in a previous life. Fritz Loewe, by then a heart-attack survivor, was not with Lerner on this one, having opted for rest and leisure under a Palm Springs umbrella. Instead, Burton Lane had accepted the call to compose the songs following an aborted attempt by Richard Rodgers to do the same with the infuriatingly unreliable Lerner—who carried on like a heterosexual version of the late Larry Hart. The show's absolutely brilliant score, judged by Rodgers "one of the finest either man has ever turned out,"[19] could not withstand a chilly critical reception aimed at the libretto, "frail and rickety ... loses itself in a fog of metaphysics," according to Howard Taubman.[20]

The nail-biting, jet setting, drug-dependant, compulsive serial husband Alan Jay Lerner would spend the rest of his frenetic existence without Loewe, flitting from one hopeless new venture to the next. Except for the justly panned *Coco*, which Katharine Hepburn single-handedly saved from red ink, all managed to lose bundles of money for their respective investors. By the time his heather on the hill was as brown as old scrapbook photos, Lerner had gone through a total of eight different composers—and that many wives. In 1969, when the United States first landed a man on the moon, Lerner landed *Coco* on Broadway with a near non-score by sometime composer Andre Previn. *Lolita, My Love*, an out-of-town floporama composed by John Barry, is intriguingly described by Lerner's biographer, Edward Jablonski, to have offered "rhythmic, melodic, declaratory, versatile" songs, the score overall being "integrated with a vengeance."[21]

That was 1971. Five years later, to celebrate the nation's bicentennial anniversary, Lerner teamed up with Leonard Bernstein to write *1600 Pennsylvania Avenue*. It lasted seven fitful evenings at the National Theatre following an avalanche of total disdain by the reviewers. *Carmelina*, an admirable venture with Burton Lane music, lasted all of 17 performances. Three years later, Lerner had his final night on Broadway with *Dance a Little Closer*. This play about disarmament, with music by Charles Strouse—according to Jablonski "just the sort of musical [Lerner] and Loewe had disdained in their romantic golden years"[22]—disarmed the next morning. While at work adapting, with composer Gerard Kenny, the classic screwball comedy film *My Man Gregory*, Alan Jay Lerner, one of the greatest theatre lyricists of all time, died at 67. One of his last songs for the unproduced last project was titled "Garbage Isn't What It Used to Be."

Neither was love. At the end of the age of the romantic musical, another of its youthful practitioners, Jerry Herman, with the two big hits *Hello, Dolly!* and *Mame*, to his name, struck out with *Dear World*. Finally, Herman's penchant for feel-good show songs fell into the wrong neighborhood, prompting an increasingly impatient Clive Barnes to complain, "Looking at all three of Herman's scores, I am beginning to harbor the suspicion that he has only written one musical—and it's getting worse."[23] The first of three consecutive Herman flops, *World's* engaging score danced obliviously around the serious issues; too much Jerry Herman again got in the way of the story.

While the final offerings by both Rodgers and Hammerstein and Lerner and Loewe may have helped hasten the decline of sentimentalized treatments, a new generation of songwriters had already set into motion the incorporation of socially controversial behavior in the *main* characters. Leading the parade were Fred Ebb and John Kander, who brought their sexually ambivalent *Cabaret*, set in a risque Berlin night club of pre–Nazi Germany, to the Broadhurst Theatre at the opportune moment during the turbulent express-yourself 1960s. It was not timidly gift-wrapped in sanitized show songs like *Pipe Dream* or *Seventh Heaven*. The reviews were largely upbeat, and the Tony Awards it reaped en masse (including for Best Musical and Best Score) were well deserved.

And what for an encore? Kander and Ebb tried their hands at a more romantic work, *The Happy Time*, and they failed, especially with the critics. Martin Gottfried called the vibrant songs "old fashioned," the libretto "instantly forgettable." Richard Watts, Jr., termed it "a struggle between a brilliant production and a mediocre book," while other scribes complained of hyperactive set-heavy direction by Gower Champion.[24] With the mighty Merrick behind it all, *The Happy Time* jumped over a land mine of nasty notices and held on for an unhappy run of 286 performances.

When did cockeyed optimism exit the world of song and dance? Advance to the late year of 1979, to a time when two remaining giants, Richard Rodgers and Alan Jay Lerner, both opened shows in New York, both to critical drubbing. Lerner's *Carmelina*, with music by Burton Lane, has a commendably first-rate score. Clive Barnes liked what he heard, then went on to ask, "So what is wrong? Everything is according to formula…. It is just too old fashioned."[25]

I Remember Mama, another older fashioned workhorse, contained a handful of effective new Richard Rodgers melodics, and it was similarly burdened by its own musty allegiance to a worn-out template. In Walter Kerr's opinion, it bore "a dullness that can't be shooed away."[26] It was the dullness of a form recycled one too many times. By then, the voices of social discontent had infiltrated the American musical theatre, and they had caused a shift in subject matter away from the abiding control of conventional Judeo-Christian mores. Away from the boy next door, once assumed to be naturally interested in the girl next door.

And by then, too, a radical change in the very sound of popular music had thrown the older order into even deeper disarray, redefining, as it inevitably would, the compositional tone and thrust of songs comprising a score deemed by commercial producers most likely to succeed on younger ears.

Love was no longer a simple thing.

CHAPTER 7

The Age of Abbott

Like an angry conflagration of warring punks spilling out into a civilized crowd, two rival gangs nearly leapt off the stage and into the audience of the Winter Garden Theatre on September 16, 1959. Their gut-wrenching tensions, set poundingly to music by Leonard Bernstein, gave first-night theatergoers a ride they would never forget. The story of ethnic prejudice, star-crossed lovers and the transcendent hopes of youth, based on Shakespeare's *Romeo & Juliet*, had originally been conceived by Jerome Robbins back in 1949, under the working title "East Side Story." It finally arrived on Broadway eight years later with a book of gripping realism by Arthur Laurents, and with spare brittle lyrics by new kid on the block Stephen Sondheim.

West Side Story mined the darker realities of street life with sizzling theatricality—with a thunderbolt of a score that rode jazz and latin rhythms like a half-mad symphony forever on the verge of exploding. And it moved us with the eloquent lament of its young protagonists vowing in the end to help make the world a more tolerant place. The racially charged gang atmosphere at the center of the story is compounded when Tony, ex-member of the Jets, is pulled reluctantly back into service, then tragically falls in love with Maria, sister to Bernardo of the rival Sharks. The serious American musical play reached its apex when the world first heard "Something's Coming," "America," "Tonight," "Gee, Officer Krupke" and "Somewhere."

West Side Story was unlike all the other shows in town against which it would be competing—shows like *My Fair Lady, Jamaica, Li'l Abner, Happy Hunting, Oh, Captain!* and *Say, Darling.* The Tonys that year were swept by Meredith Willson's first and only big success, *The Music Man,* which had also pulled a perfect set of raves from the critics. *West Side Story* took only two Tonys, one for Jerome Robbins (choreography), the other for Oliver Smith (set design). Although the production ran for nearly two years and managed to turn a profit, business was never

84

In the foreground: Carol Lawrence and Larry Kert in *West Side Story*.

outstanding, as Sondheim and Laurents would both later recall. During the first months of the run, numerous "tired businessmen," routinely expecting another easy-to-take song and dancer, walked out well before intermission in displeasure.[1] Not until the musical was turned into a movie did the public come to recognize its extraordinary qualities.

The critics recognized them immediately. "The most brilliant and exciting dance show in years," announced *Variety*. Walter Kerr, one of five to issue ringing endorsements, wrote, "The radioactive fallout from *West Side Story* must still be descending on Broadway this morning. Jerome Robbins has put together, and then blasted apart, the most savage, restless, electrifying dance patterns we've been exposed to in a dozen seasons.... He has been almost sacrificially assisted in this macabre onslaught of movement by Leonard Bernstein, who for the most part has served the needs of the onstage threshing machine—dramatizing the footwork

rather than lifting emotions into song." Brooks Atkinson described it as "a pro-
foundly moving show that is as ugly as the city jungles and also pathetic, tender,
forgiving. *West Side Story* is an incandescent piece of work that finds odd bits of
reality amidst the rubbish of the streets. Everything is of a piece."[2]

It reached the summit of musical theatre history in this country, and there it
still stands. That it continues to excite younger generations is the greatest tribute
of all to its unflinching vision of inner-city strife and to the thrilling Bernstein-
Sondheim songs, as compelling and modern today as they sounded over forty
years ago when Kenneth Tynan described them "as smooth and savage as a cobra;
it sounds as if Puccini and Stravinsky had gone on a roller coaster ride."[3] Why did
Mr. Bernstein never compose another *West Side Story*—or at least something similar? How could he? How could anyone?

Looming like a theatrical muse over the entire proceedings was stage director George Abbott, whose flair for practical showmanship fairly ruled the golden
age of musicals. Indeed, Jerome Robbins, the actual force behind *West Side Story*'s
blitzing stagecraft and choreography, drew brilliantly upon the evolving pattern
of dance-driven shows that had been pioneered under the tutelage of his primary
mentor, Mr. Abbott. In a broader sense, Robbins and Laurents merged Oscar
Hammerstein's integrated book ideas with Abbott's chronic insistence on fast
moving action. By way of Abbott, in fact, Leonard Bernstein and Jerome Robbins
were grounded in a form of musical theatre that is terse, taut and fast-unfolding,
drivingly melodic and scarcely sentimental.

An avid and accomplished rhumba dancer on ballroom floors, Abbott had
co-written and directed *On Your Toes*, the first show to utilize dance as a story-
advancing instrument. He had co-authored, produced and directed the sexually
cynical *Pal Joey*. And he had staged Leonard Bernstein's two prior hits, *On the Town*
(with choreography by Robbins), which foreshadowed the dissonance in scoring
and choreography which would erupt full force in *West Side Story*; and *Wonderful Town*, another outing high on the jazz of New York City. Abbott's staging techniques had pushed the theatre inevitably towards the opening night in 1957 when
the Jets and Sharks would clash on the stage.

When people speak of the "golden age," a period that varies depending on
each person's desire to squeeze in favorite shows, they are speaking of the greater
part of George Abbott's career. Born in Forrestville, New York, in 1887, in his
impressionable youth he witnessed the dawn of the new Yankee tuner. A couple
of seasons after Mr. Abbott hit New York City and started landing acting jobs,
Jerome Kern opened *Very Good Eddie*. At the age of 38, Abbott penned the first
of numerous plays, a comedy hit called *The Fall Guy*. The next season, our seasoned trouper was directing and co-authoring his first legit play, the innovative
melodrama *Broadway*.

In 1932, he became a play producer. Three fast-paced years later, he teamed up
with Richard Rodgers and Lorenz Hart to direct the dialogue portions of *Jumbo*, sharing credit with staging director John Murray Anderson. In quick succession came a
string of successful credits in association with Rodgers and Hart: co-librettist for *On*

Your Toes; sole librettist, producer and director of *The Boys from Syracuse*; and producer and director of *Too Many Girls*. Then came *Pal Joey* and a slate of successful ventures over the next twenty years, not a few of them reportedly saved by Abbott's touch. By all evidence, Abbott had absorbed the no-nonsense pacing styles of vaudeville, for his own productions brimmed with crackling dialogue, snappy jokes and banter, and they moved with gusto and speed. His most famous mantra was, Say it in as few words as possible! He thrived in musical comedy.

The go-go Abbott style—faster, snappier, wittier—made him a master of compensatory showmanship, and perhaps for that reason he was believed by his detractors to be suspiciously lucky in the art of casting and direction. Stephen Sondheim, whose show *A Funny Thing Happened on the Way to the Forum* Abbott took to Broadway, and for which Abbott and a roster of others connected with it (not including Mr. Sondheim) won Tonys, was ill-impressed with what he saw: "I just didn't think he had any talent," said Sondheim. "I found him a completely humorless person."[4] And author Ethan Mordden, a respecter of Abbott-directed musicals ("intelligible as a whole"), yet found them typically weighted with actors delivering lines rather than "portraying characters," and typically weak on second act progress. "He gets so much done in Act One that after the intermission he has too little story to deal with and tends to irrelevant episodes or a spate of humors. *Fiorello!'s* 'Gentleman Jimmy' is one such, a charleston number that the show doesn't really need."[5]

Debatable, that. Second acts, which are often difficult to sustain because of insufficient conflict, need whatever they can get to reach final curtain without a loss of audience interest. During out-of-town work on Irving Berlin's *Call Me Madame*, Abbott, sensing last-act deficiencies, conveyed his discomfort to the famed songwriter, who went out and whipped up the last pop song hit of his career, "Just in Love." Not only did it deliver the needed lift, after the first performance of the song up in Boston audiences demanded and got seven encores!

According to Berlin's biographer, Laurence Bergreen, Abbott's dominating presence during *Call Me Madame's* pre–Broadway road tour was definitely and not delightfully felt by book writers Howard Lindsay and Russel Crouse. To his shock, Lindsay heard actors reading lines neither he nor his partner had written. He made a few cracks about it to some company members. Soon after, Lindsay and Crouse were summoned to meet alone with the director in the lobby, were they were brusquely informed that if changes needed to be made, they would be made. As Bergreen described it, the show's official book writers acquiesced to Mr. Abbott's "grim and purposeful regime."[6]

Along the way, the grim and purposeful director excelled ironically in musical comedy, and he discovered and helped launch the careers of many of its most illustrious practitioners. He cast young Nancy Walker in the Hugh Martin–Ralph Blane *Best Foot Forward*, something about a glamour girl being sent off on a publicity stunt to date a local boy at a school prom. Miss Walker was so funny that she got placed in Mr. Abbott's next funny show, *On the Town*, playing one of three young ladies who become involved in a night of flirtatious socializing with three sailors on a 24-hour leave. And Abbott took a chance, with the same show, on two young stand-up comedians, Betty Comden (who played another one of the girls) and Adolph Green. *On the Town* was the first musical to sell motion picture rights before it even opened.

Comden and Green were never funnier than when at work on an Abbott show. *On the Town* offers four big comedy numbers—"Come Up to My Room," "I'm Blue," "I Get Carried Away," and "I Can Cook Too." *Wonderful Town*, put together by the same creative team minus Jerome Robbins, contains another laugh load—"I Could Pass That Football," "Ohio," "What a Waste!" and "One Hundred Easy Ways." Nor was Irving Berlin at a loss for humor when he composed the comedy numbers for Ethel Merman and *Call Me Madame*, topped by "Can You Use Any Money Today?," a savage put-down of government waste.

An Abbott show had little time for starry-eyed strolls up hillsides laced with spring heather. In the mid-fifties he got behind a promising team, Richard Adler and Jerry Ross, co-authoring and directing their two gigantic back-to-back, one-thousand-plus-performance musical *comedy* hits, *Pajama Game* and *Damn Yankees*. Jerome Robbins shared directing chores with Abbott and dance chores with Bob Fosse on *Pajama Game*, while Fosse alone, another of Abbott's fabulous finds, designed the footwork for *Yankees*. Both shows charged out of the gate full blast, *Pajama Game* with "Racing with the Clock," *Yankees* with "Six Months Out of Every Year!" Both scores stressed high energy, and both shows earned raves. "Fast, raucous, and rollicking," wrote John McClain of *Pajama Game*.[7] Robert Coleman termed *Damn Yankees* "The town's newest dynamic darling!"[8]

During a career that lasted into his one hundredth birthday (evidently, a fast-paced life can be a healthy one, too), Mr. Abbott's crowning achievement was surely the 1959 smash, *Fiorello!*, based on the political career of New York's beloved Mayor Fiorello LaGuardia. Abbott not only directed the show but co-scripted it with Jerome Weidman. It won the expected Tony Awards (tying for many, including Best Musical, with *The Sound of Music*), and captured the Pulitzer Prize for Drama. Let George do it! Jerry Bock and Sheldon Harnick, who created the songs for *Fiorello!*, did. The near-perfect score, arguably Bock and Harnick's finest work, contains the haunting "When Did I Fall in Love," the wistfully funny "I Love a Cop," and the angry anthem, "I'll Marry the Very Next Man." "Under Mr. Abbott's invincible direction," declared Brooks Atkinson, "the whole show comes to life with gusto."[9]

Snap, crackle and Abbott. Of some 24 new musicals he would work on during his most prolific and successful period—from 1936 until 1962—all but six were box-office lush. That's batting .750. His proteges by then were breaking out on their own. Fosse would direct and choreograph *Red Head* and *Sweet Charity*; Robbins had already left his celebrated imprint on *The King and I*, *Bells Are Ringing*, *West Side Story* and *Gypsy*. And before retiring permanently to the New York City Ballet—there to share the reins with another hoofer who had once also worked on tuners, George Balanchine—Robbins put his touch on *Funny Girl* as well as on yet one more smash, *Fiddler on the Roof*.

Tom Bosley, center, as Mayor Fiorello La Guardia in *Fiorello!*

They all mastered an intuitive understanding of what it takes theatrically to make a musical *work*. Who can say how many shows that met with failure might be better known today, might even now be playing the regionals or community playhouses, had they initially been fitted into better working order by George Abbott or one of his pushy proteges? The form needs, many have argued, book-based solidity in order to work. Yet on a more critical level musical theatre thrives, in fact live or dies, on *production* far more often than the idealists are willing to concede. And it is the director who is usually best equipped to give it the benefit of a production that can well spell the difference between failed work of art and audience-pleasing diversion.

Raised during the hurly burly years of vaudeville, whose assorted stage gimmickry he no doubt memorized, Mr. Abbott came to Broadway with a big bag of shtick that helped a number of marginal tuners bake and fake their way into the black. *Billion Dollar Baby*, a 1945 outing at the Alvin Theatre that met with variable notices and turned a profit on a mere 219 curtains, had book and lyrics by Comden and Green, music by Morton Gould, and a Donaldson award for the director. *High Button Shoes*, completely rewritten during hectic out-of-town travails, had banal lyrics by Sammy Cahn and music both very good and not so by Jule Styne, composing his first songs for Broadway. It had one big radio hit in "Papa, Won't You Dance with Me." And it had Abbott. "For a musical that's not very good," wrote Louis Kronenberger, "*High Button Shoes* is a very good musical, indeed." Another money maker.[10]

Much the same could be said of Mr. Abbott's next venture, *Where's Charley?* Another amusing mediocrity, *Charley* gave songwriter Frank Loesser his first crack at show scoring. The book and direction were by Abbott. The dances were by Balanchine. The mixed reviews were by the regulars. The real force behind a lush two year stay at the St. James Theatre, so said expert watchers, was dancing star-comedian Ray Bolger. "He is great enough to make a mediocre musical show seem thoroughly enjoyable,"[11] remarked Brooks Atkinson. In fact, as Steven Suskin reminds us in his tome *Opening Nights on Broadway*, "this was the third consecutive poorly reviewed show that Bolger built into a hit."[12] The others? *By Jupiter* and *Three to Make Ready*.

Despite generally unfriendly reviews, *Look Ma, I'm Dancin'!*, for which Hugh Martin wrote the songs, Jerome Lawrence and Robert E. Lee collaborated on the script, earned a little money for the investors after only 188 performances. Count among its redeeming assets George Abbott, who produced and co-directed; Jerome Robbins, who co-directed and choreographed; and star Nancy Walker, who gave the exasperated reviewers at least one reason to smile. Chirped Robert Coleman, "Rack up another hit for George Abbott.... Nancy Walker is terrific, a one-woman show all by herself."[13]

Abbott would work wonders through the 1950s turning two disparate projects, each built on shaky foundations, into marginal money makers. *New Girl in Town*, the so-so Robert Merrill tuner based on Eugene O'Neill's "Anna Christie," with a book and direction by Abbott, was no doubt aided by his clever embellishments along with the glitzy footwork fashioned by Bob Fosse. *Once Upon a Mattress*, adapted from the fairy tale *The Princess and the Pea*, was a kind of children's musical for adults that luckily had the Abbott touch and, most of all, the services of bright new funny face, Carol Burnett. *Mattress* had a mildly amusing book and one of the weakest scores ever to sneak into a New York house—the music by none other than Mary Rodgers, daughter of Richard, the bargain basement lyrics by Marshall Barer. A tad more talented than her collaborator, Ms. Rodgers did pen a trio of sweet tunes, the most memorable one being "Normandy." Problem is, some savvy listeners, mystified by the presence of only one such strong number, are even more unimpressed when they hear in "Normandy" a clear resemblance to "My Funny Valentine," a tune composed by Ms. Rodgers' famous father.[14] How good a musical? Once Carol Burnett departed the company, *Mattress* folded almost instantly.

The same outwitting of mediocre materials nearly repeated itself when Abbott and Burnett returned to Gotham five years later, this time with a vehicle that could boast a more interesting book and a real—at least, half real—score. It was called *Fade Out, Fade In*, and in it Burnett played aspiring screen actress Hope Springfield.

Music by Jule Styne and words by Comden and Green gave Carol plenty of reasons to shine at first—until the songs stop shining. "Pretty commonplace in its ingredients," registered Richard Watts, Jr., one of five favorably inclined first-night reviewers, "but it has enough enthusiasm, relish and gusto to make it entertaining."[15]

Abbott's direction no doubt helped keep it alive for nearly 300 performances, and it might have easily lasted longer had its star not departed so prematurely. There is only so much that expert stagers can do with substandard stuff when their Carol Burnett or Ray Bolger decides to bolt, and bolt Ms. Burnett did, following a taxi accident, dozens of poorly attended performances missed during sick time, and a sudden TV offer to star in her first series, "The Entertainers." *Fade Out* producer Lester Osterman, unable to sustain business without his headliner, suspended operations and went to court to get her back. By the time, four acrimonious months later, that Actors' Equity ordered Burnett to resume work in a musical waiting to reopen with her, the marketing momentum was gone. *Fade Out* faded back onto the boards the following February, only to begin a slow second fade, this one lasting just two months. You may be the best director in the world, but you need the necessary materials and performers and luck to make you *look* like the best director in the world.

Broadway's grand master faltered on a few occasions during his heyday years, although even his failures tended to log respectable runs. He was brought in during out-of-town gnashing of teeth to replace original director Agnes de Mille on Cole Porter's musically beguiling *Out of This World*. Abbott could not come up with the pizazz to salvage a rambling treatment by novices Dwight Taylor and Reginald Lawrence of the Amphitryon legend. Insiders considered the affair too controversially stacked with g-strings and sex jokes to find patronage in the early 1950s. Cole Porter's excellent score strained for connectedness in a curiously set-deficient context. Musicals need to establish immediately a strong sense of place, without which all the breaking-into-song comes off as so much premature ejaculation. Out of the muddled work came one of Porter's most haunting refrains, and it didn't even make it into New York City—"From this Moment On."

Mr. Abbott did not, on average, fare nearly so well with more serious material. You will recall his rescue work on the belabored Rodgers and Hammerstein fizzle *Me and Juliet*. Again, here was a poorly reviewed work that barely managed to earn a little money for the investors. The much superior *A Tree Grows in Brooklyn* gave Abbott another sentimental story of the sort he ordinarily avoided. A man who preferred strong melodies, no doubt he fell under the steady enchantment of Arthur Schwartz's tunes, set finely to words by Dorothy Fields in her prime. Abbott co-wrote the libretto with Betty Smith, author of the 1943 novel of the same name upon which it was based. Herbert Ross was signed to direct the dance routines. Shirley Booth was cast to play the wife of a sporadically employed heavy drinker in a working class neighborhood. The critics mostly loved the show, and they all adored Miss Booth like autograph seekers, calling her role the performance of a lifetime. The songs were fresh and vibrant and emotionally in touch with the story. The music for "Halloween Ballet" is extraordinary.

Zero Mostel and director George Abbott backstage during a performance of *A Funny Thing Happened on the Way to the Forum.*

"George Abbott comes through with one of the most impressive jobs of his career as co-author, director and producer," declared Hobe Morrison in *Variety.* "Audiences will generally lap up the show's weepy moments as well as its comedy … which makes *Brooklyn* the box office sock it is."[16] Yet the whole "sock" thing lasted far less than a year at the Alvin Theatre. What was so wrong with it that four other raving critics also failed to see? Otis L. Guernsey, Jr., one of two lone dissenters, saw this: "Miss Booth gives light and contour to a gloomy, flat piece of work."[17] The lackluster fate of *A Tree* remains one of the more curious enigmas of musical theatre.

As the golden era of musicals passed into history, George Abbott and his grim purposeful regime would wrestle with many more properties that did not add luster to the master's unparalleled track record. *Anya* had songs by *Kismet* creators Robert Wright and George Forrest based on the musical themes of Sergei

Rachmaninoff. It had a book by Abbott and Guy Bolton. Yes, *that* Guy Bolton. Dismissed by the newspaper judges as dated operetta, it lasted for a couple of weeks. *Tenderloin*, which opened in less than a year following the premiere of *Fiorello!*, was a follow up collaboration with the same creative team—Bock, Harnick and Weidman—obviously intended to duplicate the success of the first show. True to tradition, it did not. Regarded by Bock and Harnick fans as a notable failure, *Tenderloin* may have been compromised out of its original milieu by Mr. Abbott himself. Ken Mandelbaum suggested a sell-out to the balancing imagery of virtue: "They had to devote as much time to the dull good characters as to the highly entertaining bad ones."[18] The time was 1960.

During the more liberal years which followed, Mr. Abbott stumbled with two politically charged works. *Flora, The Red Menace* was Abbott's *105th* show, and it was the first musical by John Kander and Fred Ebb to reach Broadway. Liza Minnelli played an innocent young all–American woman getting conned into joining a communist cell. During traumatic out-of-town tryouts, a telegram went out for Mr. Abbott's famed salvage services. Though he heeded the cable, he did not work the magic either with script doctoring or fresh direction. The show pulled off a couple of raves before fading fast, leaving behind an original cast album that is coveted by collectors. A few of the better songs promise fine things ahead for the team, still then in search of a definitive voice.

The Education of H*Y*M*A*N K*A*P*L*A*N (1968), which Abbott directed, involved a lot of people who did not go on to enjoy Abbott-blessed careers: songwriters Paul Nassau and Oscar Brand, choreographer Jaime Rogers, librettist Benjamin Zavin, producers Andre Galston, Jack Farren and Stephen Mellow. Was it the material or was it the director? "A parade of forties–early fifties musical comedy cliches and virtually a parody of the kind of direction that George Abbott provided at the time,"[19] quipped an impatient Martin Gottfried. The dauntless Abbott returned the following year with another sad embarrassment, *Fig Leaves Are Falling*, a turkey he was talked into trimming after Jack Klugman, who had initially agreed to direct, opted instead to pursue acting auditions in Hollywood.

Abbott was back in 1976 with the book and direction for a Richard Adler bomb *Music Is*. Music it wasn't, although it earned the distinction of *doubling* the attendance record of *Fig Leaves Are Falling*—by four performances. And back again in the 1970s, when he staged an unsuccessful revival of *Pajama Game* and saw two of his earlier successes, *Pal Joey* and *Where's Charley*, successfully restaged by others. And in 1982, a very good year for George Abbott, who directed the return to Broadway of *On Your Toes*. And in 1987, not a very good year, when Mr. Abbott, on the eve of his 100th birthday, revived his first Broadway directing assignment, *Broadway*. It ran three nights.

All curtains must fall. Although the profession had outlived Mr. Abbott, it had never passed him by, not by a hundred workable gimmicks of stagecraft. His practical form of populist entertainment would continue to guide and inspire younger generations of directors and writers when faced with the same vexing hurdles that invariably arise out of troubled librettos: What to do when they don't pan out nearly as well on the stage as they seemed to in print or in the misleading format of the productionless staged reading? Harried directors and fretting producers have been known to resort to any number of tricks utilized by the old master to turn a borderline work into a workable hit. (Example: Joseph Lapine's deft saving direction for the ponderously theme-heavy *Into the Woods*.)

When did the so-called golden age of musicals end? Let's mark the night in 1962 at the Alvin Theatre, when George Abbott, nearing his 75th birthday, opened his last bona fide hit, *A Funny Thing Happened on the Way to the Forum*. That night, the master of musical comedy staging turned over the reins of change to a much younger talent, Stephen Sondheim, who would prove to be quite revolutionary himself, in a strange, counterproductive way. The beginning of some kind of an end was set into motion when the deceptively older-fashioned *Forum* opened, giving Sondheim, until then regarded primarily as a lyricist, the precedent he had all along needed to establish his own composing credentials. Thereafter it freed Sondheim from having to collaborate with and suffer the commercial preoccupations of other composers who favored popular songwriting styles.

Before we reluctantly depart the golden age, a few words from a couple of the four scribes who delivered strong endorsements for George Abbott's final success. From Walter Kerr: "There's nothing but the comedy going for it, and our clowns need to pile up twenty or thirty gags on top of one another before the pyramid topples and you break up as it does ... and I find it kindly of director George Abbott to have given us an admittedly lowbrow and unpretentiously merry good time once again."

And from Robert Coleman: "You'll either love it or loathe it. In our book, it looms as a hot ticket. A riotous and rowdy hit."[20]

It ran for 764 performances. It made money. And people are still producing it in theatres big and small all over the country.

CHAPTER 8

Your Own Thang

Rock—the most stressful word in musical theatre. Mention the words "rock musical" and a shrieking chorus of the insulted and ignored, the bitchy and the beleaguered will come out from behind their old-time original cast album collections to tell you everything that has gone wrong with Broadway. Listening to the diehards rant on about past glories, *pre-rock*, one could easily—and prematurely— conclude that nothing much of value has transpired on Times Square since, say, the latest revival of *Very Good Eddie* or Ken Bagley's most recent Cole Porter Revisited release.

The saga of what went wrong, and the attendant trashing of rock music, is riddled with neurotic generalizations and with incredible across-the-board dismissal of some fine shows that continue to get written and produced. Imagine someone standing along the shore and pointing to a bottle floating aimlessly upon the sea, and blaming it for a catastrophic tidal wave. That about describes the level of reason exhibited by those wounded disciples of Kern and Porter and Gershwin and Arlen. It has been over forty years since Richard Rodgers and Oscar Hammerstein, of all people, slipped into *The Sound of Music*, of all shows, one of the first fifties-style rock songs ever sung in an American musical, "No Way to Stop It." And, still, the old guard is trying to stop it, still woefully whining about the so-called demise of great show songs carved in Cohan. They persist in ignoring an axiom ages old in theatre: Popular music invariably finds a way into stage shows. It may take it years after first basking in *Billboard* top 20 status, but it happens. It happens because that's what audiences want.

No, there was no way to stop it. There never was. Does the music of today sound like Gilbert and Sullivan? Does it sound like Victor Herbert? It does not even sound much like Jerome Kern. Contemporary songwriting helps push the musical forward in interesting new directions, some quite exciting. Without such a dynamic, *West Side Story* would never have been written. Neither would, in its time, *Very Good Eddie*. Fascinating to contemplate what Dick and Oscar *might* have done with their "No Way to Stop It" inclinations had their partnership lived on. Certainly, at the very end they still asserted their talents in a timely fashion, if only in the passing phases of traditional scoring. In *Flower Drum Song*, almost hidden behind a lotus leaf, a cute little ditty—"You be the rock, I'll be the roll"—pops out to test the waters for maybe all of a minute.

And in *The Sound of Music*, "No Way to Stop It" was not the only evidence of shrewd commercial sensitivity to the present. "Edelweiss," the very last song that Dick and Oscar wrote together, so perfectly captures the folk idiom that many people today mistake it for an authentic folk song, not realizing that its actual genesis was not along the River Rhine but in an American song and dance show. Now, *that's* craft.

Richard Rodgers wrote about songs reflecting the times in which they were written. He and Oscar would soon, however, have lost out to the long-haired set. Something drastic was on the rise: Rock and roll would jump the logical evolution in show music by virtue of its blunt anti-establishment agenda. Narrowly focused as most of it would become on a disillusioned society of youthful rebels, only the young could get away with singing its songs of protest and disdain. And the musicals which encompassed their strident attitudes were limited in topic and characters. Older Broadway songwriters were knocked off their feet by the radical shift in tone and rhythm.

Before the guitar poets came to town, younger stage composers had already tinkered in twang. In 1956, one year following the release of *Blackboard Jungle*— the first movie to feature rock music ("Rock Around the Clock")—critic John Chapman attended the opening of the vibrantly mediocre *Mr. Wonderful*, produced by Jule Styne and composed by relative newcomers Jerry Bock, Larry Holofcener, and George Weiss, and issued the first warning signal. Chapman called it "the loudest show ever to be presented in a New York playhouse. The management has got the theatre's stage miked up to within a fraction of an inch of chaos. If your hearing is normal, the best way to attend *Mr. Wonderful* would be to bring two hearing aids, plug one in each ear and turn everything off."[1] The pop-flavored score contains a number, "Jacques D'Iraque" that rocks almost unconsciously— as if by creative accident—to the dynamic new beat of the times.

Charles Strouse and Lee Adams spoofed Elvis Presley's pelvic action in "Honestly Sincere," a number composed for their 1960 hit, *Bye Bye Birdie*. In the same show, they merged standard show music with basic fifties rock and roll in "The Telephone Hour." Their strong score for the unsuccessful *Golden Boy* rode the rhythms not of rock but of jazz and pop. And their 1966 offering, *It's a Bird, It's a Plane, It's Superman*, which despite decent notices failed to fly, flirted too with rock and roll in the edgy "It's Super Nice" and "We Need Him." Alas, the best songs they created for Clark Kent came straight out of standard musical comedy. The real revolution to come would depend upon younger songwriters.

More full of guitar work, though hardly a rock show, was the fairly joyless *A Joyful Noise*, starring John Raitt in fine voice, which opened on December 15, 1966.

Whatever it really intended to be in the beginning remains a riff of a puzzlement. Oscar Brand and Paul Nassau had composed their songs in the folk and Nashville vein. As recording dates and opening nights approached, they were pressured to make things sound more "Broadway" by producer Edward Padula, working to placate record company executives and investors clamoring ironically for a more contemporary sound. Most felt the watered down results were neither authentic, defined or tuneful. Actually, the resulting split-personality score is at its most appealing in the earlier segments when its more traditional numbers are *seasoned* with Nashville; at its least interesting towards the final refrains, derived wholly from generic country and folk songwriting patterns.

In the spring of 1967, less than a year following the opening of *A Joyful Noise*, flower children of America were boarding Greyhound busses and hitchhiking with do-your-own-thing strangers to San Francisco. Meanwhile, back in New York, Jule Styne, Adolph Green, and Betty Comden were watching their gospel-blues *Hallelujah, Baby!* slowly succumb to an indifferent box office. Clearly, Styne the old pro was vaguely in touch with the newer sounds. With a guitar, a little weed and longer locks he might have found his way to San Jose.

Rock and rollers who endeavored to remake Broadway in their own image had to be around sixteen going on seventeen—with dirt under their arms, good bodies, and a natural contempt for society. From its inception, the music that Elvis Presley made nationally famous, one Sunday night on the Ed Sullivan TV show, railed implicitly against '50s conformity; it blew away class distinctions and pointed to a new kind of sexual freedom before those words even existed. Then came the war in Vietnam, and in the increasing public protest against the sending of American troops to help fight it, the young songwriters found a righteous cause to fuel their discontent. In musical stage shows, their street-wise polemics allowed scarce time for dramatic development or for character delineation. They, their contemporary music and their sex appeal were the main attractions.

If the mediocre *A Joyful Noise* marked the first real departure away from standard Broadway scoring, it was off–Broadway's *Your Own Thing*, the following season, which officially rose the curtain on the new rock musical. And in such a trite way. Hester and Danny Apolinar's libretto had a twin brother and sister singing team shipwrecked on Manhattan Island. The sister, Viola, cross-dresses in a devious effort to join a typical all-male rock group, and is soon getting eyes from Olivia, believing "him" to be one cool dude. In the end, Olivia settles for Viola's twin brother, who bears a good-enough resemblance to Viola in drag. Apart from the silly retro 1920s plot, the songs of *Your Own Thing* are unmemorable.

Move ahead three months, and enter Galt MacDermot, who would achieve the dubious distinction, in this book at least, of king of rock musical composers. In his youth, he played the organ at church, wrote rock and jazz tunes and performed in dance bands. Besides the five full Broadway scores he would create, he also contributed background music for productions of *Hamlet, Twelfth Night, The Tale of Cymbeline*, and for plays by, among others, Tennessee Williams. Like most musicians seeking gainful employment, MacDermot was indiscriminate in his

Hair.

choice of material, especially, it appears, after he joined ranks with Gerome Ragni and James Rado, all with a keen ear for the unfolding flower-power era, to create *Hair*. And that is when Cole Porter sycophants began hyperventilating over the future of original cast albums.

With a book by Ragni and Rado, the latter of whom also penned the lyrics, *Hair* was actually a laid-back revue of attitudes held by longhairs of the day. It hit a resounding nerve with younger audiences and trendy adult patrons at the Biltmore Theatre, where it ran for 1,750 performances. *Hair* sang publicly of the most private thoughts—from politics to penises, masturbation to sodomy—topics ordinarily confined to peep-hole films and cut-rate group-therapy. It exploited almost every aspect of Hippiedom with an earthy eloquence never before exactly seen on a Broadway stage. The critics all fell positively in line, as if partly in fear of losing cool credibility in the modern world. Theatre professionals were not so pandering. When Richard Rodgers walked out of *Hair* during the opening night intermission, he walked out on the biggest hit of the season.[2]

Hair sent out a call to disillusioned young people everywhere. Next to snub the establishment by way of Times Square exploitation was the shocking *Oh,*

Calcutta, a nude revue produced by the otherwise esteemed London critic Kenneth Tynan. Without his prestigious stamp the cast may have ended up in handcuffs on opening night; during extended periods of the show, they bared their all. The public responded in droves, the critics with snickering derision. As people like Clive Barnes saw it, Mr. Tynan's sleazy trick had only sex on its mind, whereas *Hair* offered redeeming drugged-up moments of hip masturbatory wisdom. "Voyeurs of the city unite," admonished critic Barnes. Opined Walter Kerr, "Anything [here] will do so long as it meets two requirements: that the actors undress and that they engage in simulated sex play."[3] Armed with a wide ranging set of potent songs by the Open Window's Peter Schickele, Stanley Walden and Robert Dennis, about which more later, Tynan's artsy strip-tease ran past six nasty reviews to hang around for a three-year run, at one point transferring up to the larger Belasco Theatre.

Times Square—yeah, man, it was a changin'. Society's downtrodden souls suddenly were all over the boards. *The Me Nobody Knows* let actual kids from poor New York city slums sing eloquently of their fragile dreams for a way out. The show's best choruses—"Dream Babies," "Light Songs," "How I Feel," and "Something Beautiful"—were fashioned from early-'70s light rock sentiments. Credit Gary William Friedman and Wilt Holt for the sensitive score. Generally disagreeable notices, however, pointed to book problems. "Its materials are by school children who are not necessarily poets," pointed out the reserved Mr. Kerr, "but two hours of plainness ... can wear down the best will in the world." Clive Barnes "loved it," characterizing its young affecting cast as "the me nobody wants to remember."[4]

When the oppressed take to the stage, the results can be oppressive. Rare was the show like *Purlie*, which had gospel-clapping fun up its sleeve. And although most of its songs by Peter Udell and Gary Geld were borderline forgettable, the rousing "I Got Love" got loads of airplay. *Purlie* pushed on past mixed notices for well over a season and ended up in the red. Another look at the problems of black people, Micki Grant's *Don't Bother Me, I Can't Cope*, reportedly offered more humor, maybe the reason why it lasted for over two years and became the longest-running "gospel" musical. Whatever the show's timely charms, Grant's songs were pedestrian stuff—certainly when compared to the better popular music heard on radios in 1972. By then, rock musicals were already starting to sound derivative and dated.

There was one remarkable exception. In the 1960s, John Lennon had caused public outrage when he smugly asserted the Beatles to be more popular than Jesus Christ. Maybe true for a moment in time, until a couple of very young and audacious Englishmen by the names of Tim Rice and Andrew Lloyd Webber put the savior on the map with controversial showmanship. Their daringly titled *Jesus Christ Superstar* blazed a bold new trail in stage shows. It had Rice's direct, unadorned words and Webber's jarringly youthful rhythms (he was only 23 years old at the time). Garishly theatrical though it may have been, at the center it held up to unsparing scrutiny the exposed nerves of the characters. Musically, the

Jesus Christ Superstar: Jeff Fenholt (center) played the Savior and Marta Heflin (at Fenholt's feet) was Mary Magdalene in the New York production.

harrowing climax achieved around a bloody cross was as engulfing as an acid rock concert in full amplified frenzy. The work gave legitimacy to the rock musical.

Other composers with similar passions followed suit. Peter Link and C.C. Courtney gave us the finely realized 1969 off–Broadway pleasure *Salvation*. Stephen Schwartz showed up in the spring of 1971 with the pleasant *Godspell*. Now, the light of hip Christendom was shining down on New York audiences. Schwartz would enjoy follow up success with two more shows, both composed in a mellower light-rock vein for mainstream crowds and younger ears, and he would be rewarded with profitable patronage. Hardly a risk taker of any sort, Schwartz's music tended towards bland derivations of top 20 favorites. In *Godspell*, he let the Jesus story carry the show, and carry the show it did—for six years at various venues from the Cherry Lane Theatre in the Village where it opened, to the Promenade, another off–Broadway house, and finally to the Broadhurst Theatre on Broadway. The elevating "Day by Day" became a bona fide hit, and, for Schwartz, a popular reputation ensued, complete with a growing crowd of younger fans who could point to a composer roughly their own age. Seven road companies toured the country at one time. When it returned in 1988 to off–Broadway, *Godspell* didn't last even a year. By then, all the bell-bottomed Jesus hippies had turned their attentions to other pursuits.

A number of rock composers tried duplicating the Rice-Webber marketing strategy by first putting out albums of songs from their respective works-in-progress in order to establish commercial credibility and snare the interest of stage producers. It rarely worked, nor did various other treatments of the story of Christ find any success in New York. The era actually favored lighter fare, and the harsh sound of angry guitar players soon gave way to less strident forms of popular music.

Grease, billed as "A New '50s Rock 'N Roll Musical," seized on the sympathetic atmosphere in 1972 to launch a record-shattering eight year run, not broken until *A Chorus Line* came along. *Grease* began life at Chicago's Kingston Mines Theatre, moved the following year to the off–Broadway Eden Theatre, and on to the Broadhurst in 1972. The musical spoofed early fifties rock and roll with affection. To its eternal advantage, it presented likable young teenagers hardly at war with the world or society, just caught up in their own innocuous after-school pastimes and dating rituals. The most tense plot turn concerned a single girl whose fear of an unwanted pregnancy proved luckily unfounded.

And, of course, there were newer composers more pop than rock oriented who also benefited from the drastic changes in show scoring. *The Wiz*, a slickly packaged African American version of *The Wizard of Oz*, was a Tony Award winner for Best Musical and Best Score, loved by younger crowds and the young-at-heart during its long commercial harvest at the Majestic Theatre. The mostly cool reception from the press would not keep them away, nor would it discourage Hollywood from making a not very good or successful movie of the whole thing. The modern-sounding songs of Charles Smalls came winningly out of Motown and Disco. Smalls was one of few African Americans ever to compose for the stage. He

Dorothy (Stephanie Mills) and the Scarecrow (Hinton Battle) in *The Wiz.*

proved himself a more than worthy candidate for additional assignments, which, alas, never came around.

Stephen Schwartz struck more gold on his next two projects, *Pippin* and *The Magic Show*. Professional evaluators much liked *Pippin*, but they did not much like its successor. It's hard to know what there was to like about *Pippin*, the tale of a young man who drops out of college in the late '60s and tries to find himself. *Pippin* lumbered aimlessly across the boards while the spaced-out hero searched for the meaning of life and delivered some cool-sounding philosophies—cool, at least, to himself, and maybe to the younger patrons out in the seats. Both *Pippin* and *The Magic Show* enjoyed very long runs.

Berkeley to Broadway: Pimply-faced charisma camouflaged reams of inferior shows. The young in all their restless energy and charm have a way of pulling in voyeuristic crowds. And the best rock composers of the day weren't even composing for Broadway at all, unlike their counterparts in earlier times. McCartney

The "Togetherness" number in *Promises, Promises.*

and Lennon might have summoned forth something very novel and substantial had they gotten the urge—or the call from a persuasive producer. So too might have groups like the Doors or Yes or The Moody Blues, all of whom, grounded in serious music training, possessed the complex intensity to score dramatic properties. Producer David Merrick reached in this direction when he engaged popmasters Burt Bacharach and Hal David to write the songs for his 1968 hit *Promises, Promises*, the energizing adult musical comedy based on Billy Wilder's film *The Apartment*, with a book by Neil Simon.

Those younger guitarists and keyboard players who did compose for the stage served, for the most part, as their own book writers. Some no doubt shunned the association of veteran librettists. Some no doubt (as Paul Simon would later mistakenly conclude) felt they had the talent to do it all. Fie on anyone who dared question their hip take on the state of the world and how to get high! The spotty to miserable results of their literary labors should not surprise anyone who has charted the ups and downs of a musical or two. Most of these musicians, to their credit, got hooked on theatre and tried cementing careers in it. Sadly, most all of them ran up against their own obsolescence fast, like so many once really neat records withering away under the indifferent sun in cardboard boxes at flea markets.

There is nothing quite so unwanted as yesterday's sex symbols. Galt MacDermot of *Hair* fame switched collaborators in 1971, opting for the services of playwright John Guare and director Mel Shapiro (of *The House of Blue Leaves*), a shrewd commercial choice on both counts. With words by Guare and a book by Guare and Shapiro, MacDermot hit a second home run with *Two Gentlemen of Verona*, which Joseph Papp and his New York Shakespeare festival first presented under open skies in the summer of 1971 before moving it indoors to the St. James Theatre. Loved by everyone, it won Tony Awards for Best Musical and Best Book, and enjoyed a healthy run. Whatever all the happiness was about does not come through on the cast album, rife with forgettable tunes, barely passable lyrics (no wonder Guare was never heard from in this capacity again) and a pleasantly laid-back air that sounds like half the cast was stoned during original cast recording sessions. Shakespeare never sounded so mellow.

The Prince Charming of guitar tuners, Mr. MacDermot returned in less than a year with the first of two spectacular turkeys. Number one: *Dude*. It had a pulsing subtitle, "The Highway of Life." It had book and lyrics by *Hair*'s Gerome Ragni. It had all the thematic cohesion of two spaced-out junkies mumbling on about good and evil while really looking for the lay of the night. It ran head-on into hostile reviews, made a quick U-turn and hit the road for nowhere-man after six showings at the Broadway Theatre. Who killed the sixties? Maybe the rock musical did.

Not to halt Galt; he retooled to go cosmic—enough with that whole earth stuff. He turned in his bell bottoms for astral attire and landed back on Broadway in seven breathless weeks with a singing space-age monstrosity, *Via Galactica*. He'd actually been working on it all along, supplying music for the two shows simultaneously in progress. *Via Galactica* brought forward yet more new MacDermot collaborators: Christopher Gore and Judith Ross on book, Gore on lyrics alone. They advertised it "A musical of the future … Road to the stars," promising the "bite" of *Hair*, the "charm" of *Two Gentlemen*. Headlined the posters, "Someday: The earth will be perfect. Humans will be beautiful and all the same color. And making love will be easier than making friends." And yes, it seemed hip to expect, this would amount to the first day of the rest of our musical theatre lives.

Back on earth, director Peter Hall indulged in state-of-the-art pyrotechnics. Some, however, saw just tacky Florenz Ziegfeld effects where they should have seen the far-out cosmos. The space-age reviewers registered near total disdain from their astral chairs at the Uris Theatre: "*Via Galactica* is a strange kind of bomb," reported Martin Gottfried in his *Women's Wear Daily* write up, "a plastic one, perhaps in keeping with the super motel decor of the house and the futurism of its setting. Watching this new musical is like watching a show at Disneyland." Walter Kerr moaned hiply, "*Via Galactica* was a musical about the future that had none." Describing one of its cumbersome set pieces, Kerr riffed, "a giant crane moved the clamshell trash ship slowly about the vast stage, portal to portal. But the people inside it were good as strapped to their seats, unable to do anything but relay those foursquare lyrics…. We spent the evening staring at what seemed a steady rainfall of tapioca."

The young purveyors of adolescent insights, so ill-grounded in stage craft, it would appear, were doomed to self-destruct after their first or second high in a Broadway show. Rock musicals sooner than later lost their limited novelty with the public. They were never, in fact, as big or disruptive a force as many have since claimed. Nor did they outlast the 1970s, as author Stanley Richards predicted they would in his book *Great Rock Musicals*.[6]

Nor did they doom traditional book shows. Through the late '60s to the late '70s when guitar-driven novelties were in vogue, shows with standard scores continued to hold their own. In 1969, second only to *Oh, Calcutta* in business was *1776*. After that came, believe it or not, *Coco*—yes, *that Coco*. And in 1970? Neither of that year's biggest winners rocked at all: *Company* and *Applause*. In 1971, when *Jesus Christ Superstar* and *Two Gentlemen of Verona* opened, both were upstaged at the ticket windows by a revival of the delightful chestnut *No, No, Nanette*. In 1973, *A Little Night Music*, composed by Stephen Sondheim—a man not known for frequenting heavy-metal clubs—was the only show that year to turn a profit. Stephen Schwartz's *The Magic Show* took box office honors in 1974, with *Candide* in revival form falling a far second. The year of *The Wiz* went not the Wiz, but to a couple of musicals with conventional scores: *A Chorus Line* and *Very Good Eddie*. Advance to 1977, when a slate of hit non-rock musicals—Strouse and Adams's wonderfully old-fashioned charmer *Annie*; Cy Coleman's mainstream *I Love My Wife*; and the revival of the bombastically romantic *Man of La Mancha*—did not suffer for lack of over-amplified blasts.

This brings us, ruefully, to the class of '78, the year when rock and roll and the theatre went their own separate ways. Joseph Papp, New York's most with-it producer, delivered another big one at his Public Theatre in *I'm Getting My Act Together and Taking It on the Road*. So big that within six months it moved to the Circle in the Square in the Village, where it stayed for over a season. Emerging feminist attitudes ruled the songs, composed by singer-songwriter Nancy Ford, who starred in a musical biography built around her life. Gretchen Cryer fashioned the book and the thoughtful lyrics, which simmer and smart with predictable discontent: Anything approaching the "I Enjoy Being a Girl" school of powdery self-glorification deserves class-action disdain. Relationships (heterosexual, that is) are doomed. Gender roles are out of date. And so on. Ford and Cryer did let up a little towards the end with the joyful "Happy Birthday."

Five years before Joseph Papp took an interest in their work, Ford and Cryer had faced critical scorn and instant box office doom with *Shelter*. And before that, they had distinguished themselves off–Broadway with *The Last Sweet Days of Isaac*. Following *Act*, they would never grace another stage with their promising songwriting talents.

Let us consider 1978 for another reason. Several of the creators of successful rock musicals earlier in the decade failed to reinvent themselves outside the twangy guitar zone with follow-up projects. Stanley Walden, one of the three who had written the fine songs for *Oh, Calcutta*, came back in 1978 with *Back Country*, based on *The Playboy of the Western World*. He got no farther than the Wilbur Theatre in Boston. Geld and Udell of *Purlie* fame were represented with *Angel*, based on *Look Homeward, Angel*, in a five-performance blowout at the Minskoff. Micki Grant contributed some numbers to *Working*—a show that did not work— and also wrote all the songs for her own solo flop, *Alice*, an adaptation of the Lewis Carroll classic which got lost through a looking glass in myopic Philadelphia. Gary William Friedman and Will Holt, who had composed *The Me Nobody Knows*, saw their second Broadway bid, *Platinum*, turn to copper in thirty-three performances at the Mark Hellinger Theatre. The story that Friedman and Hold tried telling, of a famous movie singer from the swinging 1940s striving to make it as a rock artist, incurred scathing notices. At the end of his professional patience, Walter Kerr grumbled, on the verge of asking for a refund, "I have a feeling that if *Platinum* could just get rid of its book, its songs, its microphones and its almost arrogantly messy setting, it would be light miles ahead."[7]

The critics were running low on goodwill towards androgynous ponytails. Only the year before, they had endured the public embarrassment of having to face *Hair*, that mother of all rock musicals, in a far-from-flattering comeback mode. *Hair* floundered like an aging heroine in search of a fix, just as it would do years later, on both occasions failing miserably to recapture its original sex appeal. Many of the same reviewers who had been so infatuated the first time around now, ten years later, eyed the thing uneasily—as if it were some aging lover at the door with sleeping bag in hand. Members of the Fourth Estate could only smell the aroma of stale coffee, cheap incense, and used condoms, and they ran for the exits to dash off their sheepish apologies for critical indiscretions gone awry. "Nothing ages worse than graffiti," confessed Richard Eder. While Douglas Watt still had praise for Galt MacDermot's fine score, he could not bring himself to feel the lure of hippiedom anymore. "It and the '60s seem, at least at the moment, as dated as *Irene* [1919] and the first-world war…. It's gone, kids, gone, lost in a marijuana cloud as we tiptoe uncertainly through the saintly '70s."[8]

Saintly? Like their parents and grandparents who may still secretly thrill to the tunes from *Irene*, the younger generation of *Hair* enthusiasts will likely in years to come still savor its funky songs, so vividly evocative are they of the turbulent anti-war years and of a rebellious youth culture not without its shining moments on the picket lines. *Hair* reminds us of a time when the young believed they could love freely in communal harmony and change the world for the better … long before they grew up to covet BMWs and vote for politicians whose self-serving behavior they once detested.

Of surviving cast albums from the era, the most surprising of all in unexpected quality is the unbelievably eclectic *Oh, Calcutta*. Long-overdue kudos are herein offered to the three members of the Open Window credited with composing the songs: Peter Schickele, Stanley Walden and Robert Dennis, three very creative guys who drew musical inspiration from everyone from the Doors to the Beatles to Gershwin. Their constantly changing tempos keep you guessing—what *next*? Santana? Lawrence Welk? Subtle keyboard arrangements for "Dick and Jane" envelope you hypnotically, much like the Doors do on "Light My Fire." "Green Pants" rides the rhythm of old Broadway jazz. "I Like the Look" is so rousing a waltz, you swear that Richard Rodgers, not on weed, could have composed it!

By the end of the '70s, the strident cry of the downtrodden, both real and self-imagined, had pretty much vanished back into the real world, while musical theatre moved ahead in a more conservative non-politicized fashion. Interestingly, now it offered audiences a wider array of sounds. Rock had made a subtle impact on show scoring. At the same time, the rock haters started suffering post-rock-musical-stress syndrome every time they heard something that did not conform strictly to the George M. Cohan template. Conveniently, they overlooked the history of how the theatre every so often catches up with popular music and finds ways to take dramatic advantage of it.

Back, one last time, to 1978. A modest watershed of a musical opened that year and played a very long time. It earned excellent reviews, and while its music wasn't rock, neither was it Berlin or Blitzstein. In contrast to some of the politically strident shows of the '70s, this show depicted the lives of fairly ordinary citizens, happily making ends meet and finding contentment in small town day-to-day pleasures. The critics deemed it blandly agreeable. "Indeed, it is, depending perhaps on your family," pointed out Clive Barnes, "just good family entertainment." Douglas Watt placed it "very much on the sunny side of the street." Christopher Sharp called it "more fun than a beer-toting hayride at a mardi-gras…. This show, in fact, could help make ungarnished heterosexuality fashionable again."[9]

And what was that musical of 1978 that marked a return to a decidedly more mainstream view of life? *The Best Little Whorehouse in Texas*.

CHAPTER 9

The Roads He Didn't Take

One of the great ironies of musical theatre evolution was the strange sad saga of Oscar Hammerstein's prodigious protege, Stephen Sondheim, who would spend a life virtually deconstructing the populist notions of dramatic craft for which his great mentor had stood. Sondheim staged his futile revolution in a succession of increasingly independent works of abstract texture and fringe appeal. Not without precedent, his act of mutiny paid homage to the emerging "concept musical," a form favoring the exploration of ideas over character-driven narrative, which Hammerstein and Rodgers had pioneered in *Allegro*.

Sondheim's misleading genius for lyric writing would dazzle a growing legion of fans for whom he became a refuge from everything that in their minds had gone wrong since the noisy invasion of rock musicals. "Sondheimaniacs," as they would come to be known, coalesced around a shared conviction that Mr. Sondheim had singlehandedly kept alive the best—the only valid—musical theatre traditions dating back to Kern and Porter and Rodgers. They united in lockstep behind the work of a man who came into his own, ironically, during the heyday of the do-your-own-thing twanger in two acts. Sondheim's best shows opened when stages were full of protest, drugs and nudity. It was a traumatic era for Ethel Merman and Mary Martin aficionados. Instead of getting Gershwin or Arlen or Harburg at the Orpheum or the Biltmore or the Mark Hellinger, they got Grant and Gore or Mac-Dermot or the Apolinars, Ragni or Rado or Rice.

During the volatile '70s, when street-wise punks took to the boards like a tidal wave of protestors; when out from behind ghetto shacks, detention halls and massage parlors came society's underdogs to sing their songs of misfortune, a great American art form rooted in vaudeville and operetta stood at the precipice of collapse—and there are those who believe it did collapse, period. These in-your-face nouveau entertainers, blasting away on amplified instruments gave real meaning to the observation—musically captured in the opening lines for *Pipe Dream*—that it truly takes all kinds of people to make up the world.

And all kinds of musical theatre, too. While the microphone idols sang about person-to-person inhumanity, about unjust wars and group sleepovers and corporate greed, here came Stephen Sondheim, who ten years earlier had sympathized with dispossessed gangs in *West Side Story*, now spinning his own sorry-grateful lyrics about rich city dwellers panting in marital combat; about aging Broadway hoofers surveying stale dreams; about aristocratic Europeans gliding through romantic interludes; about American businessmen encroaching upon the outer limits of Japan in a distant century. During those turbulent '70s, a time of selfish personal introspection and psychobabble gone amok, Broadway had the sound of flower power and the sound of Sondheim. And if that didn't do, there was Tynan's flesh revue across town, set to music of remarkable variety from Jerome Kern to Jim Morrison.

Some fifteen years before all of this, audiences had been left in awe by the pointedly spare, ingenious lyrics of a new show called *West Side Story*—lyrics by a person they'd never heard of named Stephen Sondheim. He seemed, without doubt, the lyricist of the future. Yet Sondheim's first successful assignment had come to him simply by default, thanks to Comden and Green turning down the project when first approached to supply the lyrics. That project put the 27-year-old neophyte on the map. With music by Leonard Bernstein, some of whose original lyric ideas Sondheim reworked into his own finished verse, the numbers, like "Jet Song" and "Cool," bristled with blunt clarity.[1]

Audiences knew nothing of the troubled man behind such brilliance. Stephen Sondheim, born the only child to prosperous parents in the garment and dress design business, grew up in a posh New York household full of servants, cared for by everyone but his parents. And when his father, who had taken Steve some Sundays to ball games, left his mother for another woman, the bitter and controlling Mrs. Sondheim tried seducing her own son more than once, and indoctrinating him against his philandering father. The embittered divorcee and her precocious son lived out a sadistically symbiotic relationship. For years Sondheim experienced fits of panic around women drawing too close. In time, he established a semi-permanent homosexual union with a younger fledgling composer, although it too languished in the end.

"What she did for five years," Sondheim is quoted in the biography of him by Meryle Secrest, "was treat me like dirt, but come on to me at the same time."[2] When faced with pacemaker surgery, Mrs. Sondheim wrote to Steve, "The only regret I have in life is giving you birth."[3]

The one thing this mother dearest did give her son—a gift of fate she later jealously regretted—was her society connections. In her work as an interior decorator, she had come to know Dorothy Hammerstein, wife of Oscar, and thus did the young Stephen get introduced on a friendly basis to one of the Hammerstein boys, James. From there, it was on to the education and inspiration Stephen enjoyed under the mentoring of Oscar Hammerstein II.

Sondheim acted in school plays and learned to play the piano, believing himself to be essentially a composer. The early lyrics he wrote were created only

Stephen Sondheim in 1963.

reluctantly to get his songs in working order. He composed his first score for a school musical, *By George*. Offered some caustic feedback by Hammerstein, the protege observed a real "ruthlessness"[4] behind the mentor's charm that few others ever got close enough to see.

Young Steve was hired, for $25.00 a week, to work in the Rodgers and Hammerstein office as general errand boy. One of the fascinating first perks was to watch *Allegro* during preparations and rehearsals. So impressed was the student by this first "concept" musical in the making (evidently more so than Dick and Oscar, who did not pursue the form in future projects) that he would spend the rest of his life, he told his biographer, "trying to rewrite *Allegro* all the time."[5] At Williams College, Sondheim composed more shows. Foremost among his early and lasting influences, he listed the Russian romantics, headed by Tchaikovsky.

If Mr. Hammerstein expected his disciple to carry forth in the integrated book musical format, his influence fell woefully short. The boy wonder blossomed with a remarkable facility for verse, but with almost no regard for framing that verse in stories capable of engaging audience empathy. In one of Sondheim's college shows which Hammerstein critiqued, the prickly protege was taken to task for giving voice to unlikable characters. According to biographer Secrest, Hammerstein "was trying to convey the fact if the sympathies of the audiences were not engaged, it did not matter how brilliant the work was. It was a point the pupil may have missed."[6]

Thus would Sondheim have to rely on the variously talented book writers with whom he associated. Curiously, he never tired his own hand at libretto construction, although during his early years he earned some decent money in television writing *Topper* episodes, and he penned a number of teleplays, only one of which, *Early Winter*, got made. In his first Broadway break, he did fabulously well in collaboration with the accomplished Leonard Bernstein and playwright Arthur Laurents, who created *West Side Story's* volatile libretto. Still, the show's brutal realism initially met resistance from a large portion of the public. *West Side Story* was nowhere near in the beginning as successful as legend would have it. Hobe Morrison spotted "inescapable drawbacks"[7] in the unpleasant subject matter and the commercially limited songs. None of them received significant airplay.

Sondheim did not consider it to be a very good show, faulting it for "serious flaws," among them, "purpleness in the writing and in the songs because the characters are necessarily one-dimensional."[8] To his biographer Meryle Secrest, he recounted, "People left in droves, because people did not go to musicals expecting experimental work. They went for an evening's diversion." After he noticed the exit of businessmen following the first song, he may have wondered about the value of rave notices. "That's when I knew my career was in trouble."[9]

Sondheim's next groundbreaking work, *Gypsy*, benefited from another first-rate libretto by Laurents. Jule Styne, signed to compose the music, delivered undoubtedly his finest score. The threesome fashioned a gritty biographical take on the lives of stripper Gypsy Rose Lee and her overbearing stage mother, Rose (played to the hilt by Ethel Merman, landing the role of a lifetime). Sondheim's lyrics bristled with the same economy of words and on-target vernacular seen in his work for *West Side Story*. Hardly romantic or even comedically reassuring, but terrifically faithful to its central premise, the musical charts Rose's mounting jealousy over her daughter's mounting success and Rose's ultimate breakdown in one of the most harrowing soliloquies ever written for the stage, "Rose's Turn."

Those early manifestations of genius stand as a hallmark to the mentor. Naturally, Sondheim strove to distance himself from Hammerstein with a body of work all his own, though he seems to have resorted to extreme measures bordering on artistic suicide. "He taught me not everything I know," he carefully explained, "but everything I needed to know in order to write for myself and not for him."[10]

All along, Sondheim harbored the self-image of composer rather than lyricist. It was a desire that, once vented, proved a mixed blessing, for when he worked with other tunesmiths his work was more accessible and dramatically focused. Of the three musicals for which he supplied only the words, two were huge hits. Of all the shows bearing both lyrics *and* music by Stephen Sondheim only two, *Company* and *A Little Night Music*, are classified as commercial successes.

Did he have true compositional talent? Of course he did. Sondheim's first complete solo score was for the George Abbott directed crowd pleaser *A Funny Thing Happened On the Way to the Forum*. Believing the celebrated director to be basically untalented, Sondheim appears never to have learned from him the importance of theatricality. In fact, Abbott's direct opposition to the opening number, "Invocation" (which had replaced "Love Is in the Air"), on the grounds that it was not hummable, indirectly led to a third new song, "Comedy Tonight," being written.

Sondheim's second solo, *Anyone Can Whistle*—also his third collaboration with Arthur Laurents on libretto—required thirty-three auditions to raise the money and only nine performances in which to lose it all. It produced some fascinating songs if nothing else, and it drew sharply uneven notices. Among them, there was a prophetic assessment by John Chapman noting a "briskly syncopated score" while bemoaning the absence of "a melody *I* could whistle." Walter Kerr, who wasn't left whistling, either, called the enterprise "exasperating." Why? Because "it isn't very musical." While in Norman Nadel, Sondheim enjoyed early acclaim: "Sondheim's music and lyrics deserve an entire review in themselves … and maybe when the season lets up they'll get it in this corner."[11]

Not yet anywhere near the sainted status he would soon enough enjoy, Sondheim turned one final time to a lyric-only collaboration with another composer. He chose reluctantly to work with Richard Rodgers, a partnership many deemed would prove classic. It didn't. The downbeat story they agreed to bring to the stage, which Rodgers later described "a sad little comedy with songs" that "simply didn't work,"[12] was based on the 1952 play *The Time of the Cuckoo*, by Arthur Laurents, who also adapted it. Acrimonious disputes soon bedeviled the trio during out of town tryouts, where audiences and industry bystanders noticed a lack of the expected Richard Rodgers magic. Additional tension was caused by the fact that Rodgers was also the producer. When he tried suggesting ways to make the heroine more sympathetic—an idea that, who knows, might have made her more sympathetic, and audience empathy is something the show desperately needed—Rodgers met icy resistance from Laurents and Sondheim.

The real-life drama came to an ugly head when Rodgers first heard lyric lines alluding to homosexuality in "A Perfectly Lovely Couple" and blew up in public, screaming, "This is shit!"[13] Rodgers ended up feeling isolated and rejected on his own project, all of his ideas for needed improvement "promptly rejected, as if by prearrangement."[14] He was driven into sporadic alcoholic binges in men's rooms. To a friend of Sondheim's, British actor Keith Baxter, Rodgers is said to have remarked that he founded the lyricist "a cold man with a deep sense of cynicism."[15]

Do I Hear A Waltz, the result, proved to be a cold, unfriendly work. Nonetheless, it contains a superb Richard Rodgers score, written when he was 62 years old. And the polished lyrics by Stephen Sondheim rank among his best work in the earlier, more listener-friendly years, before he became an idiom unto himself. The songs, however, could not overcome the listless tale of an American secretary, Leona, finding temporary love in the arms of a charming Italian antique dealer, Renato, who turns out to be a married man and who, to Leona's dismay, profits from a commission on a necklace he buys her. Nothing much seemed to have happened on the stage. Walter Kerr dubbed it "an emotional drought in Venice."[16]

That was 1964. When Sondheim resumed serving as his own composer five years later and joined forces with book writer George Furth to create *Company*, his credentials as composer-lyricist skyrocketed. Sondheim's sensibilities were well

Left to right: Susan Browning, Donna McKechnie, and Pamela Myers deliver "You Could Drive a Person Crazy" in *Company*.

suited to the approaching "do your own thing" '70s, a decade fraught with group therapy and increasing public acceptance of open relationships. And that is when the Sondheim fans turned to Sondheimaniacs, when they became a serious force, swearing eternal allegiance to their hero and in effect standing constant vigil over his protected status and hallowed image.

They had plenty to cheer about in *Company*, one of the finest stage musical scores of all time, period. Brilliant in its invention and completeness, it is nearly as riveting as Cole Porter's songs for *Anything Goes*. Orchestrated by Jonathan Tunick in the style of *Promises, Promises* (the Hal David and Burt Bacharach 1968 hit which Tunick also arranged), the songs of *Company* sizzle and explode with the teeth-gnashing ambivalence of the times. Why do couples marry? How do they survive the petty annoyances and larger traumatic betrayals they inflict on each other? Maybe they survive in the negative, on "The Little Things We Do

Together"—an acerbic little ditty about irritating neighbors and driving children crazy.

Sondheim had the critics clearly on his side with *Company*, although Brooks Atkinson perhaps best understood the musical's fundamental problem when he described the central character as being more observer than actual part of the action. Walter Kerr, after detailing numerous triumphal aspects to the work, confessed, "Now ask me if I liked the show. I didn't like the show. I admired it, or admired vast portions of it.... I left *Company* feeling rather cool and queasy.... Personally, I'm sorry grateful."[17]

Among its rapturous defenders, *The New Yorker's* Brendan Gill predicted that by the year 2000, "the pressure for tickets will have begun to abate a little."[18] In earth time, the pressure for tickets abated in a couple of seasons. It has since been produced on a number of occasions in regional theatres, more to please artistic directors wishing to flash their Sondheim credentials than to thrill impatient sorry-grateful season ticket holders.

Drawn to the provocative misfortunes of life, Sondheim composed like an existential poet riding the *Titanic* for sheer mental stimulation. By now he had begun turning his back on the principles of musical theatre championed by his late mentor. He returned one year later, following thirteen drafts, with *Follies*, the lavishly staged tribute to an old theatre about to be torn down. Co-directed by Harold Prince and Michael Bennett and choreographed by the latter, the show sparkled with another set of excellent songs that musical theatre lovers would savor over and over again—linked to a libretto that many found irritatingly undramatic, even a bit mushy. Sondheim and librettist James Goldman, working from an original idea, paid affectionate tribute to a reunion of ex-chorus members returning to the theatre where they had once performed. Some of them hope to find members of the cast over whom they had once pined. Some come seeking a rebirth of youthful dreams. Some yearn to savor the present tense. Three of the first-night reviewers fell ravingly in love with the musical's surreal non-linear charms. "Nostalgia is not simply the undercurrent of the evening," reported Douglas Watt, Jr. "It is the very subject of it ... a pastiche so brilliant as to be breathtaking at times."[19]

Follies is an utterly enthralling examination of the lingering dreams that intersect in the shadows of shared memories. Characters, double cast, confront each other in the illusory terrain of *Follies*, both as they *were* and as they *are*, and the juxtapositions are full of joy and pain, of a kind of higher mental reality. Yesterday's wishes collide with today's residual letdowns. Not everyone gets out intact. Some prefer to stay safely imprisoned within the hall of mirrors of their protective imaginations.

The average theatergoer was not a candidate for this inventive concept musical. English impresario Cameron Mackintosh, who loved the show and staged it unsuccessfully on the West End with some changes, was forced to concede that it failed on the most basic level with the public. The characters, he said, remained static throughout. "I feel you've got to take the audience on a journey."[20] On its own journey across America, *Follies* failed with the common ticket buyer, and the tour was aborted. The show lost a heap of money on both sides of the Atlantic.

Falling deeper into the thrall of ideas, Sondheim became a powerful force in his own right, his every capricious move codified in the minds of his admirers. He did relent on one traditional occasion, in service to a solid libretto written by Hugh Wheeler, loosely adapting Ingmar Bergman's 1955 film *Smiles of a Summer Night*. Sondheim composed a lush, wondrously integrated set of songs exclusively in three-quarter time, and the enchanting result, *A Little Night Music*, marked a momentary throwback to operetta days. It also gave the world the only Sondheim song that would achieve lasting recognition with the public at large, "Send In the Clowns." The principal character, newly married Fredrik, lies there next to his not-yet-ready bride, Ann, fretfully waiting for consummation with an 18-year-old woman, while gradually coming to the realization that his enduring love for an aging mistress, Desiree, means more to him. *Night Music* moved audiences, turned a profit and was added, in 1990, to the Repertory of the New York City Opera.

Ever the restless innovator, Sondheim continued to prefer risks over royalties. *Pacific Overtures*, which came next, brought with it another masterful score of bold invention, about as good as anything he would create. Too bad it arrived in the company of such a deadly dull book devoid of flesh-and-blood characters caught up in real-life struggles. Another sung essay, *Overtures* was little more than a flat, lifeless pageant of costumed oriental characters coming and going, each presumably standing as a symbol for some trenchant aspect of the unfolding East-West let's-do-business saga. Through his music and lyrics, Sondheim assumed the role of impartial witness singing intelligently to himself about all the intriguing ramifications of a plotless play. His razor-sharp songs were great work on an otherwise static affair.

Sondheim's willingness to collaborate on *Overtures* with neophyte librettist John Weidman, whose one previous credit was co-author of the book for the roundly roasted 1966 Duke Ellington 3-performance flop, *Pousse-Cafe*, made no more sense than Weidman's bloodless script. And another tedious "concept musical" by the prince of singing essays hit the rocks, dividing the critics evenly across the spectrum. Walter Kerr complained of a dullness and immobility to the show, "because we are never properly placed in it."[21] Clive Barnes so enraged overly sensitive director Hal Prince with a thoughtfully mixed review full of modified praise, that Prince shot back in letter form, "You've just closed the show and you will regret it someday."[22] The two rave notices it earned ("A remarkable work of art,"[23] sang Martin Gottfried) could hardly offset the show's austere self-indulgent intellectuality. It hung on for about half a year at the Winter Garden Theatre.

Librettos without engaging stories and characters are a problem without end in musical theatre. By now, the integrated book show was under direct attack by a new generation of practitioners seeking a fresh language. None, of course, wanted to come off looking predictable or old fashioned; so they went to extremes, following Mr. Sondheim up and down the dead end streets. Though concept musicals presented more problems than they solved, this fact of life would not deter

Mr. Sondheim from his penchant for defiant innovation. Another of his alienating attributes was a growing fetish for lyrics as intricate and dense as the crossword puzzles he reveled in creating.

At the dawn of his career, you will remember, Hammerstein's protege displayed a bent for saying a lot in very few words. (Think *West Side Story*.) As time progressed, clearly he employed more words while saying less, like a sleight-of-hand magician dazzling with a stream of distracting movements just to turn a red ball into a blue ball. Sondheim's fawning fans drove him to ever more complex displays of dexterity—past the sorry-grateful multitudes who like words that relate to their own lives and tunes they can hum after leaving the show. As *Variety* once commented, summing up its critical doubts over the prospects for Sondheim's musical about painter Georges Seurat, "*Sunday in the Park* is another concept musical in which an abstract subject—the creation of art—takes precedence over story and character.... Audiences like shows about people. They're funny that way."[24]

Sondheim is famously rumored to have boasted of a conscious refusal to compose hummable, public-pleasing tunes. Not rumored at all are the in-print remarks of his friend Keith Baxter on the subject. "It seems to me," Baxter once half-jokingly put it, "that when Steve composes a song, whenever he hears a melody creeping in, he slams his foot down and stomps on it."[25] Music industry pros were struck by the composer's indifference to popular tastes. Remarked Frank Sinatra, "Stephen Sondheim ... a classy composer and lyricist, could make me a lot happier if he'd write more songs for a salon singer like me."[26] Jule Styne once came to the point: "Steve needs to write some hits. If he doesn't, these shows of his are not going to make it."[27]

At the summit of his artistic reign on Broadway during the '70s, Sondheim seemed to shun not just popular music, but musical theatre itself. On the eve of the opening of *Pacific Overtures*, he granted a *New York Times* published interview to Clive Herschorn, theatre critic of the Sunday *Express* in London, headlined "Will Sondheim Succeed in Being Genuinely Japanese?" Sondheim snidely dismissed virtually all musicals, deriding them for having recycled old forms year after year. He argued that *My Fair Lady* was essentially a wasted venture. "Unless you can add something that will improve the original, what's the point?" He uttered disdain for anything remotely resembling a mainstream enterprise. Comparing his new show to *The King and I*, he found the latter lacking. "Let's face it, *The King and I* might just as well be about a teacher coming to teach in Brooklyn, except that she comes to Siam."[28] Sondheim displayed not only arrogance, but a strange and surprising ignorance as well, bringing seriously into question the man's working knowledge of dramatic art. Had he taken the time to think through his bizarre analogy about *The King and I* and Brooklyn, Sondheim might have realized how unique imperial oriental culture was to the musical's central conflict.

Feeling infallibly bright, Hammerstein's protege now described his late mentor as a man of "infinite soul" and "limited talent," the very opposite for Richard Rodgers.[29] And his every new work received the same rapt attention once lavished upon Dick and Oscar. Yet *Side by Side by Sondheim*, a 1977 revue of his songs, gar-nered the usual mixed reviews, and turned a modest profit on a modest run. What next? Although opera was not exactly a calling Mr. Sondheim aspired to, accord-ing to his public statements, he reached brilliantly in that direction with his most powerfully chilling work, the darkly alienated songfest of cannibalism in London, *Sweeney Todd*.

His smartest move had been to link up once more with librettist Hugh Wheeler. They derived ample inspiration from Christopher Bond's diabolical tale about the barber of Fleet Street who is unjustly imprisoned and who escapes, 15 years later, to take vengeance upon his accuser, a lecherous judge who took Todd's wife and now plans to marry his daughter. The lengthy score, laced with second-rate refrains and recitative, does offer a handful of true Sondheim classics, among them "Ballad of Sweeney Todd," "Pretty Women," "Epiphany," "My Friends," "A Little Priest." Most of all, the songs have a strong reason to be heard, effectively moving the tale along. And still the venture recouped only 59 percent of its invest-ment.

Broadway ticket windows are rarely hospitable to dark, destructive works, no matter how smartly conceived. Any wretched little yarn can be turned into a work of art—at least in the eyes of dramaturgs and drama professors. Art, in fact, can be anything it plumb well wants to be, as Mr. Sondheim would try over and over again to demonstrate. Audiences can also do whatever they plumb well wish, filling up theatre seats in droves or staying home in droves. And audiences were grow-ing tired of Mr. Sondheim's increasingly unfriendly overtures. "We are plainly in the hands of intelligent and talented people, possessed of a complex, malleable, assiduously offbeat vision," reflected Walter Kerr. "Unhappily that vision remains a private and personal one. We haven't been lured into sharing it."

Richard Eder, impressed by the profusion of "artistic energy, creative per-sonality and plain excitement ... a display of extraordinary talent," brooded over the absence of focus and empathy. "What keeps all its brilliance from coming together as a major work of art is a kind of confusion of purpose.... The music, beautiful as it is, succeeds, in a sense, in making an intensity that is unaccept-able.... There is, in fact, no serious social message in *Sweeney*; and at the end, when the cast lines up on the stage and points to us, singing that there are Sweeneys all about, the point is unproven."[30]

During and after *Sweeney Todd*, which many consider to be his finest work, Sondheim matured from spare to verbose—from the simple streetwise slang of gang warfare on the streets of New York city to the rhyme-infested wordiness of a lyric writer straining in overkill to sustain a reputation. His intricate rhymes and clever phrases come whizzing by so fast—like rattling freight trains crisscrossing each other in the night—that we are left in a daze to wonder in just what direc-tion they are supposed to be taking us. At least in *Sweeney Todd*, thanks to the more controlled Mr. Wheeler, Sondheim had a strong narrative to hold on to, and that gives audiences a clear sense of dramatic purpose. The work was added to the New York City Opera repertoire in 1984.

In his next project, working not with the helpful Hugh Wheeler, but again with the unhelpful George Furth, Sondheim knew exactly where he wanted to take us—not in any straight ahead direction, of course. *Merrily We Roll Along* is painfully remembered by those who tried putting it over for the mass walkouts long before the final curtain fell. It left everyone irritatingly unengaged. After sixteen torturous attempts to connect with the Big Black Giant, nobody came around anymore for the backward ride.

In an act of reckless ego, Sondheim and Furth had based their testy musical on a flop Kaufman and Hart play of the same name. With Hal Prince at the directing helm—as he had been with nearly all the previous Sondheim shows—*Merrily* told the story of disillusioned composer Franklin Shepard, haunted by all the moral compromises he had made on his way up the ladder. He relives scenes from his life in reverse order, surveying friendships betrayed and values discarded. The surprisingly bright, thoughtful score is even warmly sentimental now and then. "Old Friends" is one of its star numbers. A slew of engaging others, too, shine hopelessly against a lifeless landscape.

The critics were driven to exasperation, making this the first Sondheim show to be unanimously roasted. As Walter Kerr saw it, *Merrily We Roll Along* offered the writers "the one thing they seemed determined to sell: disenchantment.... There is nothing wrong with the choice. It's not our business to tell creative men what to create so long as it's got a whiff of life deep inside it. But the insistence on a single theme, a single attitude, is becoming monotonous.... They are much too innovative to allow themselves to become so predictable."

Frank Rich nearly spilled his heart out in anguish over another fractured gem: "Sondheim has given this evening a half dozen songs that are crushing and beautiful—that soar and linger and hurt. But the show that contains them is a shambles. We keep waiting for some insight into these people, but all we get is fatuous attitudinizing about how ambition, success and money always leads to rack and ruin.... What's really wasted here is Sondheim's talent. And that's why we watch *Merrily We Roll Along* with an ever mounting—and finally upsetting—sense of regret."[31]

At the midpoint in his dissident drive to reinvent musical theatre, Steven Sondheim considered giving up the profession. He felt like an outcast in his own town. "I am serious," he told his biographer, "but I'm serious in an art that is hardly worth being called one." He blamed the critics. "They would all knock every show I ever did and stamp on it and sneer at it. Then, the next time around, they would refer to me as somebody who only had flops, which they caused."[32]

Just having begun a long slow descent down the other side of a mountain precariously scaled, Sondheim stubbornly refused to retreat into sense or sanity, refused safer, more fruitful associations with veteran hands. Remarked his first and most valuable collaborator, Arthur Laurents, "The shows that Hal and Steve have done together are cold.... I've never liked the theory of alienation. I think it's an intellectual conceit.... In a show you have to care even if you hate the characters, you must have some strong reaction wanting them to succeed, or wanting them to be done in, but *something*."[33]

Considering how revolutionary he had been, and how many diverse projects he had helped bring to the stage, yet for all his derring-do Sondheim seemed determined still to explore only more ways to restate the same pessimistic view of the human condition. When you end up whistling only unhappy tunes, you are no more original than the next guy. People lose heart and go elsewhere. How ironic: most everything for which his great mentor, Oscar Hammerstein, stood—likable empathetic characters, realistic librettos, hummable songs and life-affirming themes—lay along the roads that Steven Sondheim didn't take.

CHAPTER 10

What They Did for Love

About a year after San Francisco hosted the Summer of Love, Leonard Sillman hosted a riotous new edition of *New Faces*, and in it he took irreverent pot shots at such trendy issues as gender identity, incest, free love and fake philanthropy—for starters. Even the show's signature opening number, "You've Never Seen Us Before," rocked with a cheesy early disco beat not unlike the sound to be introduced, mere months later, in *Promises, Promises* and *Company*.

"Lunch Bunch" was sung by a circle of well-heeled ladies, including *New Faces* find Madeline Kahn, drinking their way from one charity fête to the next. "Love in a New Tempo" introduced Robert Klein rattling off, in John Philip Sousa march time, a barrage of unrequited solicitations to an indifferent woman. In a tongue-in-cheek dig at Sigmund Romberg operettas, Brandon Maggart boomed forth "You Are" like Nelson Eddy on Viagra. Mauled sex-object Suzanne Astor turned Murray Grand's "Hungry" into a cry for relationship equity, offering her earlobes to his ravishing lips in return for a steak.

And they hadn't heard anything yet. In Ronny Graham's "Hullabaloo at Thebes," Klein, joined by Suzanne Astor, Trudy Carson and Elaine Giftos, pushed the kinky envelope to new levels of depravity, laughing it up over incestuous intra-family relations.

Away from rough satire, Sillman acknowledged the feminist movement in the poignant "Where Is Me," rendered by Marilyn Child in the vein of a devoted housewife losing faith in her selfless devotion to spouse.

The critics inexplicably turned against the '68 edition for being, of all things, out of touch with the times, Clive Barnes crying that it "never looks forward."[1] Perhaps the sketches, half-baked according to reviews, never looked forward. Not the songs! If Sillman was not ahead of his time, he was surely on top of it, peering down upon the new adult playground with devilish on-point glee. And a show loaded with *nine* comedy songs (many of them as strong musically as lyrically) is a rich rarity, indeed. Maybe first nighters didn't get the humor, or didn't want to. The sexual revolution, after all, was no laughing matter, not to a new generation of navel-gazers.

Sillman's '68 songfest is one of the most egregiously slighted scores of all time. The new sexual mores out of which it made comedy mincemeat were better received by the public at large in serious book shows of the day. In fact, *Promises, Promises*, one of the biggest hits of the season, was both funny and sophisticated, its songs up to the moment, its timely realism a box office draw. Neil Simon's adult libretto, based on Billy Wilder's screenplay *The Apartment*, helped the production garner five raves and play more than a couple of thousand times at the Shubert Theatre.

Enlisted by director Robert Moore to design the dance patterns was a young choreographer named Michael Bennett, who had played the part of Baby John in a touring version of *West Side Story*. He had danced in a few other shows and assisted Ron Field, in 1962, on the choreography for *Nowhere to Go But Up*. And that's just where Bennett went, too, after landing his break in *Promises*.

Pop masters Bacharach and David generated plenty of melodic relevance with their fresh, angular rhythms, so perfectly in sync with the rushed momentary pleasures of married men and their unmarried girlfriends on the run, each couple illicitly convening in one man's apartment on different nights. Out of the driving score for *Promises, Promises* came the pop hit:

> What do you get when you kiss a guy?
> You get enough germs to catch pneumonia
> After you do, he'll never phone ya
> I'll never fall in love again!

The 1960s changed the face of Broadway as they did the American social landscape. Musicals were becoming more cynical, more like *Pal Joey* and *Gypsy* than *Brigadoon* or *The Sound of Music*. The public's preferences for ambiguous conclusions and fringe characters did not escape the notice of writers and composers; they could now justify following Stephen Sondheim or Burt Bacharach, or Kander and Ebb, all attuned to the emerging amoralities. Exit the boy next door. Enter the cad from the other side of town, or the lady from the apartment down the street with a red light in the window, the lady wanting really, like everyone else, to find true love. And, all things now being equal, let that red light shine.

Another young pop composer ("Witchcraft") with a gift for the kind of syncopation that Broadway loved was Cy Coleman. He hit a note of wistful disillusionment in one of his best attended shows, *Sweet Charity*, based on Federico Fellini's masterpiece *Nights of Cabiria*. It is the story of a reluctant prostitute who may have started out, like Suzy in *Pipe Dream*, homeless, or like Suzanne Astor in *New Faces of '68*, "hungry!" but who gives up her beat for a marriage proposal from a John who is actually setting her up for a routine post-nuptial robbery.

The Bob Fosse staging pushed production over pathos. Fosse came up with the original book, but foundered so on the road over daunting script problems that he called up Mr. Simon to take over the literary chores. The sunnier take on the Fellini tale which they brought into New York City was greeted with tempered notices, most of them carping about a superficial treatment. "This is the story of a show that wants to be loved," reported Stanley Kaufman, "but *Charity* grows tedious between its brightest numbers."[2] Nonetheless, loved it was, to the tune of 608 performances.

Coleman proved to be a flexible tunesmith unattached to any particular school of musical theatre, which can be a good thing. He favored highly hummable scores and well paced entertainments. Before *Charity*, Coleman had worked with Simon on *Little Me*, a Sid Caesar vehicle featuring a sampler of hilarious Simon jokes. Dorothy Fields had provided the so-so lyrics for *Charity*, as she would for Coleman's next effort, the moderately impressive box office fizzle *Seesaw*. The book came from Michael Stewart, adapted from William Gibson's play *Two for the Seesaw*, in which the Big Apple itself—the adult bookstore version, that is—becomes a character competing with a kooky wannabe dancer for the affections of the hero, a midwest lawyer enamored of the Big City on his trip east in the early 1970s. Whatever it was or wasn't (Martin Gottfried thought it a patchwork construction that delivered good basic pleasure), *Seesaw* contains some of the highest voltage music ever to sail across vinyl. In electrifying measures, at times. If only the lagging-behind lyrics of the aging Ms. Fields, out of her element here, could have added more coal to the Coleman express train.

What really flew were the tunes of Coleman and the dances of Bennett, the theatre world's newest footmaster. *Seesaw* got good notices, and it kept audiences awake, if a touch disoriented. "The only way to make a musical of *Two for the Seesaw*," figured Gottfried, "was to make a musical despite it."[3] Despite it didn't quite work. Out-of-town troubles had prompted a 911 telephone call to Neil Simon. Taking over for Stewart, he failed to work his own wonders. Despite a score full of Coleman power, the train came to a halt short of a profitable finish line.

Cy Coleman. Like certain composers of serial partnerships, we tend to name him first, and as an afterthought almost, list his collaborators. They kept on changing. There was Carolyn Leigh on *Wildcat*, the lively Lucille Ball disappointment, and on *Little Me*. Dorothy Fields did *Charity* and *Seesaw*. Then came a stint in the late '70s with Michael Stewart, who supplied both book and lyrics for two Coleman hits, both well received and well patronized, *I Love My Wife* and *Barnum*. They came ever-so-close in *Wife* to the bed-swapping rituals of the time. Two liberal-minded couples consider sampling each other's mates for a night—all in the spirit of testing the fires of sexual liberation, singing their way through such preparatory songs as "By Threes," "I Love Revolution," "Sexually Free," "Everyone Today Is Turning On," and "Married Couple Seeks Married Couple." At the point of no return, they wimp out and remain monogamous, an outcome likely engineered by the front office to keep the box office happy. Coleman and colleagues played both sides of the street fairly well.

Unapologetically suited to the sexual revolution were John Kander and Fred Ebb, de facto hippies in white shirts and ties. They dealt with '60s and '70s sensibilities in a blase, sleep-and-let-sleep manner. They found success in giving surly voice to the offbeat characters you'll never see at PTA meetings or Salvation Army volunteer drives. Eighteen months following the short-lived fate of their first Broadway show, *Flora, the Red Menace*, came their subversive *Cabaret*. The team's single most defining work mined the decadence of Berlin nightlife in the 1930s. At its brittle core are a bisexual singer and his pleasure-loving female friend, British expatriate Sally Bowles, she pregnant with the child of an American novelist. The abortion that Bowles opts for, deciding she prefers the sinister good life abroad to kitchen duty back in the States with her new boyfriend, may be easier to accept given the context of looming Nazi aggression.

Cabaret opened up a beguiling netherworld of pre–Nazi Germany, set to music with cold existential force. Kander and Ebb found their magic key in the musical hall. Directed by Hal Prince, with Ron Field ordering up the dances, *Cabaret* sounded like Kurt Weill trapped in vaudeville. It's arresting ballads— "Why Should I Wake Up?" and "What Would You Do?—contrast soberly with lighter, more smugly shaded songs like "Don't Tell Mama" and "Two Ladies." It is a bittersweet portrait of teeth-gritting fascination, actually full of the essential grizzle, sass, pizazz and perversity of old-time musical theatre.

Above life's lower depths, Kander and Ebb did not fare nearly as well. They opened two shows in 1968, neither down to the amoral grist of *Cabaret*. *Zorba*, intended to be another *Fiddler On the Roof*, was not. And *Happy Time*, an atypically sentimental outing graced with fine songwriting, failed big time. Another bust was *70, Girls, 70*, which opened in 1971 at the Broadhurst Theatre and closed shortly thereafter. Not so romantic, it signaled Kander and Ebb's return to more mischievous terrain. Somehow, though, the sight of old folks getting away with petty misdemeanors didn't charm ordinary people who might have harbored sacred perceptions of old age. This delightful musical follows a gang of edgy senior citizens plotting to rob Bloomingdale's of TV sets and chandeliers for the noble purpose of raising their pathetic living standards in a run down old folks residence. Also, they wish to expand the facility so more seniors can join in the larceny. And what judicial reprimands are they held to when the cops catch up with them? A simple request to assist law enforcement in monitoring a younger gang of street punks. Even old folk got away with crime in the Age of Aquarius dawning.

Based on Peter Cook's 1958 British comedy *Breath of Spring*, *70, Girls, 70* delivered more comedy and melody than most shows of the day, but the musical that Kander and Ebb set sailing lasted all of thirty-five performances. Mixed notices leaned towards the brutal. Douglas Watt declared it to be "about as enlightening an affair as a New Year's Eve party thrown by members of the St. Petersburg shuffleboard club.... It had me squirming in my seat."[4] As recalled by flop-show coroner Ken Mandelbaum, "Audiences loved it.... It deserved to be a success."[5]

Kander and Ebb rebounded four years later with a return to the musical hall format in *Chicago*. Audiences loved it, and it was a success. Its unsavory heroine, Roxie, arrested and tried for murdering her indifferent lover, hires an attorney. He, in turn, turns Roxie into a sympathetic defendant by having her fake a pregnancy. Once acquitted, Roxie falls out of vogue with the public, whose attentions turn to another female charmer with murderous habits, Velma, who also beats the rap. Both women, who meet behind bars, end up behind greasepaint. Homicide to hoofing. Anything goes if the characters amuse, the songs crackle, and the pace snaps relentlessly forward, George Abbott style. *Chicago* possesses a wicked sense of humor, laughing down the tattered fates of its underworld darlings with a forgiveness that borders on Christian charity. It is top drawer Kander and Ebb at nearly every swaggering turn.

The original staging at the 46th Street Theatre, the work of director-choreographer Bob Fosse, drew evenly split notices, no praises or pans. Comparing the new windy city tuner to its natural predecessor, *Cabaret*, Walter Kerr lamented the absence of clear-cut villainy in the shadows. Clive Barnes criticized the hyper-charged dance routines and slighted the whole affair for being "one of those shows where a great deal has been done with very little." Douglas Watt was ambivalent with praise: "Cynical and stylish as a musical can be, *Chicago* is a musical built to kill…. the whole thing moves like a well-oiled machine…. Fosse and his collaborators have constructed a corrosive cabaret show in which murder and its aftermath are presented as show turns…. The existential treatment accorded that breezy, raucous, wildly American city doesn't quite jibe."[6]

Of the next six shows that Kander and Ebb would write, not one enjoyed unqualified success. *Woman of the Year*, which drew mixed reviews, shrewdly cast Lauren Bacall in the starring role, and it racked up a very impressive, though profitless, 770 performance run. *The Act*, with Liza Minnelli, hung around for 233 shows. *Rink* ("a heartless show, like its predecessors, built around nothing," in the words of Steven Suskin)[7] and *As the World Goes Round* both failed to capture any kind of an audience. In later years, the same hapless fate befell *Kiss of the Spider Woman* and *Steel Pier*.

Many of the artists who took advantage of the new liberated atmosphere could get no farther than off- or off-off-Broadway. Such was the fate for *Promenade*, a 1969 curiosity, the first show to play the new theatre of the same name. The offering had okay music by Al Carmines, a pastor at the Washington Square Methodist Church, where most of his works were first presented. Its very funny lyrics were supplied by Havana native Maria Irene Fornes. Carmines and Fornes told the story of a group of convicts digging their way out of jail, then trying to steal their way back into "higher society." The hard-working songs are Brechtian, harshly sardonic in the beginning, gradually rambling off into a sermon about societal injustice and its victimized victims. Clive Barnes deemed it "a joy from start to finish!" Walter Kerr called it "spectacularly old fashioned, expressively contemporary," lauding the score for approximating an era "when music was something to skip with, or walk with, or leap with."

Meanwhile, musicals about show business also turned dysfunctional. *Dreamgirls* in 1981, with music by Henry Krieger, book and lyrics by Tom Eyen, was a brooding Michael Bennett–directed smash. They turned the Cinderella story on its head by having heavyset Effie Melody White, one of the original Supremes, get

Dreamgirls.

the heave-ho from her agent-lover to make way for a slimmer, sexier replacement.
To its credit, the unrelentingly gloomy *Dreamgirls* at least advanced the black
musical away from the ghetto. To its deficit, it advanced the art of stagecraft to
monster Erector Set proportions, utilizing six towers and four hydraulic bridges
to facilitate cinema-like transitions. As these robotic entities lumbered back and
forth across the stage of the Shubert Theatre in Los Angeles, audiences might have
wondered if they had bought tickets by mistake for a state of the art farm equipment show—or a NASA garage sale.

Down there under all that sleek machinery loomed, somewhere, the smaller
than life characters, ranting on about their crummy fates in and out of the music
biz, with all songs consistently sung in a minor key. How much more real everything might have seemed had it been simply staged on realistic sets. Complained
a haggard Walter Kerr, "Mr. Krieger's melodies make the unthinkable mistake of
sounding all alike ... all very remote."[9]

The parade of new-won freedoms continued. Homosexuality in full bloom
arrived, the same year, before a cheering off–Broadway audience when the curtain

Left to right: Fyvush Finkel, Eydie Alyson and Andrew Hill Newman, with Audrey II (the plant) in *Little Shop of Horrors.*

finally rose on William Finn's groundbreaking *March of the Falsettos*. In it, Marvin leaves his wife and young son for a gay lover. The family psychiatrist then makes a play for the deserted wife, moving in to live with her. Marvin's queer romance comes to naught, and so he takes hopeful refuge in the relationship with his son, who learns to overcome fears of growing up gay like his dad. Finn's ambitious songs are more mental than melodic. Psychobabble never sang very well. Finn, too, seemed psychically stuck in the '60s, but without the musical resources of a Coleman or a Kander to sell his challenging tale. Fine lyrics, limp tunes.

And then came Audrey II, the plant, and her creators, Alan Menken and Howard Ashman—the most gifted new songwriting team to come along since there were gifted songwriting teams. The duo dazzled with their 1982 off–Broadway blockbuster at the Orpheum, *Little Shop of Horrors*. Based on a shoestring-budget 1960 movie by Roger Corman about a sadistic young flower shop owner, Seymour Krelbourn, the show takes spectacular and hilarious risks: by evening's end all of the leads are eaten alive by Seymour's misbehaving carnivorous plant,

Audrey II, originally acquired by Seymour as a harmless gift for co-worker Audrey, after whom he pines. Not since the lyrics greats of the golden age had there been a new voice of such witty invention as Ashman. When staged with fierce intensity, the musical is as fresh and daringly different as was *West Side Story* in its day.

Ashman parodied a range of social conditions from stereotyped '50s culture to sleazy '70s glitter. About the advantages of living on the edge, shopping cart in tow, he savaged the popular '60s song "Downtown" to write the homeless version, a perverse ditty called "Skid Row."

Horrors had something that few musicals possess: a tightly constructed libretto of escalating tension. Taut, well developed books were forever in short supply. Among the precious few writers then able to fashion viable scripts, there was Neil Simon, who applied his craft to musical theatre with *Promises, Promises, Sweet Charity*, and *They're Playing Our Song*. And he performed life-saving surgery on *Sugar*, among a number of shows to whose semi-rescue he came during out of town upheavals. Michael Stewart, who wrote the book for *I Love My Wife*, also supplied the librettos for *Hello, Dolly, Bye, Bye, Birdie, George M*, and *Barnum*. Joe Masteroff, responsible for *Cabaret's* script, also scripted the Bock and Harnick classic *She Loves Me*, not initially a hit show but one that is lovingly revived on a smaller scale, where it deserves to be seen and savored. Comden and Green, who adapted *Applause*, had loads of experience assembling librettos into working order. Complain as the critics might about over-production, hyperactive pacing, or the shallow treatment of serious material, these librettists labored in one of the trickiest of all dramatic forms. Finding ways to make the characters come alive in song and dance required a special skill not always visible to the average patron—or reviewer.

"Let it all hang out" was a popular mantra of the day. And that is what they did in the ultimate tell-all musical, born out of the 1970s when group therapy was in vogue. The show was actually built on the personal disclosures offered by two dozen dancers who had accepted Michael Bennett's invitation to talk openly in a rented studio about their backgrounds and careers. The tape-recorded sessions inspired Bennett to construct a musical play along the lines of an extended audition. In edited form, the tapes were listened to by producer Joseph Papp. He agreed to sponsor a workshop production. Bennett recruited Marvin Hamlisch to write the music, Edward Kleban to write the lyrics, and playwright James Kirkwood to work with Nicholas Dante on the non-linear book. Neil Simon later added jokes (so much for script purity). They called it *A Chorus Line*, and the rest is epic theatre history. The stunningly received 1975 triumph would achieve, in its day, the longest running record (6,137 performances) of any tuner. One touring company lasted seven years; a second, five years.

Beyond the heart-pounding mythology it so effectively exploits, how good a show is *A Chorus Line*? Only the future will tell. This celebrated work has yet to reconquer Broadway. The wrong director for a revival can sabotage almost any once-acclaimed classic, as we will soon enough see. *A Chorus Line's* greatest achievement, ironically, may have been its unintended reaffirmation of the cliche American musical—that worshiped arena where any person can ascend to show biz glory overnight. A gigantic cliche at that, as towering as Mount Rushmore, as resilient as the Fourth of July, invented over and over again in the fresh embrace of new audiences rushing forward to chase after American Dreams. You don't have to look far to find it—or tiptoe sheepishly around the young to hear it, for they, too, are forever in its thrall.

The year 1975 seems so far away. Gone are some younger names who lit up theatre marquees with iridescent promise: Michael Bennett, Edward Kleban, James Kirkwood, Howard Ashman. They flourished during dangerous times. What might musical theatre have been had they lived on? Before you sing your own mythological regrets, kindly take note that Bennett during the last ten years of his life had only one success, *Dreamgirls*, to fuel his monumental ego. He had floundered the rest of the time through a trio of failures: the variously reviewed *Ballroom*; the Jimmy Webb composed *Scandal*, ironically intended to have been, in the words of author Kevin Kelly, "a celebration of sexual pleasure,"[10] which languished through repeated workshops and which Bennett abandoned in 1983 when diagnosed HIV-positive; and *Chess*, from which he walked away after a stint as prospective director. Take further note that neither Kirkwood nor Kleban was heard from again after *A Chorus Line*; that Ashman, who teamed up with Hamlisch to create the very ho-hum *Smile*, also left behind the lyrics for two more fabulous collaborations with Menken, *A Little Mermaid* and *Beauty and the Beast*, both designed not for the stage but for the world of Disney. Each of the scores contains undeniable evidence of Ashman's genius in full bloom.

Bennett, Ashman, Kirkwood, Kleban ... all dead in their forties—Bennett and Ashman from AIDS, Kirwood and Kleban from cancer. All celebrated new age freedoms on the stage, some in their personal lives. All left behind unfulfilled promise. There are many who lament what they term the death of the American musical. They will tell you that when these men (and who knows how many others of like promise) passed away, so, to a measurable degree, did the dynamic art form they seemed destined to advance. Maybe so. The world grows father and father away from George Abbott and E. Y. Harburg. And now from Michael Bennett ... and Howard Ashman ... and ...

CHAPTER 11

Muddy Concepts

Talent. It comes and goes, gracing some ages abundantly, slighting others. It is irreplaceable. All the producing savvy in the world cannot make up for shoddy material. Let them bring in the brightest directors, the best set designers and orchestrators. If the talent at the core is not there, they are just erecting so much elaborate scaffolding over a vacant stage.

Kern. Rodgers. Harburg. Lane. Lerner. Berlin. Ashman. None was the product of a school for the privileged or the disadvantaged, nor were they weaned on government grants or "genius" awards. No, they developed their gifts for expression by absorbing and giving new voice to the cultural patterns of their time. And by honing their talents in the free market place, thus were they the inevitable beneficiaries of forces beyond their control. Culture: Would there have been a George Gershwin at all—would we today be singing "Fascinating Rhythm" or "Our Love Is Here to Stay"—had the young champion roller skater from Brooklyn who composed those tunes grown up eighty years later, racing on in-lines to the beat of Gangsta rap and chilling out between sprints at Starbucks?

The intersection between creative impulse and contemporary trends can lead to unexpectedly exciting new modes of expression. Can also lead to dithering dead ends. So, beyond the futile search for history or human genetics to explain why some eras foster greater works than others, we are still left back where we began: no given age is guaranteed x number of artists. Creative genius was never that easy to understand or replicate. And never was the American musical theatre more bereft of it than during a long listless drought through the 1980s.

Deferring for a moment to the many who continually lament the so-called "fall" of the American musical, let us focus first on the dearth of American talent. (Outsiders, waiting in the green room to appear, will have their day in another chapter.) Certainly, during the 1980s almost everything that opened on Broadway came crashing down with depressing regularity, or, worse yet, died a protracted death before tiny audiences conned into a kind of mercy patronage. Taking stock of a slew of reasons advanced for the alleged rise and fall of the Yankee tuner, all are secondary to the troubling demise of talent.

And direction. The creative depression was certainly caused in part by a Sondheim-led allegiance to the "concept musical." Ordinary ticket buyers not from the East Village became increasingly turned off by its aloof disregard for story and character. We may never know how many promising young songwriters who toiled slavishly in their misguided dreams of duplicating Mr. Sondheim's style, might otherwise have produced dramatically sound projects more attuned to general tastes. There are, it seems clear from reports and chatter, tons and tons of Stephen Sondheim sound-alikes lurking—and languishing—out there in regional theatre purgatory, silently cursing audiences who don't yet get it. Virtually none of their work had ever gotten to Broadway in successful form, not by the year 2000. How sad to consider their blind loyalties to so dubious a school.

By now, American musicals with rare exceptions no longer supplied popular songs to the public at large. Through the '70s, a fair number of shows—among them, *Annie, Grease, Pippin, The Magic Show, A Chorus Line, Godspell, Purlie, I Love My Wife, They're Playing Our Song*—generated songs the public embraced or at least heard on radio stations; by the '80s, with the lone exception of Henry Krieger's *Dreamgirls*, no other new American musical landed numbers on the *Billboard* charts. This is not to argue that shows containing hitless scores are bad (*West Side Story*, remember, was one); rather, to suggest a bench mark for gauging the overall decline in accessible songwriting during those times.

A few shows did produce cabaret standards. None was more endowed with excellence in this regard, nor a more glowing exception to the abysmal era in which it was born, than Jerry Herman's 1983 smash, *La Cage Aux Folles*. Long after his blockbuster success with *Hello, Dolly* and *Mame*, Herman took much bolder steps in a more serious direction. His thoughtful songs for *La Cage* serve to affirm the unconventional tale of a couple of homosexual men, Albin and Georges, who have lived together as a virtual married couple for many years, facing a crisis over whom to invite to the wedding of Georges's son, Jean-Michel. Georges, the more straight-acting of the pair, has mounting reservations over his lover's likely behavior at the wedding ceremony, fearing that Albin's flamboyant mannerisms will cause unease and embarrassment. This leads to the first act finale, "I Am What I Am," a roof-shattering anthem to individual identity.

Jerry Herman never composed with such genuine feeling. Tragically, after testing positive for AIDS around the time the show opened, Herman was left so devastated, believing he faced a certain death sentence, that he would not have the strength of spirit to compose another musical for nearly two decades.

Herman's "The Best of Times" will certainly grace piano bars for decades to come, as will "Song of the Sands," or "Look Over There," a quiet song which poses the question of who is more important, the person one spends a life with, who is there for that person day after day, or some distant little-seen relative who might be offended by the person's choice of mates? Who, indeed. "Cocktail Counter-

Composer Jerry Herman (lower left) and director Arthur Laurents confer with original cast album co-producer Fritz Holt (right) during a recording session of *La Cage aux Folles*. Above them, from left: co-stars George Hearn and Gene Barry, and record producer Thomas Z. Shepard.

point," "La Cage," and "Masculinity" are very funny songs, full of Herman's grasp of the ironies inherent in his subject. And what heart-lifting melody! The theatre had not been this romantic a place in many seasons.

In between *La Cage* and two 1989 hits, *City of Angels* and *Grand Hotel*, not much at all happened during the vacuous 1980s. Not much except for two proficiently engaging adaptations which captured critical favor (or sympathy) in 1985, a time when residents of the Big Apple were desperately in search of anything they could hold up to show the world they still knew how to produce musicals.

Exhibit #1: *Big River*, the Roger Miller tuner about Tom Sawyer and Huckleberry Finn. It has enjoyed scant respect, even disdain, from theatrical in-crowds, a puzzling contradiction to the heap of critical favor it earned on opening night—according to *Variety's* critical tally: 17 favorable notices, seven mixed reviews and only two unfavorable calls. Country and western star Roger Miller got roped into the enterprise by two of his most devoted fans, New York producers Rocco and Heidi Landsman, and Mr. Miller's first and only musical lasted for two respectable seasons at the Eugene O'Neill Theatre.

It is not so much a put down of Mr. Miller—for his songs are pleasantly serviceable—as it is an indication of how bleak things were in surrounding Times Square playhouses to note that, smack dab in the middle of that dismal decade, *Big River* proved to be one of only two new shows of lasting commercial value. Steve Suskin, one of numerous non–*Big River* fans, called it "the best musical of the worst season for Broadway musicals in seventy years."[1] (Other entries that year included *Grind* and *Leader of the Pack.*) In fact, Roger Miller's effort gave the Tony Awards show *something* to crow about. His folksy backwoods tunes evoke a sense of character and place, though they fail to provide much dramatic traction. The best of the bunch, "Muddy Waters," conjures up real excitement, an element of the theatre Mr. Miller seemed unprepared by nature to effect at will. *Big River* did not contain nearly enough muddy water.

Exhibit #2: Later the same season came another relative newcomer to the stage with a popular music background, Rupert Holmes. His *Mystery of Edwin Drood* arrived uptown following a summer of free performances under Joe Papp's aegis in Central Park. It too had a more than sympathetic hometown press waiting to give it every benefit of the doubt when it opened at the Imperial Theatre on December 2. Down upon it came a shower of warm appraisals. In his legit follow up review, *Variety's* Richard Hummler praised the show's "unmistakable stamp of Broadway professional expertise" and its "skillfully executed hokum."[2] Holmes, who did all the creative work, adapted the unfinished Charles Dickens novel and made some intriguing changes geared to generate additional publicity.

At each performance audiences were offered the chance to decide on the show's ending by vote. As for the songs—evidently not pre-selected by audience polling—the best of the lot is the hurricane-paced opening grabber, "There You Are!" From there on out, things on the cast album sound, at best, sporadically interesting. And there you go. You can't make a lasting impression with such marginal material. Many outsiders were struck by how marginal it all seemed when the show went out on tour. Before its one-year anniversary on Broadway, the tuner's title was shortened to *Drood* in a failed effort to rebuild sagging box office. Within months the Imperial stood dark.

Established writers with major track records also fell onto hard times during the decade of Michael Jackson and Madonna and Boy George. Kander and Ebb, as previously noted, reached Broadway twice during the '80s, with *Woman of the Year* and *The Rink*, the latter a 1984 offering which kept its glitter ball rotating over a rink full of aging skaters for about six months. Harvey Schmidt and Tom Jones, struggling to reclaim the glory that once was theirs, had already embarked on a sad journey of self-destruction, beginning in 1969 with *Celebration*, continuing through the 1970s when they saw their first version of *Colette* fizzle out in an off–Broadway house and another work, *Philemon*, turn into an off–off–Broadway dud. Following that, what for an encore? Into the perilous 1980s, when the closest they came to Broadway was a place called Seattle, where their second version of *Colette* folded faster than the first one. Ken Mandelbaum considered it a "class act," sincerely believing that to be done right it would demand "a riveting star."[3] It would not be the first musical desperately in need of a riveting star. Thereafter, Schmidt and Jones set up their own workshop and tried out a few more projects on local members of the New Haven crowd. None of their works-in-progress caught the fancy of a comped-in producer.

Much the same for Strouse and Adams. Together or apart, they managed to generate not a single success during the entire eighties. Not for lack of trying. They began in 1981 with a hapless sequel to their smash *Bye, Bye, Birdie*, called *Bring Back Birdie*. It may have brought back Birdie, but not the original fans. The loathing reviewers were in no mood for protracted 1950s adolescence: "The kind of a show that teaches one to be grateful for small mercies, such as the final curtain." That from Clive Barnes. And this from Richard Watts, Jr.: "When *Bring Back Birdie* isn't simply dragging itself across the stage in one dull musical number after another, through a series of desperate plot developments, it is busy being tasteless."[4] Donald O'Connor, whom you'll fondly remember from movie musical fame, had the misfortune of falling head-first into this albatross, a fate that may have hastened Mr. O'Connor's descent into senior citizen bus-and-truck concert tours. Chita Rivera, another *Bring Back* victim, stumbled quickly into another veiled turkey, magician Doug Henning's 1983 bomb *Merlin*, before semi-resurrecting herself later years in the long-running loser *Kiss of the Spider Woman*.

Who produced *Bring Back Birdie*? Lee Guber, a name well known among his co-producing unknowns. Directed? Not just directed but "conceived it," too—one Joe Layton. The book? By none other than seasoned librettist Michael Stewart. Sad but true, it also takes talent to create finished flops. Charles Strouse, away from Lee Adams, made three more attempts on his own during the '80s—*Dance a Little Closer* (to the lyrics of Alan Jay Lerner), *Mayor* and *Rags*, all dead on arrival.

Another unforeseen 1980s casualty was Marvin Hamlisch. Following his two big hits in the seventies, *A Chorus Line* and *They're Playing Our Song*, success totally eluded him. *Song*, the stronger of the two scores, had lyrics by Carol Bayer Sager. Too bad that Hamlisch and Sager became romantically embroiled during their collaboration. The doomed affair apparently killed any chances of their working together again. What they did for love. *Song* won both praise and scorn from a barrage of schizophrenic reviews. It has been unfairly underrated by Hamlisch haters, the folks who rightfully lambast the composer for appropriating Scott Joplin music in the scoring he did for the movie *The Sting* and publicly taking credit for it. On his own, Hamlisch did what good theatre composers once did: He turned out songs of relevance and timely popular appeal. His contemporary tunes no doubt helped his shows reach younger ears.

You can't blame Hamlisch alone for all the obstacles that came crashing down on so promising a career. The first two lyricists with whom he labored, Edward Kleban and Howard Ashman, both died at young ages. While Hamlisch and Ashman were working on the meandering mediocrity *Smile* (a show that some insist is not so bad—"perhaps the most underrated musical of the 1980s," according to Ken Mandelbaum),[5] Hamlisch was also toiling with Christopher Adler's lyrics for the 1983 London flop *Jean Seberg*. In 1993, he was working with his fifth collaborator, David Zippel, on yet another well-reported fiasco, *The Goodbye Girl*.

Which is an invitation to speculate: Did Mr. Hamlisch suffer from creative promiscuity? Without a significant other to ground him in a particular style or strategic vision, to give him simple relationship security, he has knocked about like a restless teenager surfing the Net. And thus was he prone, it would seem, to the shifting of courses at the drop of an expedient suggestion or work offer. The preparation of *Smile*, involving a parade of tentative collaborators coming and going from one rewrite to the next, was bound to have wrought the oddball result that is called the official opening night version. The great unfulfilled promise of Marvin Hamlisch is not without precedent: We should not forget the similar fates that befell people like Vernon Duke and Burton Lane.

Bright new beacons of the future died off too soon or lost their way, mired in bad projects. Others with sterling credits from the past simply stopped trying. By the 1980s, Bock and Harnick, still both very much alive, were amicably no longer speaking to each other about writing songs for musical shows. After their 1976 disappointment, *The Rothschilds*, Bock expressed publicly a desire to compose "serious" music, while his disenfranchised partner was cast asunder to seek other associations. What he did six years hence with aging Richard Rodgers was an embarrassment so unbelievably bad, called *Rex*, that a basic decency prevents elaboration.

After *Rex*, Mr. Harnick took a crack, with composer Michael Legrand, at two more new musicals—*The Umbrellas of Cherbourg* in 1979, and *A Christmas Carol* in 1981. Neither undertaking progressed from regional theatre tryouts to anywhere inside the city limits of Gotham, the only place where success matters in the eyes of everyone outside the city limits of Gotham. Another serial collaborator by default, Harnick faced further taunts from the press when he teamed up with Joe Raposo to adapt *It's a Wonderful Life*. Evidently it wasn't. Then, in 1993, he would contribute additional lyrics to an epic turkey that clucked around on the boards long enough to shock disbelieving eyes and thrill to no end the New Haven crowd. They called it *Cyrano, the Musical*. Beware the phrase "The Musical" in the title, a usual tip off that trouble stalks the company. Without Bock, Harnick was as much a retro neophyte as was Adler without his Ross.

Other once-prosperous songsmiths simply never came back (or, more likely, we just don't know about it), or they endured the indignities of producerly indifference at the reception desk, gave up and entered law, or returned to dentistry. I nominate the team of Howard Karr and Matt Dubey for the award of Most Underrated Musical Theatre Songwriters of the Twentieth Century. Creators of the 1950s Ethel Merman romp *Happy Hunting*, they became the butt of undeserving jokes by reputable scholars. There is Ethan Mordden, labeling their output "some of the worst songs ever written for a musical."[6] And there is Steve Suskin, quipping that "*Happy Hunting* was composed by a dentist, without novocaine," and gleefully recounting how Merman refused to accept "untried composer" Sondheim on her next project, *Gypsy*. "Big Merm—who personally 'discovered' Dubey and Karr—insisted on veteran Jule Styne. No more amateurs for her!"[7]

Amateurs? Dubey and Karr only came up with a pair of Hit Parade candidates, plus some funny numbers, plus some graceful ballads and a few roof-raising refrains. They were following the mold cut by Adler and Ross, who mixed up Broadway with Tin Pan Alley, as had virtually all those who went before them when "pop" music was not a dirty word. Whatever happened to Dubey and Karr? Before *Hunting*, they had worked on a single number, both clever and bouncy, "The Greatest Invention," for *New Faces of 1956*. After writing their hearts out for Merman, they pursued one more chance to work on a show bound for Gotham, called *We Take the Town*. Based on the adventures of Pancho Villa and starring Robert Preston, it closed out of town in short order when they first tried taking Philadelphia. The dentist, we presume, returned to drilling for gold, for it surely wasn't to be found on a Broadway stage. It is a cruel, inbred little world, full of bitterness among rivals that can be incredibly counterproductive.

(It was no less treacherous on the West End for Lionel Bart, who followed up his gigantic 1960 success *Oliver* with a parade of sad fizzling failures. In 1962, *Blitz* fared poorly with the critics. Two seasons later, *Maggie May* drew a little more respect and stayed around for over a year. *Twang*, pelted by ghastly notices in 1965, marked Bart's last West End production other than future revivals of *Oliver*. He tried his hand on American soil, straining futilely to rekindle the magic. In 1969, his ambitious *La Strada*, based on Federico Fellini's screenplay, sank under the angry blast of five disapproving reviews after only one performance at the Lunt-Fontanne Theatre. So much for the additional music by Elliot Lawrence, additional words by Martin Charnin. Back in England, Bart tinkered on another loser, *Costa Packet*, which never saw the light of a West End opening.)

Hal Bacharach and Hal David—as far as we know—purposely did not try writing another show for the stage. Following *Promises, Promises*, they headed back to the West Coast and came up with a set of stillborn numbers for a movie musical version of the film *Lost Horizon*. Soon after, they dwindled apart. A pity, for neither man would ever again begin to achieve on his own what he had done so fruitfully in tandem with the other. A perfectionist accustomed to studio-recording standards, Bacharach's "nerve-wracking" abhorrence of irregular stage singing drove him for a long spell away from considering future stage projects.[8] In later years, the Bacharach-David songbook was mined for two unsuccessful revues. Thirty years after *Promises*, Bacharach on his own made a second known stab at a Broadway show, teaming up with B.A. Robertson on lyrics to retell "Snow White and the Seven Dwarfs" against a 1970s New York setting. "Manhattan Girl," its working title, never made it to Manhattan.

Although *The Wiz*, a huge hit, got plenty of airplay, toured extensively and spawned a film, the real creative force behind its hit-laden score, African-American Charles Smalls, would never be given a chance to repeat his singular success.

"It is astounding," wrote Martin Gottfried in his book *Broadway Musicals*, "that despite the mammoth contributions of black singers and musicians to the performance of American popular music, only Duke Ellington and Fats Waller made names for themselves as songwriters, and only because they performed their own music.... Music publishers and theatrical producers have persistently denied black composers access to the public.... Even today, rare indeed is the Charlie Smalls who has the chance to write the music for a hit show like *The Wiz*. This is the disgrace of American popular and theatre music."[9]

Smalls's inexplicable fade was not so different from that of other composers who scored big in the '70s with shows that imported sounds developed outside Broadway, from Nashville to Motown, and then languished thereafter. A few of those composers, as already noted, embarked on follow up projects that went nowhere. Perhaps they were ill-prepared to absorb the subtle changes in scoring away from a stridently narrow rock and roll heritage. And the leading pop songwriters of the day did not demonstrate much desire to subject their egos to the unique collaborative demands of musical theatre. Barry Manilow passionately tried a couple of times with original work that did not reach a major New York house.

Then there were those once-promising talents who passed semi-anonymously across doomed stages, contributing so many wonderful songs to fallen shows: Larry Grossman and Hal Hackady to *Minnie's Boys*; Billy Goldenberg (music) and Alan and Marilyn Bergman (lyrics) to *Ballroom*; Craig Carnelia to *Working*. Grossman had composed three other flops (*Grind*, *A Doll's Life* and *Goodtime Charley*); the Bergmans had been to New York once before, in 1964 when with composer Sammy Fain they worked on *Something More*, the only musical ever directed by Jule Styne, which left most of the critics wanting something different and lasted all of fifteen performances. In the indices of theatre books, Craig Carnelia's name appears but once, referencing his association with the troubled *Working*, for which he composed with such singular inspiration. The Broadway canon is littered with great songs, most of which will never find an audience beyond the small devoted class of cast album collectors.

Other neophytes to musical theatre had arrived from country truck stops and Ivy League colleges. For skeptics with golden-age memories, the end of the line was probably spotted during a pathetically barren Tony Awards telecast in 1983, when a nice enough group of singers—Jim Wann, Cass Morgan, Debra Monk, John Foley, John Schimmel, and Mark Hardwick—took the stage and performed a few of their songs from a show nominated that year for "Best Musical of 1982," *Pump Boys and Dinettes*. The Dodger Organization, the people who gave you *Big River* three years later, got behind this hokey backwoods truck stop revue, a kind of egalitarian enterprise which found high favor in the pages of the *New York Times*, Mel Gussow judging it "as refreshing as an ice cold beer after a bowl of five-alarm chili."[10] At the Tonys, it tasted more like flat lemonade at a flea market. The yawningly undramatic numbers do deliver amiably fresh lyrics, honed with intelligence in the country school of songwriting.

The same season brought another minor work, *Nine*. It is again tempting to suggest that mediocre musicals do unreservedly well in desperate times. *Nine* was warmly received by the press. *Variety* appraised it "a triumph of imaginative staging and production glitter over thin material." Tommy Tune's choreography, wrote the reviewer, cleverly concealed threadbare materials: "There isn't much time to notice how little of consequence is at stake."[11] Whatever its on-stage merits, the score is amazingly devoid of *lyrics* (remember lyrics?). For this ornery non-achievement, hats off to composer Maury Yeston, a fully credentialed Yale music professor who tyrannized his own music (some of it quite lush and lovely) with his do-it-yourself verse.

One wonders: Exactly what does a producer of taste say to a Yeston in this regard? Had musical theatre sunk so low—were there so few decent lyric writers around—that Yeston could simply get away with it? Lyrics being the least critical of a musical's three components, he did. Arthur Kopit supplied the book, patterned after filmmaker Federico Fellini's *8½*. Dance dazzler Tommy Tune directed and choreographed (with assistance from Tommy Walsh), and the glitzy thing stayed around for a healthy run. Nine years in the making, *Nine* was one of a newer breed of super slick production workhorses that have a way of lulling audiences into a false sense of entertainment. There are few mortals around willing to sing its praises.

The Tap Dance Kid, which opened in 1983 at the Broadhurst theatre, was an almost-hit that hung on for almost two seasons before going out on tour. The suitable songs came from the piano of Henry Krieger, the okay lyrics from the pen of Robert Lorick. A likable show at heart, *The Tap Dance Kid* dances on the conflict between a young black boy who just wants to dance, please—have you a problem with that?—and his father, who does have a problem with that. The dad, a proud attorney, dreads the digressive symbolism of it all. Librettist Charles Blackwell based his sensitive script on the novel by Louise Fitzhugh, "Nobody's Family Is Going to Change." What the creators failed to do was find a more original voice. The important story they told got submerged in relentless feel-good, all-dreams-come-true refrains.

Also in 1983, the team of David Shire and Richard Maltby, Jr., ultimately famous for never having had a successful show on Broadway, came to town with *Baby*. Up till that point, they had worked on Leonard Sillman's *New Faces of 1968*, and on *Love Match*, a tuner which opened the same season in Phoenix, Arizona, and closed out of town in Los Angeles exactly two months later. *Baby* barely lasted through its diaper stage at the Ethel Barrymore. Its hard-working score, influenced by the school of Sondheim with a few nods to Stephen Schwartz and Donna Disco Summers thrown in for fresh air, sounds marooned in the cerebral self-conscious '70s. Too full of Yuppie jabber, it is not an easy listen, even though a few of the selections fly—the rhythmically inventive "Baby, Baby," and the powerful anthem to parenthood, "The Story Goes On." These are not the sort of whining rich-kid parents to whom audiences gravitate. Among a mixed set of notices, Richard Hummler wrote, "The diffused and unconnected stories of three expectant couples lack immediacy and dimension.... *Baby* has no central dramatic focus."[12] In the end, *Baby* succumbed to concept musicalitis.

Near the end of the decade, Broadway dusted off an old 1950s Edwin Lester Civic Light Opera relic, *At the Grand*, which had starred Paul Muni and got no farther out of Los Angeles than jinxed San Francisco. Its outing at the Curran showed mildly enchanting if musty promise. Especially moving was the sympathetic presence of the old man, played by Paul Muni, nearing the end of his life with a fatal illness and simply wishing to experience one last touch of magic, maybe a little love, at the Grand Hotel in Berlin. Thirty years later, they brought in Tommy Tune, a smart move. Tune transformed the creaking book into a virtual character-based revue without intermission. Maury Yeston added a few fine numbers which, on balance, complimented the effective original Robert Wright and George Forrest songs. And they produced one of the best scores of the '80s. *Grand Hotel*, the show's revamped title, enjoyed a very prosperous run.

Cy Coleman, who hadn't been heard from in almost ten years, flopped out in early 1989 with the 12-performance dud *Welcome to the Club*, then rebounded wonderfully only eight months later when his *City of Angels*, an original film noir story developed and scripted by Larry Gelbart, took the town by a whirl. Coleman fashioned his sultry refrains after 1940s big band swing. David Zippel's savvy lyrics matched the savvy music, and Gelbart's laugh-loaded book earned special praise from a majority of the reviewers.

Hotel and *Angels* may long be remembered as exceptions to a decade of thundering reversals. Numbered among the era's deluxe letdowns are the three musicals which Stephen Sondheim, eventually to be christened by *Variety*, "the preeminent figure in contemporary musical theatre,"[13] introduced during the feckless '80s. Mr. Sondheim could still produce interesting, sometimes rousing songs, could still impress with deft lyrical gifts. It is a shame he squandered so much talent in the puzzling servitude of such self-indulgent projects.

Sondheim surely hastened the demise of the concept musical with *Sunday in the Park with George*—only the fifth musical to be awarded the Pulitzer Prize, and, for non–Pulitzer judges, one of the most trying evenings ever in a New York house. Clive Barnes and Richard Watts, Jr., registered their disapproval. So did the man from *Variety*, who stated, "Dispassionate respect rather than enjoyment is likely to be the predominate reaction to *Sunday* ... another concept musical in which an abstract subject—the creation of art—takes precedence over story and character...."[14]

Into the Woods, Sondheim's 1987 offering, enthralled in its preliminary moments. There was a sense of adventure in the air as audiences embarked on a potentially dangerous journey. But once the show slipped into a second act that couldn't make up its thematic mind, the intriguing fun turned into tedious mental speculation. "It is basically a dull show that never comes into satisfying focus," wrote *Variety's* Richard Hummler. "Where the characters in the first act are active and moving forward, in the second part they're passive reactors to the menace of the murdered giant's vengeful widow."[15]

The production's biggest asset was the production itself, a clever sleight-of-hand salvage job by director James Lapine, who also wrote the libretto. Much in the spirit of a George Abbott, Lapine shamelessly hauled out a vaudevillian's bag of audience-pleasing tricks. Guffaws to slapstick can't, however, get us out of these woods. In the morass that follows intermission, one trenchant lyric idea cancels out or supersedes another, there are so many competing Big Themes knocking windily about. Courtesy of the nation's leading civic light opera companies, *Into the Woods*, the perfect thinking person's musical, has found life after Broadway before Yuppie crowds and academics who harbor serious reservations with song and dance shows but feel "o.k." about something that kind of sounds intellectual.

Mr. Sondheim narrowed his vision down to the razor-thin path of a shotgun in his next big surprise, *Assassins*. First staged in 1990 by Playwright's Horizons, it amounted to a perversely perfect end to Broadway's worst decade. As if he had not already done everything imaginable to alienate audiences, Sondheim now labored mightily to defend the diabolical choices made by American dissidents with pistols aimed at enemies both personal and political. His best number, "Everybody's Got the Right," so good that it sounded like a dropout from *Follies*, was one of only eight songs in the entire recorded score. In terms of shock appeal, they are one crazed bunch, maybe too unsettling for the average ticket buyer. *Assassins* failed to move from its Playwright's Horizons preview into a larger house. In 1992, it sold out a twelve-week London run, where the critics loved it.

By 1990, Sondheim had almost completely lost touch with ordinary people, who still preferred musicals about reasonably ordinary people. (The way things are going in modern society, however, with high school students slaughtering clasmates with assault rifles, etc., *Assassins* may turn into a hot public high school drama department staple in another five or fifty years—if any public high schools are left to produce it.) By indulging himself so, Mr. Sondheim had virtually destroyed his credibility with the public. Oscar Hammerstein's reigning protege, still trying to rewrite *Allegro*, had led the musical theatre up a dead end street—not without an entourage of idolatrous fans to insulate the master from his every misstep into the woods. Nor without the encouragement of numerous Tony Awards and other assorted prizes, honors, testimonials, and a quarterly devoted exclusively to reports and essays about his work. Bringing about the near demise of the *American* musical was a group effort.

Times Square stood eerily dormant as the '90s dawned, its once-shimmering skyline of hit show titles in neon felled by an onslaught of ineptitude and arrogance. And when boat loads of gothic sets and garish pop-rock tunes from across the Atlantic docked in New York during the bleakest period, thousands of starved theatergoers lined up to buy tickets for West End imports, eager to experience once again the thrill of strong dramatic stories set soaringly to music.

And, please, not to concepts.

CHAPTER 12

Sir Musical

Not since the music of Kern or Rodgers in better days gone by had a song so embraced the heart like a lover's reassuring smile. "All I Ask of You," that song, came late in the first act of *The Phantom of the Opera*, which opened at the Majestic Theatre on January 26, 1988, and was still playing there at the end of the century. Although the critics didn't much like the show, although insiders smugly dismissed it with words like "manufactured," "cold," "derivative," audiences felt differently. Carried to a sphere of high emotion that other musicals weren't taking them to in those hapless nights on Broadway, surging crowds rediscovered the power of musical theatre to enchant and inspire. Thousands would return again and again to the same show to reexperience the magic.

Whence such freshly aggressive music, amounting to a bold reinvention of the show song? From Englishman Andrew Lloyd Webber, son of two music teachers, who grew up favoring the Beatles, rock and roll, Puccini, Prokofiev and one famous American tunesmith: "My idea, really, was Richard Rodgers," Webber stated, "and then, subsequently, it grew into musicals in general by all the best writers and composers…. I supposed I was being influenced to compose my own tunes in roughly their style."[1] Two major sources in particular propelled Webber—one an obsession of his father's, drilled into him at an early age, that "melody was the most important thing," and the other, his devotion to Prokofiev. "I have an understanding of atonalism and dissonance—which frankly Prokofiev had, only I go farther than that. The other is that I have no fear about where I will make harmony go, so long as I can make melody take it there naturally."[2]

Take it there, naturally or not, he did, and in a big way, essentially merging three sources of inspiration—Broadway, opera, and rock. Webber developed an expansive facility for dramatic scoring which he would express through a number of impressively diverse projects, from the crucifixion of Jesus Christ to a fading Hollywood star at the love-starved end of her and filmland's golden era. Following his father's admonition, Andrew mastered the all-important gift for melody, so necessary to great shows. At the same time, he would incur the lingering disdain of U.S. theatre practitioners and critics. No composer who sought respect in that incestuous little world, headquartered in Manhattan, was ever more dreaded or despised by his own peers.

Not so shocking, really, given the quirky history of critical irrelevance in the face of imposing new work. Stravinsky's "The Rite of Spring," which premiered in Paris in 1913 to audience-wide hostility bordering on revolt, springs to mind, as do a number of symphonic and operatic works originally panned by wage-earning know-it-alls. Never, in fact, are the experts more ill-equipped to earn their pay than when constricted by fetishes or hidden conflicts of interest from recognizing important new work.

Paying customers are sometimes the first to spot that something in the air. And in this story, it was the audience that spotted the genius of Andrew Lloyd Webber and elevated him to global renown. Take a look, once more, at the 1980s, this time with your focus on the work of Mr. Webber—and other foreigners, for that matter—that was not developed in the United States. You'll hear the applause of younger, more diverse patronage, and you'll see a few theatres bombarded with long lines of anxious customers that no amount of bad press could keep away. Were those ticket buyers conned into some grand illusion, itself artistically hollow at the core? Addicted to famed opera composer derivatives turned into elevator music? Those hits from the Brits, say what you will, kept a few houses on Times Square lit year after year after year, while quite a few others stood eerily dark.

As a lad, Andrew dreamed of spending his life in history and architecture, spirited by a natural fascination for ancient ruins and old medieval buildings. His mother, Jean, gave him his first piano lesson at the prep school he attended in London. His father, who trained as a plumber and who became the distinguished director of the London College of Music, once told Andrew that if he ever composed a song as good as "Some Enchanted Evening," he'd let him know. "Well," confessed Andrew many years later, "he never did tell me."[3]

At Oxford, Andrew, then 17, met and was creatively smitten with Tim Rice, and he left school in order solely to pursue a collaboration with the older lyricist, all of three-and-a-half years his senior. "Andrew had this burning ambition to be Richard Rodgers," recalled Rice, "while I sort of vaguely wanted to be Elvis."[4] Their first Rodgers & Presley venture, *Come Back, Richard, Your Country Needs You*, was not much needed by anybody in London, where it played a single performance, and, despite that, somehow got recorded on the RCA label.

Next, they created *Jesus Christ Superstar*, writing the songs in five and a half days, breathlessly atypical for the team, although not exactly for Andrew, who during those hurricane-paced days was furiously composing up a reservoir of melody from which he would draw for several shows to come. Rice shunned clever rhyming in deference to a more literal recitative approach, a bent not fancied by his future critics. Instead, he stressed narration over lyrical embroidery. The songs they crafted bristled with a youthful vitality which carried dramatic weight. Webber marshalled the force of electronic music to build an unforgettably intense climax in the crucifixion scene, where a rock-fashioned crescendo nearly blows the rafters to smithereens. The two boys flirted with links between the ancient story and the modern pop world. Mary Magdalene's "I Don't Know How to Love Him" conveyed the mystical uncertainty of the unrequited lover, while the show's title song bore a brazen new voice never before heard on the stage, a kind of acid rock fanfare—or, if you like, an overblown riff turned up to the highest decibels.

Not so curious, at all, that Rice and Webber should have entered the theatre this way, given their religious backgrounds. Rice harbored a boyhood fascination with biblical stories, and Webber, raised somewhat dispassionately in the Catholic church, would in later years return to the roots of his faith when he composed the eloquent Christmas-oriented "Requiem." In fact, there are distinctive threads of church music that weave through Andrew Lloyd Webber refrains, investing them with a subtle spiritual dimension, though he seems either unaware of the fact or unwilling to acknowledge it.

Webber's *Superstar* melodies revealed a bold new innovator in show music. He and Rice, a perfect fit for the long-haired sixties youth culture, took the stage with audacity once they actually got there. Unable to interest a producer at first, instead of holding backers auditions the American way they raised the money to record their songs in album format. And this led to Robert Stigwood, who had produced *Hair* in London, picking up the property and premiering it on the West End, where it became the longest running British musical of its time. Still, the show was easily snubbed as a fluke of clever promotion—a rock album blown up into a headline-grabbing extravaganza. In the U.S., where the scribes split wildly in their opinions, *Jesus Christ Superstar* did not duplicate its phenomenal West End success, even though it pulled off a profitable 711-performance run. And it ran up against a backlash of conservative voices, appalled by the crass exploitation of so sacred a story. Billy Graham denounced it.

In the secular word, Walter Kerr lined up in favor of the work itself, but not of the rather overheated Tom O'Horgan–conceived production that introduced it to Americans: "O'Horgan has adorned it. Oh, my God, how he has adorned it...." Douglas Watt found it "so stunningly effective a theatrical experience that I am still finding it difficult to compose my thoughts about it ... It is, in short, a triumph."[5]

In 1976, Webber and Rice revamped and expanded an earlier effort, another Bible adaptation called *Joseph and the Amazing Technicolor Dreamcoat.* Its wonderful songs drew on early Beatles romanticism. Originally done in 1968 in a fifteen-minute version as a children's oratorio, *Joseph* was lengthened to forty minutes in 1973, then by another quarter of an hour for a West End debut three years later. From there it was shipped across the sea and presented at the Brooklyn Academy of Music in 1976. Then to Broadway, five years later, where it received notices both very good and very bad. Christopher Sharp scolded it for being—horror of horrors!—"essentially children's theatre."[6] Its tunes are entrancing, its lyrics hip. Its New York run lasted an impressive 824 performances. National touring

Andrew Lloyd Webber.

companies—with whom singer Donnie Osmond has been a headliner—now and then continue to draw appreciative family audiences.

Rice and Webber returned to New York, in 1979, as daringly as when they first called, now with a musical about Argentina's Eva Peron, a woman of beauty and ambition who slept her way up the political back-bedroom ladder to become ruler of the nation. *Evita's* music was steeped in torrid latin rhythms, and, like *Superstar*, sung-through. This Webber-Rice opera derivative would have profound long-term effect on how musical theatre came to be created and sold to the public, especially to younger crowds and opera fans. Without dialogue getting in the way, all the picky literalists who squirmed in their seats over the sight of a character "breaking into a song" were spared the ordeal.

The Rice and Webber treatment of Ms. Peron's story is a blistery tour-de-force not welcomed by a lot of folks who happen to *like* characters "breaking into a song," who happen to insist on likable protagonists to root for and believe in.

Evita shrewdly succeeded despite its coldness where most other musicals of a similar psyche fail. Why? Here was a compelling take on one of life's most sobering realities: Some of the most effective and revered political leaders are themselves amorally ruthless. *Evita* conveyed this vexing irony with brute theatrical force. It was, to be clear, refreshingly unlike so many crippled shows that stagger into New York City, having been nursed over by hordes of script doctors and vacillating producers desperately settling for bubble gum because all else on the road seemed not to be jelling, and still in search of a purpose. *Evita* knew, minute by minute, exactly what it was about. Harold Prince's brilliant uncompromising direction helped underline that clarity.

"Don't Cry for Me, Argentina" sings like an authentic national anthem that has existed for years. By accident, not until minutes before it was about to be recorded during the final pre-production studio session for an album of the songs did Tim Rice come up with the title line—a spur-of-the-moment idea to replace the original words, "It's only your lover returning." The song was revved up to '70s dance-club tempo, and it became an international disco hit *eighteen* months before the show ever opened, which helped jump start the box office. Other songs, too, were danceable: "Buenos Aires" was built on the cha-cha, while "On This Night of a Thousand Stars" drifts sensually on the slow rise of a carioca beat. Together, the hypnotic, story-advancing songs comprise Webber's most unified work, validly dramatic at every turn.

The 1978 opening left West End critics gasping for superlatives. The British may be a more realistic lot. A year later, the musical came to America and got some kind of a cold shoulder. *Variety* saw 6 pans and 2 inconclusive notices; not so *More Broadway Opening Nights*, which pulled one rave out of the pile, one mixed, one unfavorable and only two pans. Let Clive Barnes speak for the fractured reactions: "*Evita* is a stunning, exhilarating theatrical experience, especially if you don't think about it much. I have rarely ever seen a more excitingly staged Broadway musical.... The fault of the whole construction is that it is hollow. We are expected to deplore Evita's morals but adore her circuses."[7]

Andrew Lloyd Webber was by now the more ambitious of the pair. Webber set up his annual Sydmonton Festivals, conducted on his own property, to try out work-in-progress on a circle of trusted friends and associates, invited to offer critical feedback. All had to swear not to share the goings-on with outsiders. And by now, Rice and Webber were increasingly at odds with each other's differing attitudes about work and play. Webber composed relentlessly. "A perfectionist," said his biographer, Gerald McKnight, "he worked long, exhausting hours shaping and selecting melodic frameworks and orchestrations for his compositions. The excitement for him lay in using fresh, original sounds."[8] Rice resisted taking part in time-consuming sessions around a piano. He deemed vacation time, friends and travel as equally essential to his well being. Once he tried his hand at being a disk jockey. Another time he took a holiday to Japan, where he had spent a year of his boyhood attending religious schools while his dad worked in the country.

Before they wrote *Evita*, Rice had declined to become involved with Webber on *By Jeeves*, which Webber ended up writing with Alan Ayckbourn. After *Evita*, when Webber turned to the poetry of T.S. Eliot for the stimulus to compose his first mega hit, *Cats*, he approached Rice about working on one of the songs, "Memory," which needed additional words to supplement some Eliot lines. Rice again declined to tango—not just once, but twice. Recounting this impasse, in itself a precarious act of memory, calls to mind how suddenly motivated certain individuals will become through perceived rivalries. After alternative lyricist Don Black supplied a set of words for "Memory," not judged suitable, and after director Trevor Nunn came up with words which Webber loved—well, then, here came Rice with a cat-like change of heart. He spent three whole draining days on his own lyric for "Memory." Too late, Tim. Trevor's entry was quite wonderful, and since Trevor was given ultimate authority to select which one to use, Trevor chose Trevor. Mr. Rice felt royally rejected, and he aired his bitter hurts with the press. "I was extremely annoyed," he told a *Guardian* reporter.[9]

Without Rice, Webber continued his reinvention of the musical into epic pop opera pitch, making it in subtle and not-so-subtle ways something distinctly different from the American musical play which had blossomed through the 1950s. Wisely, too, Webber moved quickly away from rock into a more eclectic arena—into the amplified fusion of popular music with quasi-classical idioms. This had the effect, horrifying to some, of coarsening the entire enterprise into a spectacle of manipulated sound. Though the music emanated from a single soul, the electronic glitter and all the garish arrangements gave it a kind of ponderous grandeur. Webber's devout critics may be actually bothered more by the technical enhancements and the bravura performances than by the actual songs themselves. Nonetheless, millions of theatergoers around the world heard real music and were moved.

Cats is many things to many people—fantasy, revue, allegory, even fledgling book show struggling for breath under the hulk of a monster junkyard set so real, it's a legal wonder no theatre where *Cats* played was ever shut down for safety code violations. At its purry core, *Cats* is an ingenious musicalization of Eliot's trenchant verse about the imagined ways of various felines. The freshly wrought tunes, full of gaiety and pathos, are an honorable match. Charm and fantasy much compensate for a rambling music hall format, starring Grizabella, the aging glamour cat whom some reviewers have taken to be an over-the-bed prostitute waxing lyrical over better, more admired days. Between the slumping sections that feel padded, there are unforgettable moments, like "Jellicle Ball," about as mystically enchanting as anything the stage can offer.

The exalting "Memory" saved the show from premature oblivion in a real junkyard. Producer Cameron Mackintosh was ready to close down his pet shop when—like a little lost kitten finding unexpected favor in the lap of an admiring stranger—"Memory" swiftly catapulted into hit status on Brit radio stations. *Cats* became a box office darling. At century's end, it was still charming Broadway audiences at the Winter Garden, where it had opened on October 7, 1982.

In 1985, Webber took on writer Don Black, whose "Memory" lyric he had also rejected, and they took a worldly look at the sad little heartbreaks of expedient relationships in big city environs. They titled their gem *Tell Me on a Sunday*, and it was presented as the first of a two-part evening, *Song and Dance*. Skipping over the dance half (Webber's arranged variations on Puccini's "A Minor Caprice," a wow in itself that deserves more appropriate discussion in the pages of dance tomes), *Tell Me* packs a well-honed wallop. Black's lyrics are high grade, fresh, insightful, witty—piercingly to the point. Webber's music is just as fresh and sharply contemporary, following trails forged by artists from Helen Reddy to Donna Summers.

This being a one-woman show, the songs are all sung by the heroine of the piece, a young British woman who goes to New York, via Los Angles, in the fragile hope of finding a glamorous life complete with Mr. Right. She finds it fleetingly through dalliances with four men, and her sweet resignation in the end to a fruitless journey is ingratiating and not a little noble. "Capped Teeth and Caesar Salad," "You Made Me Think You Were in Love, "The Last Man in My Life," and "I'm Very You, You're Very Me" are a few of the score's captivating treasures, tracing the heroine's funny-sad romantic adventures and letdowns. *Tell Me on a Sunday* unfolds with taut efficiency.

The original treat, another Cameron Mackintosh–backed show, lasted for only 474 performances, a niggardly run by Webber standards. Unlike the maestro's other hits, *Sunday* was not a spectacle, nor was its heroine a bigger than life character from extraordinary circumstances. She was a real person in the present tense. And when it came to composing songs for real people in the unexotic here and now, Mr. Webber seemed afflicted by a strange handicap. Give him something fantastic, like, say, an old steam engine racing against a cold-hearted electrified locomotive for champion of the tracks, or a theatre phantom possessed of a chorus girl, and then the Andrew Lloyd Webber box office opens extra windows. And the theatre gets rented forever, making the Nederlanders or the Shuberts, landlords formerly known as producers, very happy.

About the little puffer with a heart of steam, it chugged like an aging star on the comeback trail through *Starlight Express*, another show high on cinematic stagecraft, topped out by dazzling laser-beam effects. Webber's pop score, with lyrics from several hands lead by Richard Stilgoe, is one energizing amalgam of rock, soul, funk and pop, all cleverly in tune with the action, and all rendered in funky good taste. Every cast member appeared on roller skates for the entire shindig, swooping out at times over the orchestra seats on special stage-level ramps. They rolled across the Gershwin Theatre a respectable 761 times before New Yorkers would no longer tolerate the roller derby of novo musicals from Great Britain. In less snooty places like Las Vegas and London, they were still whizzing across the ramps at century's end.

Then came Webber's triumph, *The Phantom of the Opera*. He and this gothic tale were made for each other, and in his passionate adaptation, assisted by Richard Stilgoe, Webber matured by dazzling degrees. The story itself holds strong fascination; there is probably a phantom of the opera in all of us—that part of our lovesick soul that has ached for someone we will never have. The disembodied voice of this phantom stalks the Paris Opera House, bellowing forth his capricious demands to its new proprietors: Do what I say! Make *Christine* the star! Retire your aging prima donna! Replace her with *Christie*, or suffer the wrath of my certain revenge! And by measures ever more ominous as the threat builds, the theatre lights go out, performances are shuttered, a chandelier comes tumbling (kind of) down over the audience and, finally, a hangman's rope drops around the neck of Christine's rival suitor, Raoul.

Even then—there is at least one other stage version out there, by Maury Yeston, with limited box office appeal that some critics prefer—it is hard to imagine Webber's *Phantom* enjoying such long-lasting patronage around the world without the soaring melodies which he created for the fine lyrics supplied by Charles Hart, supplemented by additional verse from Richard Stilgoe. The power of music turned this bizarre tale into a heart-pounding experience. "Think of Me" invites us into the strange sadness of the heroine. The "Phantom" theme assaults us with the masked antagonist's deranged infatuation with Christine. "Prima Donna" lavishes false praise, ever so flamboyantly, on a fading star about to be replaced by the Phantom's favorite singer. "All I Ask of You" plays to our deepest romantic longings. "Masquerade" raises a shrill salute to the costumed hypocrisies behind which we so sheepishly hide, and to the fleeting nature of the physical beauty we so foolishly pursue. "Wishing You Were Somehow Here Again" overflows with hopeless nostalgia. "The Point of No Return," a dark tango, hovers erotically on the brink of forced seduction. Webber's charts play out almost like a symphony, the variously shaded refrains mirroring the Phantom's demented agenda as it impacts the lives of all who inhabit the Paris Opera House. When, at the last moment, the Phantom feels inevitably driven to remove his mask, thus exposing the deformed side of his face before a crestfallen Christine, he in effect presses us all up against the tragedy of his doomed desire, and the empathetic moment affects a powerful catharsis.

Detractors claim that *The Phantom of the Opera* is no more than a cunning theatrical contrivance; escaping them, somehow, is the heart-wrenching story of unrequited love it tells, and with such potent words and music. Among the complaints, we are told it has "no conflict," the music "sounds all the same," the story "repeats a one-theme obsession ad nauseam," the falling chandelier "is what really pulls the audiences in," and without the spectacular stage effects "there would be no show." Some of these same complainers report quality sleep during the one obligatory visit they made to see *Phantom*.[10]

Many of them anxiously await the long-planned, regularly delayed revival, in revised form, of Cole Porter's *Out of This World*. Some claim that Kurt Weill never got a fair shake; others, that some obscure musical produced in the early '80s marks the last decent act of musical theatre in the twentieth century. While arguing the demise of a great American art form, they fail to acknowledge that musical theatre has traveled a circle amidst shifting influences—from the early days of the century when shows from abroad dominated the New York theatre scene, through decades of home-grown success, to a time, one hundred years later, when European influences again hold sway.

Alan Jay Lerner, one of the few remaining pros from the golden age to hear some of Webber's early work, spotted a major new voice in the air: "Webber's childhood was steeped in the classics, which becomes more and more apparent the more one listens to his music. Influences abound, but they are filtered through a very distinctive musical personality, which gives his music a sound of its own."[11] Lerner lived long enough to attend a performance of *Cats*, whose score he found "remarkably theatrical."[12] Near the end of his book, *Musical Theatre: A Celebration*, he opined that, compared to "one-of-a-kind" Sondheim, who "cannot be imitated except by cloning... Webber, on the other hand, speaks in the popular musical language of the day, more literate but, nevertheless, contemporary through and through; and form, in these particular times, is apt to cast a longer shadow than content."[13]

Just as the music of Jerome Kern has endured for nearly ten decades, so, too, will the finest melodies from *Cats* and *Evita* and *Joseph* and *Phantom* live on. And there will no doubt come a day, many years hence, when fans of the Broadway musical will ruefully reminisce over the time when Andrew Lloyd Webber ruled the commercial stage. Having discovered in his absence a new-found appreciation, they will sing his songs in their staged concert readings and regional revivals. They will wonder why they ever denigrated his contributions in the first place. Now, at last, they will speak of songs like "Think of Me" with the same affection and respect reserved for Kern and Rodgers, for Gershwin and Porter.

All the negative reviews in the world cannot kill a good tune—or show—once the public gets a hold of it.

CHAPTER 13

A Helicopter Lands

Cats. The Phantom of the Opera. Les Misérables. Miss Saigon. Four mega hits from the Brits, all introduced to America through the early 1990s, were still on Broadway at the end of the century. Following the premiere of *Miss Saigon* on April 11, 1991, however, for the next ten years nothing new from Britain turned a profit in a New York House. This said as much about the fleeting nature of creativity as it did about the variable fortunes of producers—in this case, about Cameron Mackintosh, the young impresario who had a hand in all four imported triumphs. Had the West End wizard of record-shattering productions lost his magic touch?

Like his countryman Andrew Lloyd Webber (with whom he shares the birth year 1948), Mackintosh hummed American show tunes in his youth. Just short of his eighth birthday, he got "dragged" off to see the English musical *Salad Days.* "People singing and dancing seemed sissie to me, but of course I was captivated." He returned on his birthday, and, after the performance, marched down the aisle to introduce himself to the composer, Julian Slade, who played the pit piano. Slade escorted eight-year-old Cameron backstage, a career-defining moment. "I saw how scenery came in and out," he told Barbara Isenberg of the *Los Angeles Times,* "and I wanted to put things like that together."[1]

Did he ever. By age 19, Mackintosh, who regarded *My Fair Lady* as the greatest musical ever written, got a job in London as assistant stage manager for *Hello, Dolly.* By his late thirties, he conquered the stage with a savvy for marketing musicals worldwide not before or since equaled. Flushed with global conquests, Mackintosh became the most successful theatrical producer ever, hyping shows into international household names.

At the summit of his producing fortunes in the late '80s, Mackintosh liked pointing out how most every new musical he saw (or was pitched, via demo tape) could have been composed during the last forty years. Too staid, too old fashioned,

149

he implied, unlike the more contemporary work he believed he was producing. (His smug assertions did not always hold, for strewn among the Mackintosh-sponsored scores under scrutiny herein are tunes that sound like they could have been written forty years ago.) Mackintosh pushed his image as visionary presenter of *new* work. New or not, it was packaged in spectacular state-of-the-art fashion. The producer immersed his audiences in orgiastic displays of modern stagecraft technology, some of it so complex as to outdo special effects in today's movies.

In skeptical reaction to the pyrotechnics involved, critics of the Mackintosh touch argued that they drag down the art of musical theatre to a lower level of crowd-pandering spectacle, and that audiences, promised fireworks, are hauled in for the wrong reasons. It's a dubious charge, for without the critical goods—the stories, the characters and the songs—none of the shows could have prospered so. And if Mackintosh is guilty of extreme showmanship, he is hardly the first impresario to have bolstered his commercial prospects by investing in lavish productions. *The Wizard of Oz*, with a book and lyrics by L. Frank Baum himself, was in 1903 the premiere event at the new Majestic Theatre, and contained "brilliant scenic effects," beginning with a cyclone on stage, as reported by the *New York Times*. "It cannot be said," remarked the anonymous reviewer, "that the authors have shown any great originality, but they have thrown old and well approved materials into a pleasing shape."[2] Florenz Ziegfeld did much the same years later when he threw girls, glitter, and scenery into his opulent revues.

If *Peter Pan* can fly across the apron, why can't a chandelier fall or a helicopter land? The theatre, a rather schizophrenic place caught between make believe and in-the-flesh immediacy, has by tradition called on leading engineers and artists to help make its illusions more believable. At the same time, it continually struggles with its more theatrical urges—born out of vaudeville, blown up in musical theatre, egged on by the intimacy shared by audience and actor—to break free of naturalism and simply *strut*. And simply mug. And simply resort to another amusing aside. And simply cakewalk and charm us for the hell of it.

And therein lies a delightful dichotomy. After all, each night ushers in a different performance. If we don't exactly look for the strut, well ... when it pops up, cane in hand, hat cocked across glinting smile, we can hardly resist the encouragement it seeks. And we laugh and applaud. It can show up anywhere at anytime, smack dab in the middle of something otherwise serious, as it does in the second act of Mackintosh's *Miss Saigon*, in a bulldozer of a razzle-dazzlement called "The American Dream," a number tenuously irrelevant yet oh-so irresistible. It cares only about pleasing a crowd of people, about showing off and stealing unexpected attention, so nakedly single-minded is it, daring us to deny ourselves the pleasure of its audacious company.

Let's be adult about this. Broadway musicals at heart are like children of irresistible charm who simply refuse to grow up, refuse to behave along rational lines. They leap at us across the footlights with grimacing faces and wiggling outstretched arms, with fingers snapping up a breeze of infectious goodwill. They're forever competing to keep everyone laughingly on their side, in their camp, no matter how insignificant their reason for being there. George Abbott, not a Pirandello or a Beckett, knew this. He loaded the stage with juvenile merriment, with zany crossovers and far-fetched chases. If it worked, if it moved the show along, in it stayed.

A producer like Cameron Mackintosh has history on his side when he orders realistic sets and yet shamelessly allows party crashers into the proceedings: songs barely related to the story that might make the hit parade just in case the show has nothing as good to offer or its fireworks backfire; popular personalities known for dispensing charm in a void, as insurance against flat dialogue or saggy direction. History on his side: Senior vaudevillian Danny Kaye did major compensatory work in a Richard Rodgers late-career bust, *Two by Two*. That stolid old hack work based on the Noah's ark story drew almost every sort of critical reaction known to the theatre. When Kaye broke a leg, did the show fail to go on while he recovered? Of course not. The show went on *with* crutches. And what a hoot it was. Rodgers, however, did not laugh, recounting how Kaye, a "one-by-one vaudeville act," would goose the chorus girls with crutches or purposely run into others, slapstick style, or make up his own lines as the spirit moved him and sing his numbers in unusual tempos. At selected curtain calls, Kaye addressed his adoring fans, "I'm glad you're here, but I'm glad the authors aren't!"[3] By that time, in fact, insiders guessed that without Kaye's outrageous antics, *Two by Two* might not have drawn the crowds it did. The 343 performance run made a few pennies.

Another professional cut-up, Carol Burnett, was credited for turning the ho-hum *Once Upon a Mattress* into a hit. Sobering to contemplate how many not-so-good-musicals, originally dismissed by the Fourth Estate, prove better than initially thought when, through different casting or fresh direction in revival format, they engage as never before. 'Twas always thus: In 1927, the Gershwin brothers struck out on the road with *Strike Up the Band*, an austere anti-war tuner with a book by George S. Kaufman. Three years later, Morrie Ryskind rewrote the libretto, safely reducing it to a silly satire about a war between the U.S. and Switzerland over tariffs for imported cheese. The salvage operation pulled in the old-time comedy team of Bobby Clark and Paul McCullough, who made a big amusing difference. The smaller pit orchestra, lead by Red Nichols, included a stunning array of then-unknowns: Benny Goodman, Gene Krupa, Glenn Miller, Jimmy Dorsey and Jack Teagarden! Strike up the band they did, to a revamped George Gershwin score remarkably influenced more by Kern than by Gershwin. The reconfigured version turned a tidy profit during a 191 performance run at the Times Square Theatre, thanks not exactly to the craft of drama.

Cameron Mackintosh likely learned early the critical importance of "production values" and trained himself to survive accordingly. The "living theatre" is forever vulnerable to the quality and the vision of each individual staging. Producers can't always pick their stars—but they can pick the scenery and the chandeliers. Some go amusingly overboard in desperation to build critic-proof hits. More drops. Bigger turntables. Glitzier this or louder that. By the time Andrew Lloyd Webber's epic feline fantasy *Cats* purred into New York city, the scenery

Cats: Maria Jo Ralabate is "Rumpleteazer" and Roger Kachel is "Mungojerrie."

itself represented a new plateau in set decoration. Not only did it transform the stage of the Winter Garden into a bigger-than-life junkyard, its beguiling surrealism spread vividly across the proscenium, inviting patrons to break through the fourth wall and take up residence with Grizabella and her motley crowd. Mackintosh and Webber likely concluded that all that gargantuan set construction had *something* to do with the show's great success around the world. Well may it have. What followed from the pair kept the stage crews working overtime and the wings loaded with computers.

In the middle of it all stood Mr. Webber—not only the composer, but the co-producer. And so he was viewed by the New York provincials as a co-conspirator with Mr. Mackintosh in an insidious drive to transform Times Square into a theme park of overproduced thrill tuners. Webber was tagged a hack whose real genius lay in self promotion and the shrewd selection of directors who could convert his hamburger into filet mignon. Worst of all, he was a musical plagiarist. Guilty as charged? If so, at least he had the good taste to lift from the right sources. In the words of his brother, Julian, "Andrew will never take from anyone whom he does not respect, I can assure you."[4]

Soon enough, a well-followed hate-hate relationship between Mr. Webber and the press turned into a sideshow of competing put-downs between critics on both sides of the Atlantic. Those songs by Andrew, carped his enemies, were floridly sung and amplified, and they all sounded alike. Between Webber's refrains and Mackintosh's scenery, the scribes had a field day's worth of targets to shoot at. Their irritable notices became ever more entertaining. Walter Kerr—one of a trio of writers, you may recall, responsible for a progressive highlight of the '50s, *Goldilocks*—spent many a Sunday column in his capacity as drama critic for the *New York Times* articulating major reservations with Webber's work, while Frank Rich, the *Times'* daily reviewer, took care to reiterate at every turn his impatience with Webber. They disagreed on *Cats*. Kerr quipped, "You will get all the colorful extravaganzas I've mentioned, and more. You will also get tired."[5] Rich conceded, "It believes in purely theatrical magic, and on that faith it unquestionably delivers."[6]

Then came *Starlight Express,* which drove to exhaustion Mr. Rich, who termed it "the perfect gift for the kid who has everything except parents."[7] And then *Phantom*, whose songs he grudgingly succumbed to, reflecting, "...as always, they are recycled endlessly. If you don't leave the theatre humming the songs you've got a hearing disability."[8]

Meanwhile, back on the *Times'* Sunday food and theatre beat, Mr. Kerr likened *Phantom's* musical reprises to "steady drip molasses," the soft landing of the chandelier to a free-falling tart of sorts: "It sways a bit ... looking for all the world like the biggest cream puff you ever saw, then it begins to float down like a sigh, flowing gently as chiffon ... it does a little zig zag of a curtsy and alters course to head for the stage, where it makes a perfect, perfectly genteel three-point landing. So much for terror."[9]

At the pinnacle of his reign, Webber, now serving as his own producer, wrote a show called *Aspects of Love*. On the Walter Kerr scale of stage bakery, it would probably amount to a heap of shapeless, tasteless baking power. Ironically, the composer tried telling an old-fashioned tale sans laser beams and fog machines. Vacillating Tim Rice, perhaps still smarting over his rejected "Memory" lyric, first said yes to the project, then no. Without Rice, *Aspects* unleashed a soggy sea of anemic melodies and some of the most non-existent lyrics ever written. It brings into grave doubt the listening abilities of the English, who were said to have embraced it upon first hearing when it opened to divided notices in London. *Aspects* was totally snubbed by the annual Olivier theatre awards, failing to receive a single nomination.

When Webber tried getting the Americans to embrace it, Kevin Kelly of the *Boston Globe* was left in utter shock, writing, "Andrew Lloyd Webber's *Aspects of Love* has come to town with the hope of pleasing critics who hated the mechanical glitz of *The Phantom of the Opera* (not to mention *Cats* and *Starlight Express*).

It was thought to be a chiselled cameo, a light tangle of romance and sex rather than melodramatic torment through a glass darkly.... But as the opening song in *Aspects of Love* has it, 'Love changes everything.' On the Broadhurst stage *Aspects* instantly turns affection to aggravation, enthusiasm to ether."[10]

The original cast CD is rife with ponderous first-draft twaddle, with half-composed songs sliding off into recitative purgatory. Even the big ballad, "Love Changes Everything," warbles on like a windy old church hymn stripped of verse. Alas, that turgid Sunday school tune belongs back in Sunday school. Further observed the rueful Kelly, "After a wildly successful career (with, I think, deserving acclaim for *Jesus Christ Superstar*, *Phantom of the Opera*, and as the British say, pots of gold) Andrew Lloyd Webber now looks like a beggar. His talent is being more severely questioned than ever before. Is he just a hat-in-hand manipulator, an exploitive on-the-run tunesmith, or really an honest contributing member of musical theatre? *Aspects of Love* suggests the former, but then, luck changes everything."[11]

Does it ever. The British did not hear music for very long, either, and *Aspects* shuttered early on the West End. According to *The Times*, Mr. Webber had purposely opened *Aspects* in London rather than New York in order to escape the likely wrath of his nemesis, Frank Rich. Said executive producer Pete Wilson, "British critics don't close shows."[12] Nonetheless, those same critics were blamed for the fast fade of *Aspects*. The Webber magic was suddenly losing levitation. *If the public was tiring of spectacle, neither was it in any mood for a belabored sung-through story of intermingling amoral relationships. On Broadway at the Broadhurst, it lasted barely a season.

Cameron Mackintosh did not build his fortunes exclusively on the efforts of Andrew Lloyd Webber, whom he called "the most talented man whom I shall ever work with in my life."[13] He also had in his stable the formidable French team of Alain Boublil (lyrics) and Claude-Michel Schonberg (music), whose musical *Les Misérables* Mackintosh had seen during its uncertain infancy in Paris in 1980. He fell in love with its rather traditional music, and he reshaped the show for British audiences—before whose raving admiration it opened in 1985—by implementing script changes and adding a prologue and five news songs. And he ballyhooed it into a huge international hit. Across the Atlantic, it was greeted with the usual ambivalence. Clive Barnes found the songs "monotonous"; Howard Kissel, "drivel";[14] Frank Rich, "profligately melodious."[15] On balance, the show won over a slight majority of the media judges. "It is a smash," declared *Variety's* Richard Hummler. "Magnificent stagecraft is joined to an uplifting theme of heroic human commitment and to stirring music."[16]

Les Mis is an infinitely inspiring achievement—simply one of the great musicals of the twentieth century. It builds heroically on the transforming power of compassion and forgiveness, and it is a triumphant affirmation of all things theatrical and life-affirming for which Oscar Hammerstein stood. First and foremost, it is a well made musical play. Secondly, its strong, classically nuanced score effectively propels the story forward, even though in cast album format the

Michael Maguire, at the center of a student revolt in *Les Misérables*.

mediocre numbers pale on their own. What compels us the most is the spiritual journey of Jean Valjean, at the outset a petty thief spared a return to prison by a compassionate priest who, instead of turning him in for lifting some Chinaware from the chapel, tells the police it was a gift. Valjean then goes forward to similarly forgive, aid and inspire others, including a young brigade of French revolutionaries who fail in their quest to bring down the government. Ultimately, we are moved by the imagery of the oppressed struggling to break free, and by their penultimate song of faith that their cause will one day prevail. The first-rate stagecraft puts us there; the drama is bold and believable and complete. That *Les Mis* has won the hearts and souls of millions around the world, and continues to do so in return engagements, is in itself good news for the future of a medium that more often of late has wallowed in social decay.

Boublil and Schonberg gave Mackintosh another epic work of history to market worldwide in their extravagant opus *Miss Saigon*, fashioned loosely after *Madame Butterfly* and set in the final days of the Vietnam war. It nearly allowed for the bombing of the theatre, probably just too expensive for Mr. Mackintosh's budget. So he settled for the landing of a helicopter on stage to dramatize the tense final moments of the American evacuation of Saigon as invading Communist forces ring the city.

"The helicopter has finally landed on the Broadhurst theatre," wrote Laurie Winer in the *Los Angeles Times*, "and, as promised, it is the very best helicopter that ever played a Broadway house. What we did not expect from *Miss Saigon*, perhaps, was the awful power of the scene, the stunning agony of the Saigon evacuation in 1975, with soldiers scrambling into the big chopper and Vietnamese rioting to climb aboard, only to be left clinging on the cabin fence of the U.S. Embassy."[17]

Mackintosh exploited this impressive engineering feat for theatrical suspense, holding it off until midway in act two. The illogical placement, accomplished during a forced flashback scene, reflected a major problem with *Miss Saigon*. For all of its sporadically gripping history, this momentous musical becomes a slave to its own calculated excesses. Another incongruity was the second act eleven-o'clock blockbuster, "The American Dream," a fabulous neon-lit sendup of Yankee consumerism, complete with Cadillac car as centerpiece, elevated to bombastic irrelevance in a manner that would please the great Ziegfeld himself.

The musical's rambling narrative bears a structural heritage to *Show Boat* and gives it a certain intangible stature. To its disadvantage, however, *Miss Saigon* must ride the hollow weight of an implausible romance between a Saigon prostitute, Kim, and her GI john, Chris. Once separated after Chris is evacuated in the helicopter, unaware that he has impregnated Kim, the two are free to lyrically long for each other, and the lovely hooker never lets up in this department. Her lonely plight does epitomize some terrible truths about that tragic war; she is forced to commit murder in an act of political defiance, in order to retain custody of the son she conceived in the brothel with Chris, and in the end, faced with a visit by Chris and his new American bride, Kim takes her own life in order to insure a future for the boy with his real father.

This precarious proposition fails to fuel the libretto with natural force, so we are left to find our pleasure in the politically charged subsidiary scenes and amidst the sleaze of Vietnamese night life and American-inspired greed. What Jeremy Gerard of *Variety* called "one of the baser and cynically exploitive musicals of our time, a girlie show with a phony conscience,"[18] what Laurie Winer termed "engaging...insulting...never boring,"[19] is, nevertheless, a musical that now and then rises, as few do, on the terror and heartbreak of its most historically traumatic moments. To experience this is to come face to face with the theatre's ultimate power. Moreover, not since *West Side Story* had there been so dramatically compelling a score, a score so varied in mood from lyrical to raucous, and of sweeping orchestral passages of such cinematic force.

The producer, Cameron Mackintosh, ruled the box office for a heady 15-year spell, and still rules the box office with the same four shows. Sir Cameron and Sir Andrew, knighted by the queen of England for their sterling contributions to the economy, saw their most prop-heavy shows sell the most tickets. And when either the props or the scripts and songs stopped working wonders, they would try pointing out that, really, they had never exactly set out to blow the world away with floating staircases and falling choppers. And so they granted that small could be fine and beautiful, too. What to do, however, after giving the public the spartan

Aspects of Love and getting hissed at in return? Forge ahead with *Aspects II*, or more big rig construction?

Sir Andrew opted to recall the hard hats. He pounded out a slavishly literal adaptation of Billy Wilder's 1950 screen classic, *Sunset Boulevard*. At least in so doing, Webber and his collaborators, Don Black and Christopher Hampton, retained the taut structure of Wilder's savagely witty tale. Critically lambasted when it first opened in London, following changes the musical moved to New York, there to be awarded with split notices, most everyone agreeing on two big attractions: Glenn Close, cast as Norma Desmond; and her grand old automobile, an item coveted (in the story line) by none other than Cecil B. De Mille when one of his underlings calls the Desmond residence.

Sunset Boulevard won a few Tonys, but not enough customers during an extended New York run to leave town flush when it went out on tour, sans automobile and heavier set pieces. Close was out and Petula Clark was in when the show came out to the West Coast, by which time, according to bi-coastal critics, it had much improved. Most striking about the production was a skeletal first act building towards a rarity in musical theatre—an actually much stronger second half. Almost everything after intermission is superior, including the glaringly uneven score, which then delivers its two great moments: the surreal "Too Much in Love to Care," sung by characters Joe Gillis and Betty Schaefer on a vacant soundstage reminiscent of a Gene Kelly movie; and "As If We Never Said Good-bye," sung by Ms. Desmond upon her flamboyant arrival at the Paramount lot, where she is reverentially greeted by gawking still-employed admirers from the past. The latter song offers one of the most mesmerizing moments to be spent in a theatre, though in the west coast tour perhaps it was the extraordinary coincidence of Ms. Clark, herself not heard from for many years, playing Ms. Desmond which gave this unforgettably rhapsodic song such double-edged power.

On the fundamental level of dramatic entertainment, *Sunset Boulevard* delivers resoundingly well. So, why did it fail to stay around for years and years like other Webber blockbusters, either in New York or London town? Maybe in a word: underdevelopment. You could argue that Sir Andrew made a fatal mistake by producing the show himself; that, had he lured Mackintosh into supervising the project, he and his cohorts might have been pushed towards a more original or consistently engaging treatment, or to supply stronger songs overall. Particularly weak in the music department is Webber's flaccid appropriation of American jazz. And the literal treatment tended toward the obvious: Stage characterizations bordering on the one-dimensional paled next to their film counterparts. Notwithstanding these reservations, here is a musical that is hard to ignore, and the compelling story it tells is likely to keep it on the boards for years to come.

Webber next declared himself newly committed to an even kinder, gentler musical. In protracted collaboration with Alan Ayckbourn, he went back to work on their 1975 flop, *By Jeeves*, based on the stories of P.G. Wodehouse, and presented it in his home country to promising critical endorsement. High on the euphoria of opening-night cheers, Webber told *Time Out*, a weekly British entertainment magazine, "The days of the operatic musical may well be numbered."[20] His shoe-string staging of *Jeeves*, declared a hit in England before they decided it wasn't, did not strike the same sentimental chord with American reviewers when Webber brought it, like a child in need of special handling, to the Goodspeed Opera House, itself a safe retreat for the fallen giant of Big Apple monster hits. Visiting critics from New York were quick to recognize a charming set of songs attached to an evening of jokes and vaudeville bits they didn't much like. "Can a Lloyd Webber show fly if the scenery doesn't?" asked Ben Brantley, noting isolated pleasure for the songs. "Simple, cheerful ditties are not what Mr. Lloyd Webber usually aspires to."[21]

Variety's Matt Wolf fell in love with the score, "the evening's most attractive aspect ... with 'Travel Hopefully'—Lloyd Webber in Stephen Schwartz mode—heading the list of songs I would gladly travel to hear."[22] Another gem, and there are several, is "Half a Moment," which lifts the heart with the effortless rapture of a Richard Rodgers melody. It is all we can ask of any composer, with or without falling chandeliers. *By Jeeves* flirted with a New York opening, its producers fondly eyeing the Helen Hayes Theatre for a spring 2000 curtain. It toured a few regional venues without strong success, adding to its portfolio additional praise and scorn. And in the year 2001, it finally made it to Broadway, where it failed to click.

Webber's next project, the Harold Prince directed *Whistle Down the Wind*, was the first of his shows ever to be premiered outside London. Enthusiastic D.C. crowds greeted its world premiere at the National Theatre, but only a few critics shared the enthusiasm. Some panned the production, citing major "second act problems." Fearing a hostile New York press, into whose clutches the show was headed, Webber aborted the planned opening, took his latest erector set back home and evidently made it a more complex structure before trying it out on his fellow countrymen. "Does *Whistle Down the Wind* mark the end of the British musical boom?" asked *Variety*. "While one certainly hopes otherwise, it's difficult not to feel that the levitating freeway of Peter J. Davison's oppressive and rather scary set isn't the only thing headed nowhere.... This *Whistle* takes a promising idea and then so systematically botches it that one's primary emotion is dismay."[23]

Another botch job in the works was Sir Cameron's latest venture, *Martin Guerre*, from the team who gave us *Les Misérables* and *Miss Saigon*. A kind of singing albatross that hung around Mackintosh's neck for nearly ten years, its London opening was postponed for new orchestrations and other last-minute adjustments. When finally the moment of reckoning came, *Guerre* faced a savage reception. Among the more perplexing failures noted by the incredulous reviewers was that the element of suspense contained in the source material had been entirely deleted.

Loaded with loot and obsessed with making a heavy bird fly, the most successful producer who ever lived shut down *Martin Guerre* for yet more revisions. It reopened months later and still failed to fool the public. After languishing on the boards another twenty months, *Guerre* closed down a second time, *seven million dollars* in the red.

More rewrites, an almost totally new set of songs, and in 1999 it faced opening night number three. A sympathetic Matt Wolf, critiquing for *Variety*, expressed modified admiration. "It's third time lucky, in every area except the fundamental one of affect, for *Martin Guerre*, the long-running financial failure (and Oliver Award Winner) that has been resurrected more times than the musicals errant hero.... For all the onstage savvy, *Martin Guerre* continues to buckle under an inbred ponderousness that drags the tale down even when the voices and amazingly full-throated cast come together to soar."[24] Second only to unpredictable weather patterns are the theatre fortunes of big-time producers.

The British Boy Wonders had not put up a successful new musical in nearly ten years. In 1998, when Webber's *Sunset Boulevard* closed on both sides of the Atlantic, suffering losses estimated to reach $50 million, a revival of *Jesus Christ Superstar*, also produced by Mr. Webber, resurrected neither the savior nor the composer, and it closed early the same year, having recouped about 15 percent on a $6 million investment. Massive staff layoffs ensued at Webber's London producing arm, Really Useful. The composer put his wine collection on the auction block, where it was projected to yield a cool $3 million. And his Belgrade home at Eaton Square, valued at a handsome $25 million (chandeliers presumably not included), was offered to the highest bidder.

Mackintosh would continue pouring millions into his do-or-die obsession. "I think [*Martin Guerre*] could be Claude-Michel's finest score,"[25] he told an Associated Press reporter. Was it simply a matter of misguided infatuation with material that no amount of showmanship could overcome? "Listen," he told *Variety*'s Matt Wolf, "whether or not *Martin Guerre* is one of those [blockbuster] shows, we won't know for 10 or 20 years. If the theatre were only driven by how much money a show made, we would have no theatre."[26] For the producer who had casually juggled huge international hits in the palm of his hands, the new century beckoned ominously. *Guerre* was slated to open on Broadway in the spring of the new millennium. En route to a an aborted premiere, it played the Ahmanson Theatre in Los Angeles to large, ostensibly polite subscription-heavy audiences.

Some of them were no doubt left mildly aghast at the clumsy enterprise, surely one of the most dubiously constructed and difficult-to-sit-through musicals ever put on the boards. Only the most religiously insecure are likely to find solace in its theologically oppressive premise, centered around a drought assumed to demonstrate the wrath of God, and a man, Arnaud du Thil, who pretends to be Martin Guerre, returning to his wife after seven years and ending the rainless ordeal (as evidently fakes can also do) only to be challenged by the real Guerre who shows up to bring down act one's curtain. If only they had told the story with the linear suspense of the original tale instead of falling victim to their obsession with its medieval implications (as metaphor for contemporary global conflicts), none of which have much resonance with today's audiences. With all the millions Mackintosh had spent on rewrites, why he failed to address such a fundamental dramatic issue remains a puzzle. A few quite lovely songs do break through, like welcome rays of sunshine over a blighted landscape.

Barring a box office turnaround, years from now Mr. Mackintosh may still be ordering up yet better orchestrations for *Guerre*, presiding over cast changes, consulting with designers and hydraulic lift operators, and polishing off press releases touting impressive new script changes and song interpolations by famous-at-the-moment artists guaranteed to pull in the crowds and prove the critics wrong, once the *new* version opens. Were *all* new ill-fated shows so lucky. Getting that kid to grow up can drive a producer nearly nuts.

CHAPTER 14

Desperate Openings

At the end of the twentieth century, New York musical stages were not infrequently populated by the edgy characters who once cluttered the streets around them: hookers and pimps, drug addicts and assassins, accused child molesters and jailed cross-dressers, confused young self-proclaimed "artists" railing against a world refusing to keep them. Modern-day victims all, they sullied the very legit houses once reserved for a higher grade of dilettantes, rogues and charmers.

In order to preserve civil sanity and tourism, the New York Police Department in collusion with the Walt Disney Company shoveled Times Square free of sleaze, a heap of which appears to have taken up residence in stage musicals. For $75 or so, you could now be entertained by the freaky characters who once solicited, assaulted or terrified you out on the streets. So ridden, in fact, with low life had the boards of Broadway shows become that Frank Rich, gasping for normalcy among the singing wounded, spotted a wealth of "family values" to embrace in *March of the Falsettos*, a gay-themed musical of notable depth, if limited charm. "All things considered," Rich concluded, "I decided that the most welcome choice would be ... the William Finn musical in which the hero, Marvin, sings in his first number of his overwhelming desire to be part of a tight-knit family, a group that harmonizes."[1]

The central characters in modern musicals no longer bore much resemblance to men and women who once sang in showers and ended up in each other's arms rather than at each other's throats. Cy Coleman's 1997 perversity, *The Life*, a trade-talk tuner about cash for sex in old Manhattan, invited us into the sugar-free world of senior street walkers on the rickety rebound, varicose veins and all. These ladies of nocturnal pleasure longed only to climb the American ladder of opportunity and land better paid work for themselves in upscale districts working as, well, *quality* call girls.

Some saw Mr. Coleman's tawdry romp as the revenge of the evicted, now returning to give the Disney makeover the finger. Alas, *The Life* overestimated the public's tolerance level for riffraff. Aging prostitutes who blow back into town on Greyhound busses don't stand a chance in a song and dance show. Unlike *The Best Little Whorehouse in Texas*, in comparison a cheerful affront to standard morality, *The Life* exposed audiences to a flogging, a fatal gun fight between rival pimps and other assorted felonies committed in seedy YMCA-type rooms. The frictions come to a head when Queenie murders violent pimp Memphis for having forced her into his stable, after Memphis fatally stabs Queenie's ex-boyfriend, Fleetwood. Veteran streetwalker Sonja offers to take the rap for Queenie, who exits town on the next bus out for a place called Freedom. Left to survey the bejeweled wreckage were bemused ticket buyers, not enough of them to keep Queenie and cohorts on the beat at the Ethel Barrymore beyond a promising and prolonged 465-performance run.

It is not so hard to understand the approval of critics and crowds envisioned up front by Cy Coleman, lyricist Ira Gassman, and book writer David Newman, with whom both Coleman and Gassman collaborated. Nor why the regional theatres who participated in the musical's unwieldy development were said to have mashed the thing into so many disparate shapes. Given general audience preferences those days for bohemians of all stripes (think *Rent*), *The Life* no doubt was designed to push edgy realism to its next level of marketable depravity. The intriguing idea had come from Gassman, whose terse, evocative lyrics demonstrate a vivid intimacy with his subject. So vivid, indeed, that listening to the cast album is akin to eavesdropping on a conversation between pimps and prostitutes in a skid-row room rented by the week.

The sheer audacity of the enterprise tickled a number of critics, from whose pens flowed isolated praise. "Gritty and raucous," sang Clive Barnes. "It starts out in high gear," wrote Richard Zoglin of *Time* magazine, "and keeps topping itself."[2] *Variety's* Greg Evans complained of a vacillating libretto: "A musical that cannot make up its mind—is it a carton? A gritty slice of Times Square? A Bob Fosse ripoff? All of the above?—*The Life* wears its patchwork construction as obviously as its pimps wear wide-brimmed hats."[3]

The Life earned more Tony nominations than any other musical the same season, and lost out to a much stodgier work, *Titanic*, which also ended up in the red. The Peter Stone–Maury Yeston conceit about the fatal first crossing of the 1912 luxury liner proved a stilted work of wasted dramatic potential. Intended to offer the jaded theatergoer a disaster thrill ride, *Titanic* is far from a thrill—more like the last dying gasp of the concept musical hitting its own iceberg. Stone's leaden libretto offers engineering facts, and its stock characters are meant to depict the strict class distinctions that favored salvation for those with pricier accommodations. As the doomed ship slowly floats toward fatal difficulties, we gawk at those smug travelers, wondering, when the moment of final descent arrives, just how far downward the boat will tip and how it will toss them to their fate.

Maury Yeston's proficient if hackneyed songs—above which "Autumn" soars as the one exceptional number—gaze upon the action through a Steven Sondheim lens, full of chattering pretense. Once this voyage finally goes down, some of us can only wonder how a musical this awful could have stayed afloat nearly two seasons on Broadway. Twenty or thirty years sooner, it likely would have landed in the orchestra pit on opening night.

The tepid reviews it received ("cerebral without being particularly imaginative or insightful,"[4] as Ben Brantley termed it) did not dissuade the masses from initially patronizing it in droves, certainly not after it landed a Tony Award for best musical. Still, its run was no more prosperous than the tragic inaugural voyage it depicted, and when it docked in Los Angeles to begin a national tour, Don Shirley of the *Los Angeles Times* tossed more jeers at its ponderous airs, calling *Titanic* "a white elephant, with too many superficial characters, cliched dialogue, pompous and plodding music, and a clean crisp design that verges on sterility and pales in comparison to the illusions of the recent movie."[5]

In 1997 when *The Life* and *Titanic* opened, so did two other ambitious new shows, *Steel Pier* and *Side Show*. Based upon reviews, reports and cast albums, both musicals seem worthy of our attention and certainly of future regional and community theatre stagings, from which they would likely benefit. John Kander and Fred Ebb's romantically engaging *Steel Pier* is the bittersweet tale, set in the '30s, of one-time celebrity Rita Racine, a reluctant participant in the dance marathons run by her husband Mick Hamilton. Their marriage is kept a secret to the public for business reasons, which creates a problem when Racine falls unreciprocally in love with one of her dance partners, stunt pilot Bill Kelly, who in the end encourages her to break free of her imprisoning routine and follow her muse. That she does. *Steel Pier*, with a terrific score, was loved by a grateful few, among them *Variety* and the *Wall Street Journal*. Donald Lyons of the latter found Kander and Ebb to be in "splendid form," judging the work as belonging with their two masterpieces (*Chicago* and *Cabaret*), "not as a poor third but as a rich third."[6]

Sadly true to form, Kander and Ebb once again struck out with sentimental work. Their prior offering, the bisexual dirge behind bars, *Kiss of the Spider Woman*, had lost money as well, although it enjoyed an artificially prolonged second trip to New York City to the tune of 907 performances, largely paid for by the since-fallen Canadian mogul Garth Drabinsky. *Steel Pier* offers the superior score—one of the team's best.

Three nights after *Titanic* bowed, and two nights following the premiere of *Steel Pier*, Henry Krieger came to town with *Side Show*, the challenging portrait of a pair of Siamese twins romantically involved with two men, themselves not joined at the hip. (Perhaps they will make that the sequel.) The offbeat *Side Show* won over more critics than any of the other three major Tony contenders. "Astonishingly effective," exuded Vincent Canby. "It demands faith in a faith that is not one's own. Which is why *Side Show* is so haunting. Even as you wonder as I do—whether the Siamese twins are a significant metaphor for the human condition, you have the suspicion that you are seeking a way to avoid facing questions too primal to answer honestly ... almost as disturbing as [the 1932 movie] *Freaks*."[7]

Steel Pier.

Not so for Greg Evans, who saw synthetic naturalism in "the safest, most tolerant bunch of carnies imaginable."[8]

The generically prone score for *Side Show* may help explain the variable reactions. Krieger's music does not venture far beyond catchy showbiz tunes—good enough—and ersatz contemporary free-flowing ballads in which the composer, who seems forever stuck in Motown, tends to lose melodic definition. Bill Russel's on-point lyrics are the real star here, plumbing this almost unthinkable tale with insight and reflection. Ultimately, audiences on the outside may not be ready to identify with the indelicate notion, at which this show is aimed, of a Siamese twin cohabiting with her lover, no matter how sympathetic one can feel for her bizarre predicament.

Line 'em up. Knock 'em down. All four shows lost money. *Titanic* folded two days shy of two years on the big boards. *The Life* closed within fourteen months, also disappointing investors. *Steel Pier* lasted all of two months and four days, and *Side Show* lasted only a few weeks longer than that, its ballyhoo ending up $6.8 million in the red. *Side Show*'s producer, Rick Lyman, at a loss for words in the presence of a *New York Times* reporter, could not recall a show that had earned such glowing reviews and still failed to pick up an audience. Some cited the subject matter as the prime culprit. All things in the living theatre, however, are subject to surprise reversals. A new director and a different cast—Madonna, maybe?—and, who knows, *Side Show* could be back on the Times Square midway.

The dismal 1997 plight of our thundering foursome only added more dissonance to the siren song of the disenchanted, souls like Englishman Mark Steyn, author of *Broadway Babies Say Goodnight*. For many years, in fact, musical theatre scholars and followers have agreed that the art form is headed for the cemetery. Indeed, if it is dying, then like a lyric from Rodgers and Hammerstein's *Me and Juliet* states, it just keeps on dying. One thing is certain—quite a few singing corpses still strut the boards nightly and take in unprecedented sums of money at the box office. The year 1998 was reported to be Broadway's biggest season ever. Even if the "golden age" has long since passed into collective memory, there are all the younger fans of *Phantom* and *Rent* and *Miss Saigon* who are not losing any sleep over the touted end of an era through which they did not live. Older patrons may see a hopeless landscape; the younger kids see a tomorrow full of unknown excitement.

The ones losing the sleep are all the producers who can see—and more often than not, *do* see—ten or twenty million dollars vanish overnight. Just cause for final taps? Hardly. It has always been a crap shoot for producers and their pet projects. Throughout the entire twentieth century, hit shows were the exception, not the rule. A season full of turkeys is not exclusive by any means to the modern era, a fact of life conveniently ignored by the Broadway-is-through crowd. *Hello, Dolly* was the only new tuner to make money in 1967. In 1968, fourteen shows opened, and only two beat the odds. In 1973, Stephen Sondheim, atypically beating the odds, was the only composer that year to have a profit-making work (*A Little Night Music*) in a New York house.

Wait a moment, you say, those were *not* golden age years. All right. Open your eyes to the revered fifties, in particular to 1958, when only *one* American-produced show, Rodgers and Hammerstein's *Flower Drum Song*, made any money to speak of. And not much. The same lackluster season, one import, the David Merrick presented *La Plume De Ma Tante*, satisfied the backers, while a small revue featuring previously written work, *A Party with Betty Comden and Adolph Green*, ended up in the red after only 82 performances. Through the 1951–52 season, eight new tuners reached Broadway boards, including such obscurities as *Courtin' Time*, *Paris 90*, and *Seventeen*; according to *Variety*, success rained down only on *Top Banana*, though this is disputed by Steve Suskin in his book *Broadway Opening Nights*, which lists the Phil Silvers hoot as plummeting from boom to bust once Silvers left on vacation and was replaced, and ending up in the debit column after 350 performances.

It was never as easy as memory may suggest. However, when the question is rephrased—why such a bleak track record for *new* American musicals in modern times?—the answer points to a gloomier set of circumstances rooted in escalating production costs and the rapidly changing demographics of American society. About the latter, there is plenty to ponder that surely has vexed many a producer up against sudden death when only moments before he dreamed of the Big Hit.

(It will be accepted herein, at face value, that these big guns do not purposely set out to produce turkeys.) Once upon a Broadway, in a nation of people more patriotically joined together by common values and goals, there existed a well-educated middle-brow class, easily targeted by fairly homogenous work.

This was the time before well-merited civil rights marches, before the divisive war in Vietnam and the Stonewall riots and provocative tomes by Gloria Steinem, much of it heroically addressing unjust repressions, when there flourished a common consensus, outwardly honored at least, that men belonged with women in monogamous union. Musical stages favored such an ethos, because, overwhelmingly, audiences subscribed to that ethos. Infidelity and personal selfishness rarely prevailed over the once-populist image of the heterosexual embrace at final curtain. How long has it been since any new American musical dared present this sort of love framed in its final stage picture? *Will Rogers Follies* did feature, somewhat insipidly, Mrs. Rogers as a contented stay-at-home Hollywood celebrity housewife. And *Will Rogers Follies* ended up in the red. Happily ever after is not a theme that resonates on New York stages anymore. Ironically, it *did* in Jerry Herman's wonderfully relationship-affirming *La Cage*, whose final curtain falls on a happy homosexual couple.

So, musicals turned away from traditional romance. In the early 1990s, Lucy Simon and Marsha Norman's *Secret Garden*, which won a Tony Award for its libretto and stayed around for a decent run, pushed its heartfelt inclinations as far as the transforming effect of an orphan girl over a sick cousin and an ill-tempered uncle. Nowadays, audiences seeking adult fare on New York stages will much sooner patronize difficult and/or unfulfilling relationships set to words and music, as witness the success of such shows as *Evita*, *Miss Saigon*, and *Rent*; near-hits like *The Life* and *Jekyll and Hyde*; and gutsy revivals on the order of *Chicago* and *Cabaret*.

Stephen Sondheim hastened the movement to a more unsparing realism with *Sweeney Todd* and *Assassins*, in effect daring all others—devoted proteges and envious imitators—to match his mayhem with their own versions of Genet and Sartre. Down a neurotic little trail they slithered, too experimentally ambitious for the commercial New York stage. Other writers struggled as never before to be both anti-sentimental and humanistic. Those who found the spectacle in disorder usually fared the best. Musicals about troubled individuals caught in dangerous liaisons could ride the demographic spectrum without displeasing a theatre full of liberated men and women, themselves no longer in thrall to the older mores, but now more prone to go their separate ways once outside the theatre. What the public would accept in the revival of a romantic musical they showed scarce tolerance for in newer work.

Jonathan Larson found the spectacle in a group of self-centered and selfish young East Village artists, squatters with artistic aspirations, held socially and sexually together—and, let's kindly add, rather affectingly—by the residual dating rites of post–'60s free love. One year before *The Life* came to town, Larson's *Rent*, patterned to a degree after Puccini's *La Bohème*, traveled much the same tough turf, except that its principals (Larson insisted) were all young and sexy, whereas Cy Coleman's circle of aging flesh vendors were by now all flabby, frayed and forgotten.

In the world of *Rent*, the alluring young protagonists, plagued by a host of contemporary ills from drug addiction to STDs, believe that society owes them free rent. After all, *they* are artists. What sets them vocally off is the threat of eviction from the space they have occupied in a building owned by a former classmate turned real estate developer, Benny. Having recently married a woman of means, Benny now wants to turn the space into a cyberstudio. And he also wants to dismantle an illegal tent city of homeless people in an adjoining lot that he also owns, another act of avarice deserving further condemnation. The harassed Benny offers to let his ex-classmates stay put if only they can dissuade Maureen, one of their own, from leading a public protest against his plans to 86 the tent people. A nice enough compromise for those who can stomach such absurd deal-making.

Since all the characters in *Rent*, painted in vivid hues according to comfortable stereotypes, are young and confused and beautiful and cling so poignantly to the last threads of adolescence, they can get away with a lot in a theatre. Larson has given their brash insolence credibility in his better songs; numbers like "Seasons of Love" help banish whatever reservations one may have with the show's central conceit, spread out over two rather long acts. When the musical shines, it's a corking good rock and roll concert for the non-thinking boomer. And that's entertainment.

Rent shared 1996 season kudos with another inventive show, this one imported from the New York Shakespeare Festival unit, *Bring in 'Da Noise, Bring in 'Da Funk*. A retrospective portrait of the black experience in America, conceived by George Wolfe and Savion Glover, with a book by Reg E. Gaines and music by Daryl Waters, Zane Mark and Ann Duquesnay, *Noise* surveys everything from slavery to rap, mostly through the rhythmic language of dance and percussion. The CD is full of evocative atmosphere and drama. Some considered it superior to *Rent* ("a joyful, energizing evening, a pure pleasure," wrote *Variety*'s Jeremy Gerard).[9] However, Wolfe did not die on the eve of the show's opening, as did Larson on his, and the press, sensitive to the premature death of so promising a new voice in musical theatre, seemed morally bound to favor *Rent*, even though they tempered their glowing notices with polite caveats for the musical's ill-shaped book and superfluous songs.

By following the recitative trend in modern musicals, initially made fashionable by Andrew Lloyd Webber and Tim Rice, Larson allowed himself the rambling, undisciplined result. The device of sung dialogue has cast a pall over traditional book shows, making them sound more old fashioned to younger ears, and it can lull a lazy or self-indulgent composer into creating something second-rate. (Look what it did to Webber on *Aspects of Love*.) Never will dialogue set to music substitute for great songwriting. *West Side Story*, an old fashioned book show with plenty of spoken lines, remains about as compelling today as it was when first performed over forty years ago.

About economics, another leading factor in the bum luck of many new shows: A fair number of newer musicals are credible artistic successes, simply incapable of generating the longer runs necessary just to break even at the box office today. Soaring production and promotion costs have pushed ticket prices to ridiculous levels, affordable only to the well-heeled in the upper classes, closing the lobby doors to all but the most crowd-pandering amusements. Back in the early years of the century, a new Broadway tuner could recoup its costs in eleven or twelve weeks, then go out on tour for many months and harvest a bundle. In the 1950s, a musical that ran 400 performances was likely a commercial success. Today, even twice that number of shows may still not fully repay the backers. And with ticket prices so prohibitively high, who can blame the average consumer for wanting it all—music, spectacle, an extraordinary story with strong central characters caught up in exotic conflicts. Thus, the recent high degree of success with period pieces like *Phantom*, *Miss Saigon*, *Les Misérables*, and with works of fantasy like *The Lion King* and *Beauty and the Beast*, all inherently richer in theatrical terms.

Another prohibitive factor is the free flow of fresh material to the market place. No one will ever know how many good scripts and scores out in the hinterlands may never see the flick of a conductor's baton on opening night, may never benefit from the deep pockets of a committed producer. The New York theatre community itself poses ongoing problems to the development of new work. Unlike the film industry where outsiders with sellable ideas frequently break through— where 200 to 400 new movies get produced *every year* (not to mention scores of independent films)—the New York theatre district, host to maybe a handful of new musicals a season, jealously guards its borders. By smug tradition, it has refused to grant the possibility that talent may exist west of the Hudson. Moss Hart, turning down an offer by producer Kermit Bloomgarden to direct a new musical by an unknown, thought the script and score so bad that he encouraged Bloomgarden to drop the project. The show? *The Music Man*. "This kind of miscalculation," noted Alan Jay Lerner, "is far from uncommon in the theatre."[10]

"This is an industry which should support, encourage and inspire new talent and new voices," remarked Frank Wildhorn to the *Los Angeles Times*, "and yet there is this disdain and cynicism."[11] Librettist Peter Stone, while serving as president of the Dramatists Guild, came out in the mid–1980s to a local seminar for Los Angeles members, and basically told everyone seated: Don't even try to get your musicals into New York, because it's not going to happen for you. This from their leader, who embellished his give-up-your-dream advice by alluding to a circle of about thirty people, all based in New York City, who exclusively held between themselves the knowledge necessary to create successful new musicals, and who would pass down that special knowledge to selected heirs-apparent, also based in and around Gotham. This circle, it might be assumed, would include the individuals, among them Stone himself, responsible for the four well covered flops of 1997—*Titanic*, *Steel Pier*, *The Life*, and *Side Show*.

It would not include the West End wonder boys, not in light of a statement Mr. Stone made to the *Los Angeles Times* while out on the West Coast another year, then drumming up publicity for the touring company of *Titanic*. Stone referred to the long-running Cameron Mackintosh musical imports (*Cats*, *Saigon*, *Les Mis*, *Phantom*), any of which easily dwarfed in box office earnings anything that ever went to Broadway with Mr. Stone's name on it, as "the four British musicals from hell."[12]

Such provincial arrogance plays out at the Tony Awards, where a show of the reigning popularity of *Beauty and the Beast*, with a first rate score, actually lost out to the plodding and very uncommercial *Passion*. We are left to consider a possible bias against the producer, Burbank-based Walt Disney, or one of *Beauty's* two lyricists, Englishman Tim Rice, who was hired to finish a job so magnificently begun by the late Howard Ashman in the last hours of his life. It is an arrogance that until recent years refused to include for Tony Awards consideration shows mounted off–Broadway, an area that brings forth some of the most creative new work.

The same Big Apple experts who leap into a frenzy of self-congratulation over home-grown hits can just as uniformly resort to the smirking dismissal of outsiders with respectable offerings. During the same inglorious 1997 season when Peter Stone and his colleagues from the Circle of Thirty brought in their four box-office clinkers, pop composer Frank Wildhorn opened two musicals of his own, one of which, *Jekyll and Hyde*, outlasted them all. Following a long national tour that engendered passionate word-of-mouth, the Wildhorn and Leslie Bricusse adaptation of Robert Louis Stevenson's "The Strange Case of Dr. Jekyll and Mr. Hyde" began its life on May 5, 1997, at the Plymouth, where it was still playing well beyond the year 2000.

Jekyll unfolds in a bold melodramatic manner that suits the outlandish tale of a doctor's tumble into sexual chaos following his heroic self-injection of a chemical he hopes will eradicate the darker side of human nature. Wildhorn's treatment is full of dramatically driven songs; of gothic exotica; of the forebidding repressions of the Victorian era; and of the ghastly facades of early-day medical apparatus bordering on a Frankenstein lab.

In his endless tinkering with the script, forever struggling like Dr. Henry Jekyll to create a more perfect form, Wildhorn could have easily shucked aside twenty minutes of action and dialogue (most shows, in fact, could) and a couple of ballads too many that sound like pop-market interpolations. The particular touring version under review herein was by turns clumsy, exhilarating, despondent, erotic, hopeful, and, in the end, a grim reminder of how ill-equipped humankind is to root out evil from the earth. It built steadily to the promised diabolical climax in a whorehouse, and did not linger one moment thereafter.

Vincent Canby called it "an inside joke; a send up of the kind of Faustian musical theatre that even Andrew Lloyd Webber seems to have abandoned, though the joke isn't intentional."[13] Ben Brantley dumped on it for being "leaden, solemnly campy ... [a] plastic monster assembly kit of a musical ... There are a couple of scenes with real fire and many more with synthetic fog that creeps on and off the stage, rather like a wandering attention span. It is easy to sympathize with fog."[14]

Linda Eder and Robert Cuccioli in *Jekyll & Hyde.*

Then came, five months later, *The Scarlet Pimpernel*, not quite as intriguing or as foggy as *Jekyll*, but in fundamental ways a better realized work. Much funnier, too. Musical comedy rearing its long-unseen head in the late '90s? There it was, a retro comic operetta full of melody and panache and big old fashioned production numbers. Nan Knighton's deft lyrics were refreshingly straightforward. Her book stayed finely on track through the first act, though it veered into (non-fatal) second-half overwriting which needlessly slows down the narrative. Too, like *Jekyll*, *Pimpernel* pitched a couple too many of Wildhorn's generic ballads. His best tunes, some calling to mind the more robustly melodic patterns of the golden era (i.e., *Kismet*), were as seductive as they were rousing.

Douglas Sills, the show's acclaimed star and a showman of the first order, lived up to his role in high camp fashion, only to regress over the course of the evening from amusing light foppish touches to belabored exaggerations—not unlike the musical's second-act excesses. Pelted by a nasty avalanche of first-night notices (only two favorable nods among the dreary lot), *Pimpernel* eventually shut down to retool. And when it reopened, a number of open-minded critics, taking a second look, admitted that the musical now seemed, in fact, rather entertaining. By then, a ragged production history dogged the enterprise, and it eventually left New York a loser, retooling once more into version number three for the road.

Dissenting reviews are usually the most entertaining ones to read, and much more temptingly fun to write. Given the venomous nature of the *Jekyll and Hyde* and *Pimpernel* haters in the press (and all around the country where they would surface, in congenial alliance with one another), it is doubly reassuring to note that *Jekyll* actually picked up *four* favorable notices *in* New York city—one of them from Howard Kissel of the *New York Daily News*, and that *Pimpernel*, as mentioned above, turned some initially sarcastic reviewers into modified fans once it underwent major changes. On the road, it inspired *Los Angeles Times* scribe Michael Phillips to quip, "Forget your troubles, come on get foppy!"[15] Frank Wildhorn would struggle to achieve a legitimate foothold in a field of artistic endeavor not known for kindness to strangers. An established pop composer with numerous hit records to his name, he admitted to being an unabashed fan of Lloyd Webber, whose songs he grew up singing and idolizing. Not such a bad career move, considering that the composer Wildhorn chose to follow had grown up singing and idolizing the songs of Richard Rodgers.

Chapter 15

Revival Roulette

Broadway braces itself for an identity crisis whenever another of its "golden age" musicals is dusted off, polished up, stretched this way or that, and given a new cast and director for a return visit to the big boards. The journey backwards in time can be fraught with unforseen dangers, for what most distinguishes a show—new or old—is the production that carries it to New York City. Some revivals affirm a musical's hallowed status. Others hold ancient praise up to scorn and debate. Conversely, a musical that originally flopped may reveal previously undetected charms the second time around. Something like what they say about love.

The precarious world of the Broadway revival teaches us a lot about the elusive dynamics of a singing show, and it reduces to academic drivel much of what is taught on the subject within ivy-covered walls. When all is said and done, the producer rolls the dice and takes his chances like a day trader. When the farcical *Red Mill*, a 1906 Victor Herbert curiosity, played the Ziegfeld Theatre 39 years later, it *doubled* its original performance run despite conflicting notices. *Pal Joey's* 1952 revival, to the tune of 542 performances, handsomely exceeded its original run 12 years before. *Porgy and Bess* redeemed its lackluster 1935 reception by the belated acclaim and patronage it enjoyed through subsequent restagings. The same held true for Kurt Weill's academically valued *Threepenny Opera*, which suffered almost instant death its first time out in the early thirties.

Cole Porter's legendary *Anything Goes* went from huge 1930s hit, to barely profitable off–Broadway revival in 1952, to triumphant 1987 run—804 curtains, nearly doubling its original 1934 harvest. The ambivalently reviewed Kander and Ebb 1968 entry *Zorba* sold only a few more tickets in 1983, though this second New York visit followed a nationwide tour and was followed, in turn, by more cross-country bookings. Rodgers and Hart's *The Boys from Syracuse* and *A Connecticut Yankee* both did well in reprise. *Syracuse* declared a profit from only 135 performances. By today's bookkeeping, such a run would be floporama.

Other less talented tuners were never able to overcome initial public resistance. Mark Blitzstein's one-sided depression era polemic against corporate insensitivity, *The Cradle Will Rock*, miserably failed a couple of restagings. *Lost in the Stars*, by Mr. Blitzstein's hero Kurt Weill, stayed lost 23 years later when its comeback run exceeded the inaugural one month engagement by a total of eleven performances. While a production can overcome inferior script materials, it can rarely save a show that was not intended to entertain in the first place.

The revival producer faces two conflicting agendas: On the one hand, he has the psychological advantage of courting a more sympathetic press and audience with an already-respected chestnut, and his economic investment will be a bargain compared to the millions required nowadays to get a brand new show into working order before the critics are invited to take a look. On the other, his marketing instincts will compel him to promise a "new and improved" version of that chestnut, which opens the door to all sorts of tinkering. Most early-century musicals are considered so hokey and hastily assembled (librettist Moss Hart was great at setting up first acts full of crackling dialogue that went nowhere) that the makeovers they receive are tolerated, sometimes applauded. Often these frivolous books are overhauled in an effort to inject more "substance" into them, as if cotton candy needed broccoli on the side. Often, too, additional songs by the same composers from other of their shows are interpolated. Audiences get to enjoy the extra melodies and lyrics, the critics still carp about "silly" stories, and the producer might make a bundle. *No, No, Nanette* in revised format adapted by Burt Shevelove did much better at the ticket windows in 1971, more than doubling its 1925 attendance records. Credit Mr. Shevelove? Or the return of Ruby Keeler?

They tried revising Neil Simon's script for his and Cy Coleman's *Little Me*, a Sid Caesar vehicle that was delightful in the first place and rang up excellent critical endorsements, although it fell modestly short of turning a profit. Perhaps in revival form they were striving for less of what Hobe Morrison, in *Variety's* original assessment, referred to as "a certain kind of click American musical ... slight story material is put across with fast, loud, taut and comically punchy expertness."[1] The revamped edition attracted fewer souls. Blame the revisions?

The urge to tinker with aging librettos can lead to counter-productive rewrites; worse yet, to the virtual deconstruction of a great art form. Less skeptically treated and not so frequently tinkered with are the so-called golden age classics, considered better constructed, although they too can stumble on the comeback trail, causing us to wonder just how "golden" the age was. The wonderful Bernstein, Comden and Green 1944 treasure *On the Town* has yet to take the town a second time, and it has tried ... and tried. Other shows that share its gasping afterlife include *Finian's Rainbow* ... and *Brigadoon* ... and *Bloomer Girl* ... and Frank Loesser's 1944 hit, *Where's Charlie?* None has made it into Broadway revival heaven. Cole Porter's critically cheered 1953 hit *Can Can* got bombed by the critics who saw it in 1981 when it tried dancing again at the Minskoff Theatre. Steve Suskin blamed a humiliating 5-performance run on the same second-rate materials minus the "colorful choreography" of Michael Kidd and the star power of Gwen Verdon that had helped camouflage the failings of the original production.[2]

Many of these "golden age shows" are starting to suffer the same stigma of dated triteness and contrived story telling. A musical may fail because it is too "old fashioned"—yet rarely is this complaint logged against the great plays and comedies of world drama. Molière, Strindberg, Chekhov, Shakespeare—they have all survived fairly intact through endless reinterpretations. Few, if any, are carved up and reassembled by out-of-town script surgeons. Furthermore, the romantic musical is not an invention of Kern or Lerner or Loewe. It predated the work of Rodgers and Hammerstein by at least a century. Yet a disturbing number of the better written book shows from this era of innocence and craft are getting libretto facelifts, and there is scant evidence to suggest the operations are necessary or helpful; in fact, they may cause more harm than good.

Walter Kerr in the '70s railed against two overloaded revivals, *Irene* and *Good News*, for interpolating an excessive number of songs from other sources, in Kerr's opinion not germane to the tone or time of the respective shows. "Whenever this sort of thievery is attempted … it immediately destroys the property, and the pleasure of the property, at hand. We are not seeing *Irene* or *Good News* any more, we're having a random and ultimately indigestible smorgasbord crammed down our throats. We're also being deprived of likely future revivals of the shows from which well-known goodies have been filched; who'll want to do them for us now that their tombs have been rifled?"[3]

The variable fortunes along revival row suggest that major script overhauls can be dangerously premature; that the future remains an open end for musicals of all stripes and track records—thanks again, it would appear, to the people involved. *On Your Toes* ended up on its heels, a victim of horrible reviews in 1954 at the 46th Street theatre, but thirty years later, with original director George Abbott returning to the helm, bested its original 1936 run. Angela Lansbury played Mama Rose in a 1974 revival of *Gypsy* that got dream reviews and was ignored by the public. Tyne Daly played the same role fifteen years later, and kept the show in business for half a thousand performances. A golden age star, *My Fair Lady*, has never come close to duplicating its original *three thousand* performance harvest, nor has it even made a decent dime or two trying. Not in 1976, when Ian Richardson played Professor Higgins for one profitless year; not in 1981, when Rex Harrison himself returned to Broadway, was blasted by three negative notices, and was out of work in 119 shows; nor in 1993, when Richard Chamberlain took a stab at the Eliza Doolittle challenge in a production that struck some as being directorially capricious. Reviewing the Harrison edition, Don Nelson observed, "Perhaps revivals—a colleague calls them necrophilia—bring with them a certain second hand aura that forbids one the exhilaration of the first time discovery…. *My Fair Lady* is a great musical yet it probably can never satisfy the romantic preconceptions an audience 'remembers' from the past. Maybe that is one reason why this performance did not work well."[4]

Because these "golden age" champions can fade as fast on the revival boards as the inferior shows that pre-dated them, the temptation to tinker with them grows. Today's directors, many of whom did not witness the dawning of the musicals they set out to restage, are egged on by political correctness and by a careless disregard for the fragility of the libretto, the unseen instrument whose job it is to establish a clear dramatic road map and then to maintain order and sensible progression forward. A sound libretto will hold its own against the constant tug and pull of the songs, not all of which may truly belong, and against the distracting look-at-me asides of all those cocky kids—old and young—up there on the stage clamoring for audience adulation. Theatregoers become terribly impatient when all the frivolous fun lacks at least a context, something to firmly grasp as the ride lurches rhythmically on its way. In other words, they need to believe that the frosting has cake.

Forming the invisible spine of the story, a libretto that succeeds in holding our interest, in making us want to return after intermission, can be wrongly criticized for minor non-structural defects, such as corny dialogue or hackneyed characters, and end up being deconstructed out of working order in a desperate fit of suicidal rewriting during previews or out-of-town tryouts. In setting out to fix legitimate minor problems, they end up smashing the whole thing to smithereens. Wrote Richard Rodgers, wisely and ruefully: "When you start rebuilding a show you must always be careful that the number you may feel is delaying the action does not actually support the dramatic structure of the entire play. If you replace a song, you may find yourself with a problem in another scene fifteen minutes later. It's like pulling out one seemingly inconsequential brick from a wall, only to find the entire wall collapsing. And no one ever really knows why."[5]

Rare is the musical not cited by someone for structural flaws in the final stretch, usually caused by lack of focus, the most consistent failure in libretto construction. Failing to define up front a clear dramatic premise (one of Oscar Hammerstein's mantras), a musical play will likely languish in the final stages, thrashing aimlessly around like a stood-up boxer for lack of a compelling crisis to confront and resolve. What seemed so exciting at the outset (example, *Into the Woods*) eventually collapses into confusing disarray. Most tuners by and large move more on musical momentum than on narrative conflict, another reason why it can be difficult to reach climax: How do you resolve what you haven't instigated?

Gypsy struck Kenneth Tynan, one of its most ardent admirers, as a less engaging thrill after intermission, owing to plot redundancies, too few new numbers introduced, and the over-the-top "Rose's Turn," an excessive outburst, in his opinion, wherein Ethel Merman "sets about lacerating herself in prose."[6] *West Side Story* runs into a somewhat anti-climactic second half, too, after the momentous rumble promised and built to in the first act reaches a resounding climax. What follows intermission, while Tony's rivals sniff him out for revenge, is more contemplative and rueful in tone. So ... do you accept imperfect masterpieces or give ambitious directors carte blanche to "fix" them?

If the director's name is Hal Prince, you agree that maybe Act II could be better, and further down the road to deconstruction slides the golden age musical. I'm talking, of course, about *Show Boat*. The Jerome Kern–Oscar Hammerstein landmark musical was not a perfect work, yet it remains so fully satisfying, so rich in its own intangible qualities of spirit, as to bring into grave question the never-ending attempts to revise it. The revisionists-to-the-rescue can point for precedent to none other than Oscar Hammerstein himself, who signaled his own insecurities with *Show Boat* (though not strictly with post-intermission scenes) by the major changes he made to the show for its 1946 revival. Hammerstein eliminated three top-flight songs—"I Might Fall Back on You," "Till Good Luck Comes My Way," and the roof-raising Charleston, "Hey, Feller!"; added a new number, "Nobody Else But Me"; excised two complete scenes, and virtually removed a third by drastically rewriting it. Out, too, went "Niggers All Work on the Mississippi." The upgraded revival, co-directed by Hammerstein and Hassard Short, offered the public brighter sets and costumes, and considerably more dancing; the choreography of Helen Tamiris was said to have set this *Show Boat* dramatically apart from its original 1927 version. And the revival, according to *Show Boat* scholar Miles Kreuger, lost money on a 417-performance run.

Show Boat runs low on focus and force after the interval, though it would not be the first musical to lighten up in the second half. In his handbill program notes, Prince explained that he wanted "to restore serious incidents and clarify plot and character motivations." The Chicago World's Fair scene was axed as "irrelevant," too typical of how musicals once started up after the interval with "high energy entertainment devoid of story content."[7] Kreuger, in his book about *Show Boat*'s creation and production history—written long before the Prince rationale—saw things differently: "Following the bright and colorful spectacle of Act Two's first scene and its optimistic, dreamlike mood, the grimness of the next sequence is most affecting."[8]

Prince added scenes of exposition meant to flesh out the sinking fate of Ravenal in the second act, as if audiences would not understand the penniless plight into which he and Magnolia had slid following their marriage. Prince had Magnolia walk the streets in a manner that suggested she was servicing gentlemen to make ends meet. He reassigned "Why Do I Love You," originally written for Ravenal and Magnolia, to Parthy, who sings it to her own infant granddaughter in a crib! And he inserted several numbers not heard in the original production. Of particular interest to theatre buffs was the inclusion, midway in Act I, of the haunting "Misery's Coming Around." Queenie is given principal access to the song, and her static rendition comes off as extraneous. These superfluous changes did little to advance the action, which at times seemed to stop dead in its expository tracks.

"Misery's Coming Around" would have been better confined to the utterly magnificent recording of *Show Boat* music produced and conducted by John McGlinn, just like numerous other luscious Kern tunes that were either cut from the original production before it reached the Ziegfeld Theatre or added to the London company or to the film versions. It is one thing to have available for private listening all the songs associated with the various stage and film presentations of this great American musical. Another to have them implanted at will after the fact by the self-ordained restoration experts. To be sure, a number of dazzling compositions not heard in the original graced the Prince production: "Dance Away the Night," and "I Have the Room Above Her," among others. On the other hand, some songs were slighted. Little play time was given to the second-act jazz jumper, "Hey, Feller!" Perhaps it too, in Mr. Prince's estimation, lacked story content.

William Hammerstein, the son of the man who wrote *Show Boat*, theoretically should not have been thrilled with any of these liberties taken. In fact, as controller of his father's estate, he was overruled by the interests of Ferber and Kern when they voted to grant John McGlinn the right to record all the songs. And when McGlinn expressed the opinion that "Misery" should be incorporated into any future productions, Hammerstein promptly disagreed in the most sensible manner. "Misery is a wonderful, moving piece of music, but is was cut for a reason. When experienced knowledgeable people cut material from a show, it's because it's not working, and they're usually right. The well meaning archivists who come onto the scene years later and put back these pieces of material countermand the decision of the creators. I compliment Mr. McGlinn on the making of an historical record that serves a useful purpose by showing how a great piece of work is put together. But it must not be considered a signal for a new kind of production of *Show Boat*."[9]

About ten years later, strangely, the same Hammerstein did not resist the interpolation of "Misery's Coming Around" into Prince's renovated floating palace. In fact, the one remaining son of Oscar decided to enjoy the revamped vehicle, which had first been tested on him in the rudimentary form of a staged reading offered by Mr. Prince. "I'm impressed by what he has done," Hammerstein beamed to Michael Wright of the *Daily Telegraph*. "There's been a lot of talk about how the show has 'changed,' but a lot of that's nonsense. Many of the songs have been repositioned, but it's still the same show. Hal has made some drastic changes, but they're largely in the staging, not the script. I think they're wonderful; they help the show without fundamentally changing it."[10] So much for the duration of a belief.

The Prince version received mostly rhapsodic notices. There can be no denying the glorious perfection of its first act. And as to the second, any better? Some of critics still carped about an inbred superficiality, and the purists were not at all pleased. These adventures in rewriting have long-term consequences on a leading American art form, increasingly vulnerable to such tampering whenever it steps back onto the "living stage"—unlike a film that is fixed in celluloid, a book in print, or a symphonic score by protective conductors and musicians. Ominously, the Rodgers and Hammerstein office has begun sanctioning a disturbing number of virtual deconstructions. With or without William Hammerstein around to counter such overtures—or approve them after being courted with staged readings—the properties of Dick and Oscar are increasingly being roughed up, rifled through, cut up and pasted back together. Songs get transferred out of one show for moonlighting duty in another. Perhaps they are bothered by the failure in general of their musicals to succeed in revival. Likely not as many high schools are licensing *Oklahoma* anymore. In fact, the only R&H work that has done well in return engagements to New York City is *The King and I*, primarily the editions of it in which Yul Brynner appeared, playing the role of the king, which he inaugurated. The revival of *Oklahoma* that William Hammerstein directed in 1979, which opened just two weeks before the death of Richard Rodgers, drew surprisingly mixed notices—including an all-out pan—and earned a profit from only 293 performances. Although the Pulitzer Prize winning musical *South Pacific* is staged now and then in small playhouses and occasionally on civic light opera stages, it is largely regarded within the theatre community as a dated work. And so, fearful of an embarrassing return to Broadway, the Rodgers and Hammerstein office refused even to grant a touring production starring *Robert Goulet* the right to play in a New York house. The same office did, however, sanction a clumsy, vulgar, and not very funny made-for-television movie of the play in 2001, which starred one of its producers, Broadway veteran Glenn Close, inappropriately cast in the role of Nellie Forbush. Those who fear further damage to *South Pacific* may take solace in the sensitively wrought 1958 movie version directed by Joshua Logan. Notwithstanding the overly criticized color tints that appear during musical sequences, it is one of the finest film adaptations ever of a stage musical.

Carousel, Rodgers and Hammerstein's darkest work, finally made it back to New York after first being recycled through the British gothic musical mindset, courtesy of director Nicholas Hytner and the Royal National Theatre. Hytner sought and was given permission to make script changes, all rather minor save for a new opening scene, set in the mill where Julie labors, apparently intended to convey a grim sweatshop atmosphere. Hytner's aim was to strip away the sentiment which he assumed had built up over the years. That he did, to a degree unmagical, depriving the work of the intangible R&H spirit. Without the charming innocence that Dick and Oscar were always careful to supply, there is little lost happiness to cry over at the end.

In this gloomier *Carousel*, to which, it was smugly implied, hip younger crowds weaned on Jerry Springer and the O.J. Simpson trial would relate, "The Highest Judge of All" was dropped. Political correctness nearly ruined the evening: Bring on Mr. and Mrs. Snow, played by an African American couple, a delightful alternative. Then add stupidity to enlightenment by having a young *blond* play their *son*. Hytner's unflinching interpretation, praised by many, played it too close to the bone and too far from reality. Judging by the audience at two San Francisco performances, those younger patrons one would have expected (based upon glowing press reports and predictions) were nowhere in sight.

The Sound of Music, which made its first return to Broadway in 1998 at the Martin Beck Theatre, might have benefited from Hytner's acerbic touch. Given its abundant displays of cute moppet behavior and blasé adult indifference in the face of a mounting Nazi threat, here is a musical that cries out for gravity—or at least comically shaded characterizations—but which seems forever destined to sing and dance in the shadow of the overwhelmingly popular ultra-sweet film version which starred Julie Andrews. Lovable and fascinating Mary Martin, there in the beginning, no doubt brought her subtle impish idiosyncrasies to the role of Maria; the Marias who have followed Martin, starting with Florence Henderson and including

Andrews, rarely rise above the role of sugar dispensing machines. Came the Broadway revival, directed with a sharp eye for scenery and song cues by Susan H. Schulman, who promised by implication to remove some of the goo that had formed over the years. Schulman declared herself committed to the play's more serious political underpinnings, telling reporters she believed the original stage version was "edgier"[11] and that the movie had been "sanitized." Strangely, she also courted the status quo, putting it this way to a *Backstage* writer: "There is an expectation level among audience members that we do respect.... Seeing the production should be like a visit to an old friend."[12] So much for a vision. Alas, Schulman proved herself a wishy-washy director, unable to escape the intimidating commercial force of that Julie Andrews movie, to which, her battery of producers likely fretted, audiences everywhere would make constant picky comparisons. The recharted fate of six major songs alone illustrates how, degree by degree, the show's fragile substance has been undermined over the years by additional frosting.

In the original production, "My Favorite Things" is sung by Maria and Mother Abbess, sharing a mutual affection for a list of life's simple pleasures, and it offers Maria subliminal encouragement from the convent as she embarks on her journey to serve as a governess for Captain von Trapp's seven children. In Schulman's version, the number is replaced by the generically innocuous "I Have Confidence In Me," a song imported from the movie for which Mr. Rodgers had supplied his own words, a song that sounds like something out of *Annie* or *Sweet Charity*. The ejected "My Favorite Things" ends up in the storm scene in Maria's bedroom, as it did in the film, bumping "The Lonely Goatherd," a number that bore haunting relevance to the storm with its lines "high on a hill was a lonely goatherd" and the nervous yodeling rhythms. The banished "Goatherd" is now introduced at the Kaltzberg concert hall, replacing a deleted reprise of "Do Re Mi," which in the original version had given the song's central contribution to the story a nice circular completion.

Other subtle changes: In the original cast, the worldly "How Can Love Survive" was rendered by Max and Elsa in the captain's passive presence; now, the captain is not even present. In the original, "No Way to Stop It" began with the captain, his frustration with the looming Nazi threat boiling over, strumming angrily against his guitar. In Schulman's version, he just sings it, sans guitar. Lastly, the original featured "An Ordinary Couple," a love duet between Maria and the captain, built on the imagery of a shared belief in companionship, on the simple contentment derived from an embrace each day as the sun fades away. Forty years later, that fading sun was nowhere to be found. "An Ordinary Couple" was completely 86d, callously replaced by another Richard Rodgers solo effort written for the movie, the stupefyingly simple minded "Something Good," in which Maria oddly alludes to a "wicked" and "miserable" childhood, leading us to ponder whether our nun-on-the-run has a police record. We are forced here to endure the composer stumbling over himself in a feeble reach for insight.

Arguably minor changes? Altogether, they kept the show clearly in the world of Julie Andrews. Schulman's production moved with precision and polish from one big musical highlight to the next, drawing its vitality from the gut-grabbing showmanship of those final Rodgers and Hammerstein creations. Especially terrific were the dramatic escape scenes at the end. If *The Sound of Music* lends itself to inspired direction, Schulman's handiwork fell respectably short.

Dr. Kildare (aka: Richard Chamberlain), who joined the New York cast during the run, did not set the box office on fire with his regally austere reading of Captain Trapp. Nor did the revival need another lovely Julie Andrews sound-alike in the form of hard-working Meg Tolin. Following 540 performances, the company quietly departed the Great White Way for an extended road tour, having failed to recoup all of its $6 million investment.

The Rodgers and Hammerstein organization evidently does not take very seriously what their own Richard Rodgers had to say on the subject: "When we can possibly get them performed the way they were written, we do because we've found from experience, some of it painful, that the best way to project these things and to get a response from a live audience is to do them the way there were done originally, after we got finished correcting them ourselves."[13] Well, ironically, Rodgers didn't take his own advice either. This is the same Rodgers who, following Hammerstein's death, dropped and added songs to *The Sound of Music* (at one time making the stage version conform to the film version). The same Rodgers who betrayed his better instincts at least on one mind-boggling occasion when he, or someone in his office, authorized the tacky disco-driven *Pal Joey '78*, which featured Lena Horne in a national touring aberration that did not dare cast its cheap strobe lights on a New York stage. Mr. Rodgers may have been smarting over the poorly received revival of *Joey* in a more conventional version, only two years earlier, when Theodore Mann staged it at the Circle in the Square Theatre. The urge to stay modern can wreck havoc with proven classics.

Out of all this deconstruction, of course, looms the tantalizing promise that *Allegro* or even *Pipe Dream* might one day rise triumphantly, thanks to effectively rewritten scripts. Both shows have first rate scores, interesting characters and salvageable books. *Pipe Dream* with its quirkier on-the-edge cast would probably find a more hospitable reception in the age of ambivalence. *State Fair*, the movie, was turned into an enchanting stage musical full of many things to love, though romantically it lagged way behind the times. It struggled through an erratically patronized national tour before suffering a fast fold on Broadway. Familiar songs from *Pipe Dream* and *Me and Juliet* were interpolated, some convincingly, others not. The Rodgers and Hammerstein office has, it would appear, given up on *Pipe Dream* and *Juliet* ever finding an audience beyond the concert staged-reading format, largely patronized by die-hard fans of all things pre-guitar. And so these songs are up for grabs. So, too, increasingly, are even the more successful shows themselves.

Cinderella, regarded with little argument as the finest original musical ever scripted for television, was bartered away, song by song, to Disney, completely rewritten for sit-com audiences in 1997, and pitched deceitfully as "Rodgers and Hammerstein's." Hammerstein's lyrics were not good enough for TV's cultured crowd; in clear violation of a stipulation in Richard Rodgers' will prohibiting such posthumous alterations, Fred Ebb added new lines to "The Prince is Giving a Ball."[14] Tunes from other shows (one by Rodgers and *Hart*) were added. The strongest musical number offered did not even come from the original TV score, and the epic soulful rendition of it by Whitney Houston suggested a style that, had it been thoroughly infused throughout the show, might have given Cinderella's date with Disney a more memorable edge. The number was a deftly wrought hybrid merging two obscure R & H songs, "There's Music in You," from a 1953 movie *Main Street to Broadway* in which Dick and Oscar appeared, along with Mary Martin who sang the song, and "One Foot, Other Foot" out of *Allegro*. Whitney Houston's rendition, during the wedding scene, of the surprisingly effective result made it sound like a big potential pop hit. Not to be.

Flower Drum Song is another property arguably not in need of a major overhaul, an underrated musical comedy hit easily derided by its detractors as politically out of date—notwithstanding that the same could be said for a great many novels, films, and plays. *Flower Drum Song* was a clear winner when it opened, full of bright humor and hummable songs. Nonetheless, Playwright David Henry Hwang, one of the writers who worked on Disney's *Aida*, was commissioned to supply a new book. And that he did, returning (he misleadingly claimed) to the novel by C. Y. Lee upon which the show was based, consulting with the author, and yet delivering a harder-edged, more contemporary vision, far removed from Lee's. A pre–Broadway tryout was slated to commence in the spring of 2001 at the Ahmanson Theatre in Los Angeles. Lack of sufficient funds, however, caused the venture to be moved back to the fall and onto the boards of the smaller Mark Taper Forum.

Music theatre watchers wondered what the director would do with "I Enjoy Being a Girl," the song about a woman applying makeup and talking for hours on the telephone, which sends more people up the wall than the most misogynistic rap lyrics or violent television programs. With all the striking changes Hwang made to *Flower Drum Song* ("I Enjoy Being a Girl" was retained), unless his redesigned libretto—assuming the commercially promising production reaches Broadway—can turn a very good show into a great one, no doubt some director years from now will make a case for merely producing the musical as originally conceived and written, just with fresh direction and faces. How revolutionary!

Perhaps no single event in revival history has so agonizingly underscored the precarious life span of the libretto as did the grim fate, in 1995, of the anxiously anticipated new Broadway production of Stephen Sondheim's *Company*. The classic work was met with full houses at the not-for-profit Roundabout Theatre during its scheduled three-month run, and by a gushing endorsement from the bible of showbiz. "After a shaky start," reported *Variety*, "the show builds, expanding, finally, to greatness."[15] Not in the opinion of lesser bibles. The majority of reviewers issued pessimistic assessments, and the initial surging crowds consisted mainly of hard core Sondheimaniacs. A terse edict from Margo Jefferson of the *New York Times* called for a divorce of score from libretto: "I suppose there's no point in a musical being a musical unless the songs are worth more than the script. The better scripts aim to be timely, the better scores aim to be timeless, and it's usually a nice arrangement. But when the story begins to work against the best interests of the score, an audience has every right to wish the two would split and to their separate ways.... I would rather have seen it in concert version. Concert versions of musicals treat the script like a road we tread lightly between songs. Mr. Sondheim the composer and Mr. Sondheim the lyricist are a brilliant match. Two is all the company we need here."[16]

And that's all the world may get, if the passing years make *Company's* libretto less viable. Ms. Jefferson had it backwards: It is the score that must serve the best interests of the story, not vice versa, if there is going to be show at all. Producer John Hart had planned to move *Company* into a house uptown, until a piddling advance sale of $100,000 in response to early adds touting a move did not, in Hart's credible judgment—soundly supported by box-office traditions—justify the formidable transfer. Stephen Sondheim, no doubt smarting over a recent string of flops, lashed out at Hart by issuing a public statement "denouncing," in the words of *New York Times* writer Peter Marks, the producer's inability to do the job. "We couldn't find a producer," stated the fuming Sondheim. "We found an enthusiast in Mr. Hart, but unfortunately he has no experience as a producer, only as a money man."[17]

Sondheim revealed that, as a contingency for going forward, Hart had made repeated demands for numerous changes from content to casting. They were just the ploys of a producer seeking to stir up dissension and carve an easier exit path for himself, as the angry composer saw it. Indeed, that moment came when the show's director, Scott Ellis, fiercely refused to replace lead man Boyd Gaines with Michael Rupert, an idea of Hart's to bolster public interest. Hart was getting little cooperation from anybody. The Nederlanders, who had tentatively agreed to help finance the move, backed out, leaving Hart on his own. Sondheim saw only cowardice. Hart "didn't really want to move the show,"[18] he claimed, whining about the good old days when producers were really producers, though he omitted one key factor in his looking back comparisons—when shows were really shows. In his defense, Mr. Hart could point to a thundering absence of public interest. It just wasn't there, sorry or grateful.

What happened? The world of reality is what happened. Long term success proved as elusive for *Company* as it did, not quite to the same degree, for its spiritual antithesis, *The Sound of Music*. Neither show took the town by storm. Cynical self-analysis among the dysfunctionally wed may not hold up any better than confident sentiment on the Austrian alps.

CHAPTER 16

Cirque du Disney

Where once there were adult book stores, massage parlors and convenience alleys for lonely tourists on fixed incomes, now giggling hordes of children and parents ran across well-scrubbed streets to attend spectacular new family musicals. Where once, that mean Big Apple resembled a prison yard at recess time and taunted out-of-towners to swim in its slime and take it like a real "New Yorka'," now the folks from Petaluma to Providence stood in squeaky clean lines to see stage versions of Disney animated movie hits. Across the street at the sparkling new Center for the Performing Arts, more crowds formed in warm fuzzy bliss to patronize a musical with a heart as big and righteous as a neon-lit flag about turn-of-the-century race relations.

The streets of Gorky's lower depths in old Manhattan had been swept free of hustlers, prostitutes and common riffraff—all herded out of the theatre district into more appropriate climes like Prospect Park or the Jerry Springer audience. Fretting city officials, fearing the loss of tourism to a growing national perception that sleaze and violence were synonymous with New York City, formed an alliance with movieland giant Walt Disney to refurbish the Old Amsterdam Theatre on 42nd Street—yes, *that* 42nd Street—and help lift the neighborhood back into mainstream respectability. Times Square went to the ducks. No wonder the locals reveled in shows like *The Life* and *Rent*, which dared to depict the way things were before Mickey Mouse moved east to astonish the most jaded by proving that he could rival those envied Brits and all their confounded hits. Disney made the chancy film-to-stage leap with all the derring-do of Secretariat entering a horse race at the Toledo County Fairgrounds.

No getting around it: There *was* a void to fill. Cameron Mackintosh and colleagues, who had performed rescue work not exactly welcomed by know-it-all New Yorkers, were lately striking out with new shows. To the implicating question—what could be done to offset a growing public impression that Broadway

183

was basically a showcase for golden age revivals and all those brazen British imports which hung shamelessly around forever—had anybody else a better answer than the Disney machine? Certainly, however many new writers may have been stalking producers' suites with demo tapes in hand, they were not being "discovered" by the Big Guns who own all the real estate and would rather rent than produce.

Ah, yes, rent. Disney had enough money to lease practically every playhouse in the district, and the Mickey Mouse makeover recast Broadway as a kiddie fun zone. Lording it over the new moppet-friendly midway was Disney's regal *The Lion King*. Since taking the town by the tail in 1997, it has consistently pulled in packed houses. And the end of its reign on Broadway was nowhere in sight as the century came to a close. Epitomizing the absolute triumph of showmanship over substance, *The Lion King* offers a rare visual extravaganza that succeeds by never standing still long enough to reveal the machinery beyond the magic. It is a purely theatrical amalgam, continually hauling out new treats from the wings, by turns a children's pantomime, a Busby Berkeley spectacle, an ice show charade, high camp humor, the Village People in jungle gear, Cirque du Soleil in the air, and, of course, Disney everywhere. Never were the arts of direction and stagecraft more critical to the success of a show—nor more transparently devoid of a soul. Hardly a musical at all, *The Lion King* does not feel so much written or composed as cobbled together down a Hollywood assembly line of time-tested ingredients, all of them shrewdly employed to sustain the spectacle—and sustain it they do. No producer alive has the showmanship and marketing savvy of Walt Disney. Audiences have responded with abundant devotion.

Stager Julie Taymor's larger-than-life puppets enchant and mystify. The songs of Elton John, Tim Rice, and a host of additional contributors keep a basic ersatz jungle beat thumping. The predictable story line—the king's evil brother, Scar, who covets the thrown, kills the king and banishes his young son, Simba, who must eventfully find a way back to reclaim his place—gives Disney fans sufficient excuse to believe the evening has a purpose beyond mere amusement. A theme? Oh, perhaps the hip allusion in Tim Rice's verse to a kind of rare primitive wisdom, cosmically appealing as long as the listener refrains from contemplating present-day conflicts raging across the African continent:

> It's the circle of life
> And it moves us all
> Through despair and hope
> Through faith and love
> Till we find our place
> On the path unwinding
> In the circle
> The Circle of life.

The Lion King is likably lightweight entertainment, and Disney deserves some credit for at least introducing the stage to a whole new generation of moppets, who may gravitate in seasons to come to less pandering parades. The gushing reviews virtually all pointed to the obvious. "A theatrical achievement unrivaled in its beauty, brains and ingenuity," declared Greg Evans, reviewing in *Variety*.[1] *Los Angeles Times* critic Laurie Winer dared to register nagging qualms: "When Taymor's hand is quiet, or when it is ineffectual (such as in the insipid, floating ballet number that adorns 'Can You Feel The Love Tonight?'), *The Lion King* is revealed to be a show that renders its themes simplistic, and one with a weakness for pandering jokes."[2] Less hesitant was Robert Brustein, artistic director of the American Repertory Theatre at Harvard, expressing dismay at yet another example of New York's descent down a mindless thoroughfare of sterile family fun: "Ultimately I felt empty. What it's about is essentially kitsch.... It just seems as though Broadway is just for foreign businessmen, out-of-town tourists and 10-year-olds.... It has lost its serious audience."[3]

Although Disney's inaugural 1994 stage entry, *Beauty and the Beast*, addressed a theme of real and relevant substance—physical versus spiritual beauty—it, too, got nearly buried alive under an incessant barrage of glitz and gadgetry. It lacked the film's "visual wit,"[4] complained the *New York Times'* Janet Maslin. Quipped her *Times* cohort David Richard, "It belongs right up there with the Empire State Building, F.A.O. Schwarz and the Circle Line boat tours.... It is Las Vegas without sex, Mardi Gras without booze.... Others may look upon the mind-boggling spectacle as further proof of the age-old theory that if you throw enough money at the American public, the American public will throw it right back.... Only the primary emotions and the most elemental reactions stand a chance of holding their own against the bustle and blazing pyrotechnics."[5]

Indeed, and agreed. The producer's relentless deference to frosting, from blinding fireworks and dancing spoons to chattering costumes and endless mugging, telegraphs a chronic lack of faith in the worthy little tale being enacted. Charmingly romantic are the opening scenes, in which Belle's eccentric inventor father, Maurice, is introduced with his unique wood-chopping automobile. There is momentarily in the air the look and sound of a delicate fantasy about to unfold. Soon after, though, Maurice loses his way in the Disney forest, and so does much of a promising story, which instead subsumes itself in a penny arcade of hyperactive stagecraft. And in the end, here is a show that may leave you feeling more exhausted than enchanted.

Disney's show-stopping invasion of the Great White Way did not earn it many friends at the next Tony Awards, where, nominated for nine Tonys, *Beauty* won just one, for costume design. Its marvelous score, primarily the work of composer Alan Menken and the late lyricist Howard Ashman, with apt supplementary lyrics by Tim Rice, lost out to a second rate chamber musical by Stephen Sondheim, *Passion*, a supreme snub tantamount to, say, *The King and I* being trumped in 1951 by *Golden Apple*. While *Passion*, another typically profitless Sondheim work (this one about a soldier falling in love with an ugly woman), soon faded depressingly away, long lines continued forming outside the Palace Theatre by folks eager to experience the story of a beautiful young woman falling in love with a rather ugly beast. Five years later, it was playing to 90 percent capacity houses.

During the 1998 season, when *The Lion King* began to roar, Disney's across-the-street neighbor, Canadian-based Livent corporation, finally unveiled its own new E-ticket ride to the theme park of bigger-than-musical musicals, this one called *Ragtime*. It was a show calculated to extract big emotions from America's lingering, guilt-ridden ambivalence over the plight and place of African Americans in U.S. society. Now, Uncle Walt could gaze upon his rival across the street and see a mirror reflection of his own synthetic showmanship. The two tuners were said to be locked in a bloody duel for the heart and soul of American patronage via the Tony Awards. They ended up sharing top honors. No surprise. *Ragtime* was judged to contain the best score. *The Lion King*, however, roared off with the coveted "Best Musical" award.

The antithesis of a fairy tale, *Ragtime*, based on the novel by E. L. Doctorow, pitches with virtuous determination the major American saga of race relations, something on the order of Julie Andrews holding court in a high school civics class. It has the look, sound, and good intentions of a proficiently polished amateur musical. What it suffers from the most is Terrence McNally's sprawling free-form libretto, which juggles, not too gracefully, several stories simultaneously and treats them in stereotypical fashion, much like a patriotic world's fair pageant fraught with one dimensional characters and Big Messages. The stiffest of the lot turns out to be Coalhouse Walker Jr., ironically written to hold center stage, even though his just grievance against some bigoted firemen for smashing up his new Model T does not get fueled up until well into a meandering first act. Into the surrounding morass wanders the infinitely engaging Tateh, a widowed Jewish emigrant from Eastern Europe who dreams of becoming a movie director. His ever-pensive soul and story would have made a fine musical all in itself.

Critic Laurie Winer, in whose Southern California backyard the show made its first stateside appearance, argued that the story springs from a humanity not fairly acknowledged by everyone and that, on balance, "*Ragtime* is the work of a producer with a passion for history, unafraid of a tragic ending, and who possesses a strong commercial sense."[6] Conversely, among a panel of dissenters, there was Vincent Canby, in whose *New York Times* notice, headlined "Big and Beautiful, *Ragtime* Never Quite Sings," he lamented, "The first act begins with huge promise in a knockout title number…. With increasing frequency in the course of the show, the individual numbers appear to be illustrating emotions that have already been announced. The score, especially in its third hour, seems not to be hurtling the show forward in great leaps but stopping it dead in its tracks. You begin to feel cornered…. Toward the end of the show, the score has begun to sound like a nonstop series of personal epiphanies and gallant resolves to plug on, no matter what the obstacles, to some better tomorrow."[7]

What both *Ragtime* and *The Lion King* shared prolifically in common were undistinguished scores of plodding calculation. *Ragtime* rides high and wide on fanfaric anthems either celebrating the American promise for incoming immigrants or decrying righteously the specter of racial bigotry and injustice, all set to words as cloyingly simple minded as ad copy for a presidential campaign. Its creators, Lynn Ahrens and Stephen Flaherty, may have a unique voice of their own, but it does not sing through here. At the outset, the songs are fetchingly in tune with the syncopated rhythms of the colorful era portrayed, especially the title number, then "Crime of the Century," "Getting Ready to Rag," "Henry Ford" and "New Music." But what promises to be a journey full of rhythm and insight goes musically, and certainly lyrically, downhill as the narrative shrivels and shrinks into overstatement, from breezy to ponderous. Among a few standouts with a pulse of their own is the wonderfully intimate little "Buffalo Nickel Photoplay, Inc." In it, the human size dreams of Tateh trickle through like pure unexpected sunshine out of a big, ashen, concept-musical sky. For a moment in the key of humanity, we are actually face to face with a real flesh-and-blood person, not a cardboard articulation of the producer's strident idealism.

The musical disappointments of *The Lion King* are of a different sort, apparently induced, just the same, by the cold dictates of corporate design to achieve a demographics-sensitive diversity of sounds—from jungle chants and bongo drums to "Yeah, man!" '60s rock power. In this case, the power of a huge film studio doubtlessly deserves credit for the pleasing if pedestrian patchwork, which does not so much move the action as embroider it with atmosphere and primal energy. While the show's famous nonprofit arts director, Julie Taymor, may rightfully claim having enjoyed reasonable autonomy, the composer Elton John and lyricist Tim Rice openly acknowledged, without a trace of discomfort, allowing Disney all the revisions it deemed essential to satisfy its particular scheme. Not just revisions, but additional words and music supplied by an army of other songwriters—ten people in all, including Taymor—reportedly engaged to overcome a noticeable weakness in the original batch of John and Rice songs.

In fact, the show's musical highlight, "Shadowland," was supplied by three of them—Lebo M, Hans Zimmer and Mark Mancina. But John and Rice delivered a home run of their own in their edgy "Chow Down," an atypically fierce outburst that flirts with acid rock:

> Tell us again—gee
> It's so incredible
> That you're so rude
> When you're so edible
> When you are food!
> It's time to chow down
> Chow down!
> Ch-ch-ch-ch-ch-chow down
> ......
> I think we should begin the meal from scratch
> So many juicy segments to detach
> Be good as gold for you're as good as carved
> Here, kitty, kitty ...
> We're starved!

This howling irreverence sends the score momentarily into male-hormone orbit, away from the ersatz jungle drums and two-syllable laments of a bamboo musical, and it gives us a tantalizing taste of what the two Englishmen might have done had they been encouraged or granted permission to forge raucously ahead in this hard rock vein. Another gem from the British duo that makes you forget you're on a plastic safari ride is the hilariously fun "Madness of King Scar."

In matters of script and score development, Disney and Livent mirrored each other's control-freak producing methods and lavish production fetishes. Livent's founder, Garth Drabinsky, who dreamed up adapting E. L. Doctorow's *Ragtime*, held a competition among composers and lyricists for the job of creating the tunes, and then evidently dominated the songwriting process, note by note by note. Ditto essentially for Disney. Both organizations shunned any association, formal or affiliate, with the New York League of Theatre Producers. Perhaps the feeling was mutual. Given the snide indifference of New York theatre people to outsiders, one can imagine a reluctance on the part of Drabinsky and Disney to meet for coffee or share trade secrets with the producing colleagues of Peter Stone and his Circle of Thirty. Disney has shown a preference for English songwriters, Drabinsky for Americans. Neither is all that revolutionary, nor has either yet quite managed to duplicate, as no doubt each burningly desires, the global marketing wizardry of modern day magnate, Mackintosh. Disney is fast getting there, though, having by the year 2000 mounted a total of *six* companies of *The Lion King* on the boards worldwide, from New York to Toronto and Los Angeles, and with another two units playing on Japanese stages.

So far, Disney has reaped real profits. Not so for its smooth-talking rival across the street, who talked himself into bankruptcy, the inevitable outcome of Mr. Drabinsky's having conned his gullible investors with some of the most advanced bookkeeping deceptions ever sold a pack of angels. Before the discovery of fraud caught up with the Canadian producer, he reveled in the heady role of Broadway's promising new impresario, dreaming of becoming another Cameron Mackintosh. Madly devoted to American musicals, Drabinsky latched onto *The Kiss of the Spider Woman* in its troubled infancy, deciding he was destined to give it legs. He sponsored rewrites and additional tours, none profitable, then brought it back to Broadway for a second chance before the critics, making this possibly the shortest time in history between the opening of a failed musical and the date of its subsequent first New York revival. *Kiss*, even with better reviews, proceeded to languish at the box office—a protracted exercise in long-run image-building by a producer slipping deeper into debt. The downbeat original cast album does not inspire much of an urge to see the actual show, and none of the national on-tour engagements generated strong turnouts to witness the sullen songfest between two unlikely inmates—a drag queen and a South American political revolutionary— trapped behind prison bars in the same cell, where their disparate sexual urges ultimately collapse into an uneasy consummation.

Riding high on falsely inflated earnings, Mr. Drabinsky paid for the magnificent if needlessly overwrought revival of *Show Boat*. A man with passionate determination, he gravitated to Harold Prince, who directed *Kiss* and *Show Boat*. Besides his penchant for bookkeeping gymnastics, Drabinsky also threw blind embraces around all things American, commissioning a dizzying array of new work and revivals for future presentation, including a Dr. Seuss children's musical; an adaptation of the film *The Sweet Smell of Success*, with a score by Marvin Hamlisch; and a revival of *Pal Joey*. And he envisioned an empire of new theatres spanning coast to coast, which he in time would build, and which would house his many imagined hits. *Ragtime* was to have been his crowning attraction in the Big Apple, as well as in multiple companies touring the globe. Perhaps there will one day be a musical about this insanely ambitious Canadian. Numerous felled impresarios will identify.[8]

To his credit and before he lost control of his enterprise, Mr. Drabinsky did demonstrate the admirable resolve to put his bogus capital and personal drive behind *some* new work. The same could not be said of the Disney office, where an evident abhorrence of failure has kept them from taking seriously anything not already tested on the silver screen and fit for children of all ages. They have sponsored endless workshops and readings of new musicals "in development," none of which has progressed to opening night, while turning another animation property, *The Hunchback of Notre Dame*, into a stage tuner of uncertain merit and box office lure, which premiered quietly in Berlin in the summer of 1999. With its ability to attract top creative talent from all over the world, would Disney ever put up a new musical *first* written for the *stage*? Well, almost.... A new work already halfway in the hands of the Burbank animators, who assumed they'd be sketching it into full-blown cinematic glory, became instead the new Elton John and Tim Rice Broadway-bound tuner *Aida*. When Disney had approached John in 1994 about working on the film project, he showed such scant interest, not wanting to follow *The Lion King* with a similar assignment, that Disney countered with an offer to skip animation and go directly to Broadway if John and Rice would agree to do the songs.

The John-Rice work, based on the children's story by Leontyne Price, and also the subject of the famed 1871 Verdi opera, slogged erratically through hissing notices when first presented in an elaborate workshop at Atlanta's Alliance Theatre. The humbling glitches resulted in a rapid turnover among the creative staff. In came replacement director Robert Falls, of Chicago's famed Goodman Theatre. Falls recruited others to help rescue the ailing infant, including playwright Henry David Hwang. At the center of all the critical sniping was a split-personality musical trying to be both serious and cartoonist. "These Egyptians," wrote Charles Isherwood, reporting for *Variety*, "sound just like post-adolescents from today's hot-blooded TV dramas."[9] Revisions were implemented without the on-site participation of the composer, confined to his English abode and concert dates. John did drop one number and add another.

Songs from *Aida*, issued in a pre–Broadway concept album, failed ominously to make a decent dent on *Billboard* charts. The show was greeted by indifferent reviews ranging from cool to nasty when finally it faced the Manhattan first nighters. In a *Wall Street Journal* notice headlined "Bland as Custard … a Saccharine Dud," Amy Gamerman observed, "This musical about a doomed romance in the age of the Pharaohs is as lifeless as a mummy."[10]

Hundreds of new musicals are forever in the works, and only a handful of them, if that, will ever see an audience in the city that never sleeps. The romantic notion harbored by writers that big-time producers are looking for them is largely a myth. In truth, the more successful a New York producer becomes, the less likely will he or she be to seek out and present the work of neophytes. Disney can and does attract the most marketable and accomplished writers in the world. And yet through all the countless readings and workshops of new work by outsiders that Disney has reportedly sponsored since first taking Broadway back in 1994, not a single show has been launched on the road out of Burbank. In fact, by virtue of its association with two or three already established names (Ashman, John and Rice), Disney had not promoted any new talents at all. Par for the course. Drabinsky beholden to Flaherty and Ahrens? Just before plunging into financial infamy, he had his *Ragtime* creators at work on his new Dr. Seuss show *Seussical*; they were given an up front advance of half a million dollars. The show did not last a year in New York.

Cameron Mackintosh has yet to produce in a big way any of the budding British talents whose work he has tried out on local English workshop audiences. He has made his fortunes entirely off the efforts of just two teams: Webber and his various lyricists, and Boublil and Schonberg. Oh, but you say, yesterday's titans took real chances! On whom, beyond maybe the lucky one or two? For all his bluster, David Merrick was spineless when it came to the discovery and support of unknowns. In 1960, in association with Zev Bufman, Merrick did dabble with a trio of neophytes—Jack Wilson, Alan Jeffreys, Maxwell Grant, all of whom remained incognito ever after—in the 8 performance fizzle *Vintage '60*, for which they, along with Fred Ebb and Sheldon Harnick, supplied songs and sketches. On his own, Merrick virtually *never* worked with newcomers; there is the one obscure exception when he took half a chance by introducing to the world outside of Manhattan Edward Thomas, the ill-fated participant of a failed David Miracle. Thomas composed the music for a show that closed out of town in 1967, *Mata Hari*, with words crafted by Martin Charnin. Charnin himself had already been to Broadway briefly four years earlier when he and Mary Rogers, in association with a horde of people who came and went during stormy on-the-road rewrites, wrote *Hot Spot*, a 43-performance deadbeat staring Judy Holliday. Beyond this one fruitless gamble, Merrick never again typed out contracts for unproven talents. And, surely, he fought them off daily at the door. Merrick took on only credentialed songwriters, such as pop titans Burt Bacharach and Hal David, assigned to provide the songs for *Promises, Promises*.

Courage it takes, to say "yes" to untested stage composing talents. Only a few producers have shown it (revue master Leonard Sillman certainly did), and then only on very rare occasions and with mostly established professionals from Hollywood or the recording studio. Feuer and Martin brought to the stage Cy Coleman and Frank Loesser, both of whom came in with popular songwriting credits. Alan Jay Lerner and Frederick Loewe, who struggled individually up the theatre ladder through a number of disappointing ventures, got their first big break together when Mark Warnow (a virtual unknown himself) produced their inaugural collaboration, the flop wartime musical *What's Up*. Kermit Bloomgarden believed in pop music maker Meredith Willson. Lee Sabinson and William Katzell put E. Y. Harburg and Burton Lane over on Broadway after each had amassed numerous film and stage credits.

Edward Padula produced the first Strouse-Adams show, *Bye, Bye, Birdie*, after the duo had contributed, together and separately, to three Ben Bagley revues in the mid '50s. Before Richard Kollmar and Albert W. Selden mounted Bock and Harnick's first effort, *Body Beautiful*, Bock had already, working with lyricist Larry Holofcener, sold songs to Sid Caesar's TV series, "Your Show of Shows," and had co-composed *Mr. Wonderful*. And Harnick had worked on Silllman's *New Faces of '52* and on the Bette Davis bomb, mounted the same season, *Two's Company*. Harold Prince took a chance on Kander and Ebb, two relative unknowns with limited stage resumes but with a big song hit, "My Coloring Book," to their name. Also direct from the Hit Parade, Richard Adler and Jerry Ross ("Rags to Riches") had Prince, Robert Griffith and Frederick Brisson in their court.

Costume designer and producer Oliver Smith, in partnership with Paul Feigay, helped launched three major talents: Leonard Bernstein, then a symphonic and ballet composer, and Betty Comden and Adolph Green, two nightclub entertainers who had never worked on a Broadway show in any capacity. Edgar Lansbury in association with four other producers brought us Stephen Schwartz a couple of years after he, at age 21, had composed the title song for the hit 1969 play *Butterflies Are Free*. Lore Note raised the capital for the late off–Broadway sensation *The Fantasticks*, the work of fellow Texans Harvey Schmidt and Tom Jones, who had already supplied music and verse to a couple of New York revues, including Ben Bagley's short-lived off–Broadway effort, *Shoestring '57*.

Garth Drabinsky had shown a preference for people who know their way around Manhattan. While his reins of power were slipping fiendishly away, the hyperactive Canadian mover and shaker was overseeing fifteen new projects in various phases of development. He produced the cheerfully reviewed *Fosse: A Celebration in Song and Dance*, and daringly he turned his back on vacuous spectacle by turning to a work of grim non-opulent naturalism, *Parade*. This he accomplished by once again confusing the stage for a classroom and by slipping into a fatal co-producing arrangement with Lincoln Center. The chancy new work they agreed to present had a score by Jason Robert Brown, a book by Alfred Unry, and direction by Mr. Drabinsky's favorite, Hal Prince. (Prince had originally tried talking Stephen Sondheim into the project; Sondheim declined, wanting to work on something in "a lighter vein.") Nothing much about *Parade* could overcome the gloomy premise: Leo Frank, a Jewish businessman in Atlanta, is tried and convicted for murdering one of his pencil factory workers, a 13-year-old girl. Following a dubiously conducted trial fraught with anti–Semitism, Frank is sentenced to death. When his fate is commuted to life imprisonment, an angry mob out for revenge breaks into the jail, hauls Frank out and lynches him.

Brown's score is full of promise for the composer, too sprawling and self-conscious for the show. *Variety*'s Charles Isherwood was left utterly dismayed by the depressing affair. "Broadway has not exactly been a festive place in recent months." Isherwood sensed a black and white depiction of victim and villain: "Its moral positions are hammered home with dogged insistence, and its unhappy ending seems to be quietly present in every scene."[11]

Vincent Canby was left perplexed by the lifeless treatment. "It plays as if it were still a collection of notes for a show that has yet to be discovered." The music? "Some pleasing melodies." Lyrics? "Banal (I assume) by design in the way of commonplace speech." Candy wondered how such a sordid and downbeat little roadblock had gotten this far. And in his pondering the preparation phase, he may just as well have been describing the behind-the-scenes trials of the musical's famously fallen producer: "What was Mr. Prince thinking in allowing *Parade* to be produced in this condition? He believed in it, certainly, but something happens in the course of long pre-production work, readings, workshops and rehearsals, even to the pros. Collaborators have a way of psyching each other up, as they should do. At the same time, they can become isolated, so self-absorbed, so removed from reality and so mired in tiny details that they begin to see results not visible to the outsider."[12]

Isolated. Self absorbed. Removed from reality. Not without a few fine reviews to its name, *Parade* closed down after 39 previews and 84 performances at the Vivian Beaumont Theatre. Lincoln Center, minus the critical support of the now bankrupt Garth Drabinsky, was left solely responsible for the weekly running costs, and for losses approaching $5.5 million. Still, *Parade* might have some kind of a future in the emerging touring and regional theatre market for Broadway also-rans. There is something indelibly magic about even a musical that lasts only a single night on the Great White Way. It has *been* there, as precious few can claim. One night on Broadway is really all a show needs to pick up a Tony or two, and there were plenty of them to go around at the upcoming final Tony Awards presentation of the century.

The fate of every planned new Livent opening was thrown into jeopardy in April 1998, when control of the theatre on the other side of the street directly facing Walt Disney's New Amsterdam fell into the hands of another Disney figure, ex–Disney president Michael Ovitz, famous for a well-publicized Disney severance package amounting to $20 million. In an act of corporate sibling rivalry, Ovitz dropped $20 million into Livent, which had reported a fourth quarter loss of US$37.7 million and a loss of C$44.1 million for the year of 1997. Buying up 12 percent stock, Ovitz immediately assumed the status of potential savior, and he legally finagled himself into a position which allowed him to vote 36 percent of the company stock. Later he admitted that even he had been hoodwinked by Drabinsky's bookkeeping shenanigans and that the firm's financial health was worse than he had initially been led to believe. Touring companies of *Ragtime* were shut down, though the New York edition was still doing brisk business. Wall Street analysts figured that if it could continue drawing near-capacity houses and generate extra revenue from touring companies for another five years, it would probably pay off its herculean production costs and start reaping profits.[13] Alas, *Ragtime* failed the longevity test by two or three seasons. A gradual downward spiral in attendance proved fatally uncontrollable. Up went the notice: Following a two-year run, the show would give its final performance on January 16, 2000, losing, according to *Variety*, "much if not all" of its $10 million investment.

What irony: At the end of the century, two Hollywood moguls associated with multi-venue entertainment were competing with each other on the same street in the biggest theatre town in the world! Will Disneyland Square continue turning millions on the sale of trinkets, sweatshirts, souvenir mugs and peanuts?

Will it ever produce a show to thrill grownups? The mega-musical experience offered by the tycoons from London, Burbank and Canada has made it increasingly difficult for any show to succeed. And as long as the alternative to theme park tuners is Brecht or Genet or Sondheim, the public will continue going for Elton John tunes and warm fuzzy animals parading up theatre aisles in Ringling Bros. formation. Only when a new generation of bold assertive composers, lyricists and librettists appear to truly lead the way, will the circuses now flying high over Broadway stages begin to seem a little less compelling and necessary.

Chapter 17

Long Ago and Far Ahead

The passing of Jerome Kern in 1945 was mourned by the entire nation. The composer of *Show Boat*, Kern was only 60 years old when he died, leaving behind a towering canon of popular songs from both film and stage scores with which virtually every American citizen identified.

A special afternoon bicoastal radio tribute to Kern's passing brought to the microphones a number of nationally known singers, including Dinah Shore, Jack Smith, Patrice Munsel and Nelson Eddy. The presence in particular of teen idol Frank Sinatra reflected the timeless appeal of so many wonderful Jerome Kern standards, many of which Sinatra had grown famous singing. Announced Nelson Eddy, introducing the 29-year-old crooner:

"We might have taken more than just this hour and still not have exhausted all of the songs from Mr. Kern's many scores, nor run short of friends who wanted to do honors in their musical way. But those whom we do have here have all chosen their own Kern songs, and so I'm going to ask the young man now standing next to Patrice in New York why he has chosen his particular songs. What about it, Frank Sinatra?"

"Well, Nelson," Sinatra replied, "I'm going to sing 'The Song Is You.' In the first place, it's my favorite among Mr. Kern's songs. And then again, this is a musical tribute to him, and our thanks for his having given us all this wonderful melody. So every time anybody whistles or hums a tune of Jerry's, for me, well, he's not gone. He's in the music, in the song. That's why I've asked to sing 'The Song Is You.'"

Next came the song's lyricist, Oscar Hammerstein II. "Now, before proceeding," he began, "it is with great pride that I read the following telegram from the president of the United States: 'I am among the grateful millions who have played and listened to the music of Jerome Kern, and I wish to be among those of his fellow Americans who pay him tribute today. His melodies surviving will live in

194

our voices and warm our hearts for many years to come. For they are the kind
of simple honest songs that belong to no time or fashion. The man who gave
them to us has earned a lasting place in his nation's memory. Signed, Harry S
Truman.'"[1]

Earlier in the program, Hildegarde sang "The Last Time I Saw Paris"; Dinah
Shore, "Bill"; Jack Smith, "Who." Nelson Eddy chose "All the Things You Are,"
one of the most cherished of Kern's compositions (with words by Hammerstein),
originally written for the musical *Very Warm for May* which lasted all of fifty-nine
performances on Broadway.

For all his melodic gifts, Jerome Kern had faced the same daunting disappointments that have dogged virtually all other composers answering the call of
musical theatre. At the time of his sudden passing, he was in New York overseeing rehearsals for a revival of *Show Boat*, from which surely he drew some solace
and pride, for he had lived infamously through a series of failed ventures in recent
years. Following Kern's death, the never-perfect *Show Boat* once again opened to
generous respect for its immense attributes of melody and spirit. "It is what every
musical should be—and no other has ever been," wrote John Chapman. Declared
Louis Kronenberger, "Our memories didn't lie. *Show Boat* is great stuff.... The
story may be all schmaltz and corn and hokum, full of romantic trappings and
sentimental gestures and melodramatic flourishes. But it is all of a piece, and it
holds our interest."

"*Show Boat* is still magnificent," declared Ward Morehouse. "It was in 1927
and it was in 1932 [when revived], and it always will be. Here's a musical play with
beauty, pathos, nostalgia, panoramic patterns, and a Jerome Kern score that will
endure for as long as the theatre exists."[2]

At the end of the twentieth century, one could inevitably conclude that perfection in musical theatre writing is a rarely obtainable goal. The arguable exceptions, led by *The King and I* and *My Fair Lady*, are miraculously few, indeed. How
many musicals can claim the total mastery of a Rembrandt or Rivera, a Dickin-
son, a Balanchine or Stravinsky? The same enraptured *Show Boat* reviewers who
voted with their hearts also noted weaknesses with their minds. One was Morehouse, qualifying his essential joy: "If the story now runs down and runs somewhat to patness in its final phases, if portions of the narrative now seem a bit
labored and if a few of the present players are not up to the form of their predecessors, those faults are but minor."

"*Show Boat* continues to suffer from its old 'last-act trouble,' as its first producer, Florenz Ziegfeld, used to call it," conceded Robert Garland. "The operetta
still starts a story it never really finishes. From the moment Magnolia and Gaylord are married at the conclusion of the opening stanza, the Mississippi River saga
hides behinds its music and sings its plot around in all directions. A midway, a
music hall, a convent, a boardinghouse, and, at long last, back to the levee again."
Still, Garland granted this fabled musical gem its enduring legacy: "The immortal Jerome Kern score maintains its magical appeal. It was, it is, it always will be
Show Boat's crowning glory."[3]

The same argument could be made against the medium itself—against count-less ill-realized librettos born out of good intentions but rendered either too con-trived or too maudlin, or underwritten, or overwritten, or out of focus, or conceptually obscure, and saved time and again by songs, scenery, clowns and showmanship. The situation remained as perplexing in 1999 as it was back before and after *Show Boat* opened, and clear up through the golden age. Musical stages are littered with those charming juvenile showoffs who simply refuse the efforts of others to dress them up with proper adult attitudes.

Another giant that would continue earning respect for its songs, if not for its originally heralded book, was *Oklahoma*, the show that had pushed the "integrated musical" idea into formidable maturity. When first presented, it won glowing notices. When revived 36 years later, it was both cheered and panned. Howard Kissel complained about the "often dated material." Walter Kerr proposed dia-logue pruning: "The entertainment is now too long, by a good twenty minutes. No one should touch the music, though. All that incredible music."[4] Rarely does anyone dare touch the music. Critical displeasure is almost always aimed at *per-ceived* script shortcomings. The evolution of the book musical from the 1940s for-ward did alleviate to a degree the problem of trivial material, and more shows from the postwar era are brought back successfully than ones from earlier peri-ods. Yet creators still faced the same old problem every time they attempted some-thing new: how to wed music and story with seamless persuasion and force every beat of the way.

During Jerome Kern's day, musicals and popular music were one in the same. No wonder the composer of "Old Man River" and "Smoke Gets in Your Eyes" was so lovingly remembered at his passing. He had been a prime contributor to Amer-ican culture, helping through his music to bring people of all stripes and persua-sions together. And had he lived long enough, Kern likely would have rued the day when rock and roll and the social upheaval of the '60s hastened the splinter-ing apart of the once-homogenous class of Americans who had embraced his songs. Before the rights-obsessed cultural wars of the '60s—and before the advent of cable TV and the Internet—there was, remember, only one Hit Parade, only three major television networks, and a sense among the citizenry of belonging to only one melting pot.

During the radio tribute, after Jack Smith sang "Who," Nelson Eddy com-mented on the song's having been first introduced in *Sunny*, which opened in 1925 at the "old" Amsterdam Theatre, "now a movie house." Nearly half a century later in a parallel twist of fate, the "new" Amsterdam, having been converted back into a legit house by Walt Disney, was playing host to *Beauty and the Beast*, a stage musi-cal adapted from a film. There always is, at the last moment, someone to revital-ize and make new all over again a form of entertainment whose imminent demise has long been predicted.

How long can it survive on these last-minute rescues? The aging pop stars of yesterday—the over-the-hill rockers who may still have some hidden music inside their keyboards—have not done well in their interactions with musical theatre.

The dreary outcome of Paul Simon's hopelessly uncommercial bomb *Capeman* tells the story of the naivete (or arrogance) of a famed songwriter-singer believing that by merely composing a batch of new songs, no matter how questionable the dramatic premise, the whole thing would somehow work because of the lure of his name alone. Perhaps Paul McCartney and others of his ilk sensed the gloomy odds against setting foot in the theatre, where good songs are often wasted on unsalable material, and resisted all offers.

It grows ever more difficult to mount a new work that can bridge all the splintered audience categories in this insanely individualistic land of ours. Just as the major television networks continue to see their audience base erode as more people select from an increasing plethora of cable outlets, so do Broadway producers struggle with the demographics explosion. How to please audiences so dissidently diverse? Evidently, not on sleaze and controversy alone. Take a look at Hollywood: Despite relentless competition from the internet and cable TV, the booming motion picture industry repeatedly finds new ways to restate universal themes— *Titanic's* heroic love story; the quirky, marriage-affirming *My Best Friend's Wedding*; the soaring parental love inherent in *Life Is Beautiful*; the touching relationship of a drifting musician and a deaf mute in Woody Allen's Felliniesque *Sweet and Lowdown*.

And what had the titans of Times Square to offer audiences as a new millennium approached? More strip tease and drag. More lynchings and misogyny, drug overdoses and S&M. More offbeat losers locked in ambivalent distress. While hundreds of new multiplex movie houses went up from sea to sea, Broadway patted itself on the back for being ever so hip, making ticket buyers the unwitting brunt of its self-defeating brilliance. They got *Side Show*. They got *Passion*. They got *The Life* and they got *Parade*. And, if that was not enough, the new century just around the corner promised them two competing new productions of *The Wild Party*, each based on the 1928 poem by Joseph Moncure March about a roaring twenties orgy. The plot concerns Queenie, a sexually active chorus girl with a penchant for extra-rough love, who, called a slut by her misogynist lover, Burrs, gets even by having a party for the purpose of bedding another man in Burrs' face. To this sexual merry-go-round come society's free and fallen spirits, specialists all in debauchery—whores and underage delinquents, free spirits and boxers and scumbags. Lust, mayhem and homicide were promised. And that was the state of the adult American musical theatre at the dawning of the year 2000.

Nonetheless, at century's end, Broadway itself—if not the "musical theatre" according to purists—was not doing shabbily. Long-running hits from the Brits and film-to-stage family amusements from Burbank, California, kept theatres aglow, thanks to the return of half-way hummable tunes and epic tales of romantic consequence that resonated with a broad cross-section of the tourists who purchase most of the tickets. Thanks also to the arrival of golden age shows on return visits, shows whose older sentiments were as acceptable to contemporary crowds as are the quaint comedic charms of *I Love Lucy* reruns or a Frank Capra film.

The future remains tenuous. Where are tomorrow's Broadway babies? Not since the New York premiere in 1991 of *Miss Saigon* had there been a new block-buster import from the West End. And *Cats*, which had been around for 18 years and seen by more than 10 million persons (one of them, 670 times!), was finally slated to close, on June 25, 2000, after 7,397 performances. In 1998, Vincent Canby, lamenting the caustic reception accorded Paul Simon's *Capeman*, took time to survey the overall scene in neighboring playhouses, and he saw a bleak horizon. "To the consternation of the theatre community, it's the Disney Company, the corporate giant whose name is synonymous with faceless clout, that has turned out to be the most eccentric and successful of the new producer entities.... The success of *Lion King* not withstanding, the Broadway musical is no further along now than it was last September, or 10 years ago, when *Phantom of the Opera* opened."[5]

And so they brought on more time-tested shows from out of the past. "Yet another standout season on Broadway for musical revivals!" announced one of the hosts at the Tony Awards telecast on June 6, 1999. This time up, four shows were nominated for Best Revival—*Peter Pan, Little Me, Annie Get Your Gun*, and *You're a Good Man, Charlie Brown*. Of the musical numbers presented from each of the entries, a bright new number for *Charlie Brown*, by Andrew Lippa, the composer of one of the versions of *Wild Party*, provided the sort of polished exuberance the public still enjoyed encountering in a theatre. And of the new musicals up for Tonys, a song performed from Frank Wildhorn's third tuner to make it to Broadway, *Civil War*, strained like a cheesy warm-up number for a Jimmy Swaggart revival.

"No, This Isn't Over," a song of hope performed by the imprisoned hero in *Parade* expressing his reaction to the news of a reprieve, sounded oddly forced and out of place ... and terribly distant in tone from the rousing dance number out of *Fosse*, a high-energy retrospective of the late choreographer's work that landed a Tony for Best New Musical.

And there were more sour notes to come. When the Tony for best director of a musical was bestowed upon British choreographer Matthew Bourne for his staging of Peter Tchaikovsky's "Swan Lake," a few disbelieving gasps were heard. Bourne had won the hearts of New Yorkers with an all-male in-drag cast, and they returned the thrill by dumbfounding him with the Tony honor for his work on a *ballet*, itself ruled ineligible for consideration as Best Musical. Desperation, it's been said, is not pretty. Even less so at the Tonys. "I'm absolutely astonished," confessed the astonished Englishman. "Best director of a musical that's not even a musical!"

From what was hardly even a season. Left unastonished by the bizarre Tony telecast, watched by 28 percent fewer folks than the previous year's, were members of the cast and company of the fourth new tuner nominated for a Tony, *Ain't Nothing But the Blues*. Deprived of their promised prime-time appearance due to unforseen time constraints, they went public with their displeasure, arguing that the exposure would likely have boosted their business, and threatening to file a lawsuit. Dave Letterman, who joked about the abysmally uneventful Tonys ("I fell asleep; did *Hair* get any awards?"), made hay out of the conflict, inviting members from *Ain't* to perform on his late night show.

The last Tony Awards presentation of the century was overwhelmed by the superior glories of better seasons gone by. America's three most honored playwrights, Arthur Miller, Tennessee Williams and Eugene O'Neill, all represented on Broadway that year, were all nominated for Best Revival of a Play. The honor went to Arthur Miller, whose acceptance speech included a plea to producers to take greater risks. Miller also acknowledged the savvy of producers in finding ways to keep a rich canon of shows, both serious and sung, commercially alive. "For the marvelous revivals on Broadway, I know we are all grateful and very proud."

On November 12, 1900, an early British import, *Florodora*, with songs by Leslie Stuart, Paul Rubens and Frank Clement and a book by Owen Hall, opened at the Casino Theatre, where it settled in for a 553 performance run, bettering its London box office. Rivaling Gilbert and Sullivan, the light-hearted charmer, featured the Florodora sextette, ladies who twirled parasols, swept about in their floor-length gowns, and danced with six properly top-hatted partners. All glib garnishment for a story about the maker of Florodora perfume in the Philippines, Cyrus Gilfain, who longs to wed Dolores, the daughter of a man he has wronged. In a 1920 off–Broadway revival, *Florodora* lasted through 150 showings.

On December 6, 1999, at Lincoln Center, the last new musical of the century, *Marie Christine*, opened. It was a retelling of the Medea myth, with music and lyrics by 37-year-old Michael John LaChiusa—according to *Time* magazine's Richard Zoglin, "one of the most acclaimed of the post–Sondheim composers."[6] *Marie* was the tale, set in New Orleans in the 1890s, of a woman of mixed-race Creole parents. Haunted by her white father's rejection, Marie practiced voodoo, on one occasion turning to spaghetti the arms and legs of her maid; on another, casting an erotic spell over a Caucasian sea captain, into whose arms she rapturously slipped, long enough to bear him two children.

Eagerly anticipated by New Yorkers, it received, in Zoglin's estimation, "an extraordinary buildup from the *New York Times*."[7] That paper lavished no fewer than three major features stories on the show during previews, and then, once it opened, agonized over that which it had so passionately hyped, causing its critic, Vincent Canby, to lament a lack of "spontaneity," music that failed to "successfully embrace the primal narrative," and, in total, an evening that left him "simply exhausted and a little confused."[8]

"Just in time for the holidays," reported *Variety*, "another dark and ambitious new musical lumbers onto the stage of the Vivian Beaumont Theatre ... a fatally dispassionate musical about passion run amok ... utterly artless in its story storytelling.... What LaChiusa needs the most is a collaborator with a dramatic vision that can more artfully harness his musical gifts.... That, above all, is the voodoo missing from *Marie Christine*."[9] The reviews were discouragingly mixed; the music, they said, was difficult; and the run was not extended. Within less than a month, *Marie Christine* had closed.

Is the musical theatre dying? Personally, I do not believe it is, for the all-too-obvious reason that songs are not going out of business and doubtlessly never will. Neither will the timeless lure of dramatic story telling. Inevitably, the two will now and then find each other in stageworthy ways that move an audience to empathy and laughter or tears. It all depends, of course, on how effectively tomorrow's composers, lyricists and librettists can merge music with narrative. Some of them, probably only a precious few, will succeed. And their successes will be the stuff of a producer's dream.

The American musical can't go back. That is certain. It can only go forward. And in going forward, may it recover some of the magic lost, the talent misused, and the greater traditions left insecurely behind. Most of all, may it lure tomorrow's finest composers and writers back to the stage.

Discography

This section lists recordings and also "Scores the Scores." Virtually all show scores available in recorded format were reviewed. The following information is provided for each score:

- Title of musical.

- Date first presented on Broadway, followed by number of performances, when available. (OB indicates Off Broadway.)

- 1 to 5 star rating.

- M = composer; L= lyricist.

- One-sentence critique taking into consideration every song reviewed, the overall quality of music and lyrics, and other factors including thematic unity, variety of material, inclusion of comedy numbers, and story relevance. Every effort was made to listen to as many songs as possible, which sometimes necessitated drawing from more than one recording. Only songs known to have reached opening night on Broadway were considered; carefully excluded were any numbers cut out of town or during previews, or added to subsequent productions or film versions of the work. Generally, only scores containing a clear majority of the songs (as of opening night) were considered. The exceptions are treated as follows: In lieu of a starred rating, which for these exceptions is omitted, the number of songs reviewed is listed. These comments on the scores in *recorded format* should not in any way be construed as reviews of the musicals themselves.

- Record label and record number (all are vinyl unless otherwise noted), followed by identity of singing ensemble: OC = original cast; LC = later cast, with date given; SC = studio recording; AC = archival reconstruction.

STARRED RATINGS

★★★★★ Most honored achievement includes some twenty-five scores from over three hundred reviewed.

★★★★ Highly distinguished work.

★★★ Quality score offers definite pleasure.

★★ Serviceable to mediocre; most albums in this category contain a fair number of musical and/or lyrical assets.

★ Not all these shows are turkeys, and many contain at least one or two fine numbers. All, however, are on balance chronically weak.

Ain't Misbehavin' (1978 / 1,604p) ★★★ M: Fats Waller. L: various. Zingiest batch of uptempo numbers since Gershwin days, with raucous humor and second-rate blues ballads. (CD RCA 2965-2-RC OC)

All American (1962 / 80p) ★★★ M: Charles Strouse. L: Lee Adams. Warm graceful tunes and spunky humor, lushly orchestrated in filmland style. (Columbia KOS2160 OC)

Allegro (1947 / 315p) ★★★★ M: Richard Rodgers. L: Oscar Hammerstein II. Finely wrought work referencing simplistic conflict fails to flesh out dramatic implications. (RCA LOC-1099 OC)

Annie (1977 / 2,377p) ★★★★ M: Charles Strouse. L: Martin Charnin. Delightful tour-de-hummer brims with relentless optimism, Depression-era wit, and crackling Broadway pizazz. (Columbia 34712 OC)

Annie Get Your Gun (1946 / 1,147p) ★★★★★ M/L: Irving Berlin. Blockbuster songfest whose captivating on-point lyrics lead the way. (RCA LSO-1124 LC-1966, with Ethel Merman)

Anya (1965 / 16p) ★★★ M/L: Robert Wright and George Forrest adapting themes of Rachmaninoff. Nice lyrics fail to give wonderful music much dramatic specificity. (United Artists UAL4133 OC)

Anyone Can Whistle (1964 / 9p) ★★★ M/L: Stephen Sondheim. Early Sondheim fascinates with unique voice. (Columbia AS32608 OC)

Anything Goes (1934 / 420p) ★★★★★ M/L: Cole Porter. Breathtaking Porter-perfect songwriting on relentless parade. (Epic FLS15100 LC-1962)

Applause (1970 / 896p) ★★ M: Charles Strouse. L: Lee Adams. Enough talent, especially in the lyrics, to make this acceptably mediocre. (ABC-OCS-11 OC)

The Apple Tree (1966 / 463p) ★ M: Jerry Bock. L: Sheldon Harnick. No apples under this one. (Columbia KOL6620 OC)

Arms and the Girl (1950 / 134p) ★★ M: Morton Gould. L: Dorothy Fields. A nice little discovery of tender charms, engaging voices and pleasantly uneven songs. (Columbia reissue of Decca X 14879 OC)

Aspects of Love (1990 / 377p) ★ M: Andrew Lloyd Webber. L: Don Black and Charles Hart. One of the worst scores ever to reach Broadway demonstrates the pitfalls of recitative (sung dialogue) overkill. (Polydor CD 841 126-2)

Assassins (1990 / 30p) ★★★ M/L: Stephen Sondheim. Sondheim's daring artistry on the side of angry losers and outcasts is good for a few savagely subversive turns. (RCA tape 60737-4 RC OC)

At Home Abroad (1935 / 198p) ★★★★ M: Arthur Schwartz. L: Howard Dietz. Witty, worldly, and melodic—second-drawer Schwartz and Dietz sampler is fine enough. (Monmouth-Evergreen)

Babes in Arms (1937 / 289p) ★★★★★ M: Richard Rodgers. L: Lorenz Hart. Rodgers and Hart masterpiece. (Columbia OL7070 SC-Mary Martin)

Babes in Toyland (1903 / 192p) ★★★ M: Victor Herbert. L: Glen MacDonough. Charming old confection evokes the joys of a once-simpler childhood. (Decca DPL7004 SC).

Baby (1984 / 241p) ★★ M: David Shire. L: Richard Maltby, Jr. Babyhood versus therapy in the key of smug, slavishly Sondheim, too much of it still in diapers. (TER1089 OC)

Bajour (1964) ★★ M/L: Walter Marks. Some rousing dance music and bawdy humor can't quite camouflage the insipid lyrics. (Columbia KOS2700 OC)

Baker Street (1965 / 313p) ★ M/L: Martin Grudeff and Raymond Jessel; also, Bock and Harnick. Triteness overcomes wit in overly generic effort. (MGM E7000 OC)

Ballroom (1978 / 116p) ★★★★ M: Billy Goldenberg. L: Alan and Marilyn Bergman. Such wonderful songs, no ballroom was ever better scored or more lyrically understood—even if the drama is late-arriving. (Columbia JS35762 OC)

Bandwagon (1931 / 260p) ★★★★★ M: Arthur Schwartz. L: Howard Dietz. Classic '30s highlight, both lush and jazzful, well supported by articulate lyrics. (RCA/Camden INT.1937 OC)

Barnum (1980 / 854p) ★★★★ M: Cy Coleman. L: Michael Stewart. Dazzling, lyrically clever slice of Americana set rousingly to period music, perfectly in tune with subject matter. (CBS JS36576 OC)

Beauty and the Beast (1994 / still running) ★★★ M: Alan Menken. L: Howard Ashman and Tim Rice. Vibrantly relevant tracks convey affecting little tale in classic musical theatre language. (Walt Disney tape 60861-0 OC)

Beggar's Holiday (1946 / 108p) ★★★ M: Duke Ellington. L: John Latouche. Graphic songs of hopeless ghetto ironies produce an interesting if downbeat listen. (Blue Pear BP1013 AC-cast demo, piano only arrangements)

Bells Are Ringing (1956 / 924p) ★★★ M: Jule Styne. L: Betty Comden and Adolph Green. Sturdy, well constructed work fondly remembered for a pair of pop standards. (Columbia OL5170 OC)

Ben Franklin in Paris (1964 / 215p) ★★★ M: Mark Sandrich, Jr. L: Sidney Michales. A splendid set of warmly engaging songs in the key of romance. (Capitol VAS 2191 OC)

Best Foot Forward (1941 / 326p) ★★★ M/L: Hugh Martin and Ralph Blane. As bright, eager and frivolous as youth itself once was. (Cadence CLP4012 LC-1963, Stage 73)

Best Little Whorehouse in Texas (1978 / 1,584p) ★★ M/L: Carol Hall. Beyond a fresh premise treated with engaging humor in a country and western format, not much melody to enjoy. (MCA-3049 OC)

Big River (1985 / 1,005p) ★★ M/L: Roger Miller. Pleasant to rarely exciting country and western ditties provide authentic atmosphere, if little drama. (MCA-6147 OC)

Blackbirds of 1928 (1928 / 518p) ★★★ M: Jimmy McHugh. L: Dorothy Fields. Rollicking romp high on sass and snap comes with a few tepid blues numbers. (Columbia OL6770 AC)

Bloomer Girl (1944 / 657p) ★★★ M: Harold Arlen. L: E.Y. Harburg. Lush romantic refrains dance frivolously around the central dramatic issues. (Decca DL9126 OC)

Boy Friend (1954 / 485p) ★★★★★ M/L: Sandy Wilson. Exuberant non-stop words, music and rhythm triumph. (RCA LOC-1018 OC)

The Boys from Syracuse (1938 / 235p) ★★★★ M: Richard Rodgers. L: Lorenz Hart. Rodgers tops Hart in high-octane originals. (Capitol TAO1933 LC-1963)

Brigadoon (1947 / 581p) ★★★★ M: Frederick Loewe. L: Alan Jay Lerner. Rhapsodic collaboration conveys Scottish setting with authentic charm. (RCA AYL1-3901(e) OC)

Bring in 'Da Noise, Bring in 'Da Funk (1996 / 1,130p) ★★ M: Daryl Waters, Zane Mark and Ann Duquesnay. L: Reg E. Gaines. The black experience in America from slave ships to evasive taxis—a rare, musically indifferent bird full of its own intriguing dramatic nuances and atmosphere chronicled through tap, percussion, and hip hop. (RCA CD 09026-65565-2)

By Jeeves (1996, Goodspeed) ★★★★ M: Andrew Lloyd Webber. L: Alan Ayckbourn.

Utterly enchanting repertoire of freshly wrought old fashioned type show songs. (Polydor tape 314353 7184-4 OC-London, 1996)

By Jupiter (1942 / 427p) ★★★ M: Richard Rodgers. L: Lorenz Hart. An almost tragic reflection of two giants at the end of their collaborative journey, the result lurches from sheer brilliance to utter banalities, "Careless Rhapsody" being one of the greatest unknown ballads ever written. (RCA LSO-1137 LC-1967)

By the Beautiful Sea (1954 / 270p) ★★★ M: Arthur Schwartz. L: Dorothy Fields. Bright tunes and a couple of fine ballads prevail despite meager lyrics. (Capitol T-11652 OC)

Bye Bye Birdie (1960 / 607p) ★★ M: Charles Strouse. L: Lee Adams. Borderline work nonetheless offers some big payoffs, including early rock songs in a stage show. (Columbia OS2025 OC)

Cabaret (1966 / 1,165p) ★★★ M: John Kander. L: Fred Ebb. Variable words and music skillfully capture glib cynicism and mounting despair in the face of rising Nazi power. (Columbia KOL6640 OC)

Cabin in the Sky (1940 / 156p) ★★★★ M: Vernon Duke. L: John Latouche. From blues to swing to gospel, a modest tour-de-force rich in melody, funk and sentiment nearly ever beat of the way. (Broadway Angel CD 2DM 0777 7 64892 23 OC)

Call Me Madam (1950 / 644p) ★★★★ M/L: Irving Berlin. Zesty, pop-driven powerhouse bristles with sock and levity. (Decca DL9022 SC-Ethel Merman)

Call Me Mister (1946 / 734p) ★★★★ M/L: Harold Rome. Wonderfully honest work captures ambivalent emotions of Americans facing adjustment to life after World War II. (Columbia X14877 reissue of Decca DPL7005 OC)

Camelot (1960 / 873p) ★★★★ M: Frederick Loewe. L: Alan Jay Lerner. Almost too romantic in toto, these excellent songs both animate and smother the rather ponderous tale they serve. (Columbia KOL5620 OC)

Can Can (1953 / 892p) ★★★ M/L: Cole Porter. Moderately appealing work offers occasional flashes of the old Porter passion. (Capitol W452 OC)

Candide (1956 / 73p) ★★★ M: Leonard Bernstein. L: Richard Wilbur; additional by John Latouche and Dorothy Parker. Bernstein excels when spectacularly inventive, falters when merely mimicking old operetta traditions.

Capeman (1998 / 68p) ★ M/L: Paul Simon. If there is a venue for such second- and third-rate songs so persistently undramatic, surely it is not a Broadway stage. ("Songs from the Capeman" Warner CD 46814 SC) (Simon told the Los Angeles Times, October 1, 2000, "the best songs" were not included on this pre–Broadway, non-cast album.)

Carmelina (1979 / 17p) ★★★ M: Burton Lane. L: Alan Jay Lerner. Touching and humorous Italian tale, intimately wrought in fine underrated score, contains a few ready-made standards waiting to be discovered. (Original Cast OC8019 OC)

Carmen Jones (1943 / 502p) ★★ M: George Bizet. L: Oscar Hammerstein II. Sporadically affecting adaptation conveys sensual atmosphere in staid terms. (RCA LM-1881 ST)

Carnival (1961 / 719p) ★★ M/L: Bob Merrill. A pity such charming numbers share the stage with such clinkers. (MGM E39460C OC)

Carousel (1945 / 890p) ★★★★★ M: Richard Rodgers. L: Oscar Hammerstein. Towering craftsmanship and magic wrapped around a dark tale constitutes about as good a score as was ever conceived. (MCA-37093 OC)

Cats (1982 / 7,397p) ★★★ M: Andrew Lloyd Webber. L: T.S. Eliot; additional words by Trevor Nunn. Ingenious musicalization of Eliot's verse, full of mysterious enchantment and old British musical hall charm. (Polydor CATX001 OC-London)

Celebration (1969 / 110p) ★★★ M: Harvey Schmidt. L: Tom Jones. Compelling creativity in modern jazz-oriented songwriting generates fertile excitement. (Capitol SW198 OC)

Chess (1988 / 68p) ★★★ M: Benny Anderson and Bjorn Ulvaeus. L: Tim Rice. Strongly crafted pop-rock tracks of pragmatism pack a chilly existential wallop. (RCA/CAS 7700-4 RC OC)

Chicago (1975 / 923p) ★★★ M: John Kander. L: Fred Ebb. Glibly cynical, the underworld struts in smug guilt-free syncopation and outrageous levity across the boards. (Arista AL9005 OC)

A Chorus Line (1975 / 6,137p) ★★★ M: Marvin Hamlisch. L: Edward Kleban. Average, hardworking numbers soar down the final stretch. (Columbia 33581 OC)

City of Angels (1989 / 878p) ★★★ M: Cy Coleman. L: David Zippel. Winning mixed bag charts a sultry '40s big band agenda. (Columbia C46067 OC)

Coco (1969 / 332p) ★ M: Andre Previn. L: Alan Jay Lerner. One fine ballad and two funny numbers can't save a sadly pathetic collaboration, in which a very average composer brings down a great lyricist. (Paramount PMS-1002 OC)

The Cocoanuts (1925 / 276p) (5 songs heard) M/L: Irving Berlin. A winning set of contemporary songs. (Box Office/JJA 19744 AC)

Company (1970 / 706p) ★★★★★ M/L: Stephen Sondheim. Brilliant ground-breaking achievement evokes the age of ambivalence with unsparing realism. (Columbia OS3550 OC)

Cradle Will Rock (1937 / 14p) ★★★ M/L: Marc Blitzstein. Arresting new song forms, brutally realistic, wasted on a biased anti-business polemic parading as Broadwayized opera. (MGM SE-4289 LC-1964)

Dames at Sea (1968, OB 575p) ★★★ M: Jim Wise. L: George Haimsohn and Robin Miller. Old-fashioned Times Square tunefulness aplenty warms the heart. (Columbia OS3330 OC)

Damn Yankees (1955 / 1,019p) ★★★ M/L: Richard Adler and Jerry Ross. Well crafted, formula-driven songs strong on beat, short on unity. (RCA LOC-1021 OC)

Darling of the Day (1968 / 32p) ★★ M: Jule Styne. L: E.Y. Harburg. Styne and Harburg sustain graceful, witty collaboration for only half the distance. (RCA CD 09026-63334-2)

The Day Before Spring (1945 / 165p) (5 songs heard) M: Frederick Loewe. M: Alan Jay Lerner. Lovely, thoughtful, and perhaps too reflective. (Bagley Revisited PS1337 SC)

A Day in Hollywood, A Night in the Ukraine (1980 / 588p) ★★★ M: Frank Lazarus. L: Dick Vosburgh; additional music and lyrics by Jerry Herman. Incredibly uneven offering, for which all share blame, delivers big wonderful tunes and hilarious verse. (DRG SBL12580 OC)

Dear World (1969 / 132p) ★★★ M/L: Jerry Herman. A plethora of rousing refrains vaguely addresses the intriguing premise. (Columbia ABOS3260 OC)

The Desert Song (1926 / 471p) ★★ M: Sigmund Romberg. L: Otto Harbach, Oscar Hammerstein II and Frank Mandel. Fluttering, mushy operetta too true to staid traditions. (Columbia CL831 SC)

Destry Rides Again (1959 / 472p) ★★★★ M/L: Harold Rome. Excellent, torridly paced songwriting tribute to old West mythology. (Decca DL9075 OC)

Do I Hear a Waltz? (1965 / 220p) ★★★ M: Richard Rodgers. L: Stephen Sondheim. Sharp lyrics, superb music, and nothing much seems to happen. (Columbia KOL6370)

Do Re Mi (1960 / 400p) ★★★ M: Jule Styne. L: Betty Comden and Adolph Green. Typical mixed bag from Styne, Comden and Green offers plenty to enjoy. (RCA LSOD-2002 OC)

Donnybrook (1961 / 68p) ★ M/L: Johnny Burke. Bland lyrics and melodies soon turn good-natured pleasantries to boredom. (Kapp KD-8500-S OC)

Don't Bother Me, I Can't Cope (1972 / 1,065) ★ M/L: Micki Grant. Neither can we with songs like these. (Polydor PD6013 OC)

Dreamgirls (1981 / 1,522p) ★★ M: Henry Krieger. L: Tom Eyen. Tough muscular numbers of contemporary black angst turn redundantly gloomy. (Geffen GHSP2007 OC)

Dubarry Was a Lady (1939 / 408p) (6 songs heard) M/L: Cole Porter. Another winning Porter entry in which he strains to load his lyrics with humor. (Bagley Revisited: Crewe CR 1340; and Columbia OS 2810 SC)

Evita (1979 / 1,567p) ★★★★ M: Andrew Lloyd Webber. L: Tim Rice. Seductive existential pop opera builds like a symphony on Latin rhythms and compelling lyrical honesty. (MCA MCA2-11007 SC-1979)

Fade Out Fade In (1964 / 271p) ★★ M: Jule Styne. L: Betty Comden and Adolph Green. Wonderful opening numbers collapse into lazy let's-get-the-job-done songwriting. (ABC-Paramount ABC-OC-3 OC)

Fanny (1954 / 888p) ★★ M/L: Harold Rome. Long-winded arias fail to achieve dramatic liftoff. (RCA LOC-1015 OC)

The Fantasticks (1960 / still running) ★★★ M: Harvey Schmidt. L: Tom Jones. Historic collaboration wanders a little too sprawlingly from the rhapsodic to the cynical. (MGM SE38720C OC)

Fiddler on the Roof (1964 / 3,242p) ★★★★ M: Jerry Bock. L: Sheldon Harnick. Rhapsodically enchanting—almost to the sagging end. (Columbia SX30742 OC-London)

Finian's Rainbow (1947 / 725p) ★★★★★ M: Burton Lane. L: E.Y. Harburg. From musical theatre heaven, a golden age landmark. (Columbia OS2080 OC)

Fiorello! (1959 / 795p) ★★★★★ M: Jerry Bock. L: Sheldon Harnick. Tough, tender, rousing and relevant gems sparkle with lyrical perfection. (Capitol WAO1321 OC)

First Impressions (1959 / 84p) ★ M/L: Robert Goldman, Glenn Paxton and George Weiss. A perfect partnership features equally dreadful words and music. (Columbia AOS2014 OC)

Flahooley (1951 / 40p) ★★★★ M: Sammy Fain. L: E.Y. Harburg. Joyful collaboration flies high on witty verse and wonderful music before running low on its own unique magic. (Capitol T-11649 OC)

Flora the Red Menace (1965 / 87p) ★★ M: John Kander. L: Fred Ebb. A few early nuggets from a fine new team seeking a voice of its own. (RCA LSO-1111 OC)

Flower Drum Song (1958 / 602p) ★★★★ M: Richard Rodgers. L: Oscar Hammerstein II. Vibrant, well shaded opus evokes the color and conflict of San Francisco's Chinatown at odds with its younger generations. (Columbia OS2009 OC)

Follies (1971 / 522p) ★★★★ M/L: Stephen Sondheim. Fascinating amalgam of old Broadway, '40s blues and Sondheim ambivalence sweeps dreamily across the stage. (Capitol SO-761 OC)

Forty-Second Street (1980 / 3,486p) ★★★★ M: Harry Warren. L: Al Dubin. One blockbuster follows another in this loaded compilation of songs by Warren and Dubin, the deftly clever lyrics a brilliant match for the roof-raising notes of old Broadway. (RCA CBL1-3891 OC)

Funny Face (1927 / 244p) ★★★ M: George Gershwin. L: Ira Gershwin. The Gershwins in very good form. (Monmouth-Evergreen MES7037 AC)

Funny Girl (1964 / 1,348) ★★★ M: Jule Styne. L: Bob Merrill. Nicely crafted numbers recycle appealing showbiz clichés to tell a rather depressing yarn. (Capitol VAS2059 OC)

A Funny Thing Happened on the Way to the Forum (1962 / 964p) ★★★ M/L: Stephen Sondheim. Sondheim's singular young genius is undeniably on the rise in this generally engaging album. (Capitol SWA01717 OC)

Gay Life (1961 / 113p) ★★ M/L Arthur Schwartz and Howard Dietz. The once-prolific collaborators resume in promising style, but run short of inspiration long before an embarrassing reunion runs its ragged course. (Capitol WAO1560 OC)

Gentlemen Prefer Blondes (1949 / 740p) ★★★ M: Jule Styne. L: Leo Robin. Reliably good melodies and delightful verse convey a warm movie-musical feel. (Columbia OL4290 OC)

Gigi (1973 / 103p) ★★★★ M: Frederick Loewe. L: Alan Jay Lerner. Fractured, stillborn stage adaptation of their movie masterpiece supplies two new delights, "The Earth and Other Minor Things" and "Paris Is Paris Again," and one gigantic dud which nearly consumes an entire act, "The Contract." (RCA ABL1-0404 OC)

Girl Crazy (1930 / 272p) ★★★ M: George Gershwin. L: Ira Gershwin. From this bright, breezy outing, the world got "I Got Rhythm" and a few other Gershwin gifts. (Columbia COS2560 SC)

Girl in Pink Tights (1954 / 115p) ★★★ M: Sigmund Romberg; incomplete melodies at time of Romberg's death further developed and completed by orchestrator Don Walker. L: Leo Robin. Amusing blend of old operetta romanticism and contemporary Broadway idioms make this a surprisingly good catch. (Columbia ML4890 OC)

The Girl Who Came to Supper (1963 / 113p) ★ M/L: Noel Coward. A few good numbers lost in a slough of premature achievement. (Columbia KOS2420 OC)

Godspell (1971 / 527p) ★★ M/L: Stephen Schwartz. The Jesus story reduced to feel-goodness by harmless light rock derivations. (Arista ALB6-8304 OC)

Golden Apple (1954 / 173p) ★ M: Jerome Moross. L: John Latouche. From one of the weakest scores ever to reach Broadway came one of the finest songs ever to reach the radio, "Lazy Afternoon." (Elektra EKL-5000 OC)

Golden Boy (1964 / 569p) ★★★ M: Charles Strouse. L: Lee Adams. Strong resilient collaboration tells a difficult story in a likable, pop-centered style. (Capitol SVAS2124 OC)

Golden Rainbow (1968 / 385p) ★★ M/L: Walter Marks. Strong, pulsing songs of theatrical import become redundant in slick jazz-repetitive voice. (RCA/Calendar KOS-1001 OC)

Goldilocks (1958 / 161p) ★★ M: Leroy Anderson. L: John Ford, Walter and Jean Kerr. A few top Anderson tunes distinguish an empty-headed work of reigning unoriginality. (Columbia COS2007 OC)

Goodtime Charley (1975 / 104p) ★★ M: Larry Grossman. L: Hal Hackady. Fine talent evident in the exceptional numbers makes the mediocre outcome doubly disappointing. (RCA ARL1-1011 OC)

Grand Hotel (1989 / 1,018) ★★★★ M/L: Robert Wright and George Forrest; additional M/L: Maury Yeston. Exciting work combines '30s sophistication and modern stage sounds to capture offbeat story with suitable flair. (RCA tape 09026 61327-4 OC)

Grease (1972 / 3,388p) ★★ M/L: Jim Jacobs and Warren Casey. Beguiling sense of humor keeps droll '50s rock and roll numbers on life-support. (MGM 1SE-34 OC)

Greenwillow (1960 / 95p) ★★ M/L: Frank Loesser. For all their lovely intentions, these gentle, sometimes haunting numbers are numbingly similar in virtuous design. (Columbia P13974 OC)

Grind (1985 / 79p) ★★ M: Larry Grossman. L: Ellen Fitzhugh. Promising material fails to mature through narratively weak series of downbeat ruminations. (Polydor 827072-1 Y-1 OC)

Guys and Dolls (1950 / 1,200p) ★★★★★ M/L: Frank Loesser. Loesser captures offbeat subject matter with incisive poetry and humor. (Decca DL9023 OC)

Gypsy (1959 / 702p) ★★★★ M: Jule Styne. L: Stephen Sondheim. Anger, ego and alienation inform anti-romantic songs with raw cold excitement, allowing Mama Rose (Ethel Merman) to triumph while daughter Gypsy Rose Lee remains a faceless stripper. (Columbia OL5420 OC)

Hair (1968 / 1,750p) ★★★ M: Galt MacDermot. L: Gerome Ragni and James Rado.

Funky, funny, even eloquent evocation of '60s hippie culture. (RCA LSO-1150 OC)

Half a Sixpence (1965 / 512p) ★★ M/L: David Heneker. Briskly superficial enterprise stars one charming hit, "If the Rain's Got to Fall." (RCA LSO-1110 OC)

Hallelujah, Baby (1967 / 293p) ★★★ M: Jule Styne. L: Betty Comden and Adolph Green. Stylish and sensual entertainment steers smartly clear of then typical black musical gloom. (Columbia KOS3090 OC)

Happy Hunting (1956 / 412p) ★★★★ M: Harold Karr. L: Matt Dubey. Lively deck of pop-informed numbers charge the quirky proceedings with fresh energy and humor. (RCA LOC-1026 OC)

Happy Time (1968 / 286p) ★★★ M: John Kander. L: Fred Ebb. Vexingly uneven delight steeped in vanishing '50s sentiments. (RCA LSO-1144 OC)

Hazel Flagg (1953 / 190p) ★ M: Jule Styne. L: Bob Hilliard. Recycled swing dressed in threadbare music and words. (RCA CBM1-2207 OC)

Hello, Dolly (1964 / 2,844p) ★★★★ M/L: Jerry Herman; additional songs by Robert Merrill, Charles Strouse and Lee Adams. Big razzmatazz express loaded with melody pushes good will and hoopla to the hilt. (RCA AYL1-3814 OC)

Here's Love (1963 / 338p) ★★ M/L: Meredith Willson. Warm and lyrical, Willson's good nature at holiday time falls modestly short of fulfilling. (Columbia KOL6000 OC)

High Button Shoes (1947 / 727p) ★★★ M: Jule Styne. L: Sammy Cahn. Half wonderful, half forgettable. (RCA LOC-1107 OC)

High Spirits (1964 / 375p) ★★★ M/L: Hugh Martin and Timothy Gray. Cleverly relevant score, by turns romantic and whimsical, rewards the enchanted listener. (ABC-Paramount ABCS-OC-1)

Hit the Deck (1927 / 352p) ★★★ M: Vincent Youmans. L: Clifford Grey, Leo Robin, Irving Caesar. Carelessly realized amusement offers some fine melodies ill-served by lackluster verse. (MGM MCA25033 ST)

House of Flowers (1954 / 165p) ★★ M: Harold Arlen. L: Truman Capote Lazy, lovely refrains, like poetry set earnestly to music, sleep in the shade of the banana drama. (Columbia OL4969 OC)

How to Succeed in Business Without Really Trying (1961 / 1,417p) ★★★★ M/L: Frank Loesser. Very funny, very polished, very Loesser. (RCA LSO-1066 OC)

I Can Get It for You Wholesale (1962 / 300p) ★★ M/L: Harold Rome. And wholesale it is—a disjointed mishmash whose better songs, some inventive, merit respect. (Columbia KOS2180 OC)

I Do! I Do! (1966 / 561p) ★★★★ M: Harvey Schmidt. L: Tom Jones. Rich sentimental collaboration explores the changing moods and faces of a long-lasting
marriage. (RCA LOC-1128 OC)

I Had a Ball (1964 / 199p) ★★ M/L: Jack Lawrence and Stan Freeman. High-energy
blast of '40s-era big band clichés, flashy and fun and agreeably shallow. (Mer-
cury OCM2210 OC)

I Love My Wife (1977 / 872p) ★★★ M: Cy Coleman. L: Michael Stewart. Eclecti-
cally sprawling lineup delivers ample pleasures. (Atlantic SD19107 OC)

I Remember Mama (1979 / 108p) ★★★ M: Richard Rodgers. L: Martin Charnin.
Famed composer's final work is a warm and fuzzy valentine, the generally agreeable tunes bearing paltry lyrical goods. (Polydor 411-827-336-1 Y-1 OC)

Illya, Darling (1967 / 320p) ★ M: Manos Hadjidakis. L: Joe Darion. Swaggering,
flamingo-intense one-note bore. (United Artists UAS9901 OC)

I'm Getting My Act Together and Taking It on the Road (1978 / 1,165p) ★★ M:
Nancy Ford. L: Gretchen Cryer. Laid-back '60s feminist protest and self-dis-
covery, stronger on words than music. (CBS/C SP X14885 OC)

Inside U.S.A. (1948 / 399p) ★★★ M: Arthur Schwartz. L: Howard Dietz. Moderately delightful portrait of mid–American values in the ever-melodious '40s.
(Box Office 19733B AC)

Into the Woods (1987 / 764p) ★★★ M/L: Stephen Sondheim. Out-of-control self-
help musical offers bewildering smorgasbord of radiantly sung ideas, some
hauntingly realized. (RCA 6796-1-RC OC)

Irene (1919 / 670p) ★★★ M: Harry Tierney. L: Joseph McCarthy. Smartly entertaining score for its day merges traditional and pop styles. (Monmouth-Evergreen MES/7057 LC-London)

Irma la Douce (1960 / 524p) ★★★ M: Marguerite Monnot. L: Alexandre Breffort.
Boldly inventive work addresses red-light tale with gritty attitude and ambiance.
(Columbia OL5560 OC)

Jamaica (1957 / 557p) ★★★ M: Harold Arlen. L: E.Y. Harburg. Generously stocked
mixed bag is strong on sensual poetry, listlessly weak on labored anti-consumer
satire. (RCA LOC-1036 OC)

Jekyll and Hyde (1997, still running) ★★★ M: Frank Wildhorn. L: Leslie Bricusse.
Bizarre tale compellingly told with direct melodic force and lyrical flair. (Atlantic
tape 82976-4 OC)

Jelly's Last Jam (1992 / 569p) ★★★ M: Jelly Roll Morton; additional music by
Luther Henderson. L: Susan Birkenhead. Designed to showcase the music and
life of jazz man Jelly Roll Morton, who shunned his own race, this jumping black

revue sustains a red hot pulse with grizzle, humor and cool sophistication. (Polygram CD 314510846-2 OC)

Jesus Christ Superstar (1971 / 711p) ★ ★ ★ M: Andrew Lloyd Webber. L: Tim Rice. Remarkable rock opera, stylishly spare, builds to harrowing climax. (MCA DL7-1503 OC)

Jimmy (1969 / 84p) ★ M/L: Bill and Patti Jacob. A few affecting ballads offer scarce relief from overactive, cliché-intense outing. (RCA OSO-1162 OC)

Joseph and the Amazing Technicolor Dreamcoat (1981 / 757p) ★ ★ ★ M: Andrew Lloyd Webber. L: Tim Rice. Agreeably eclectic numbers, full of graceful light-rock melodies and hip lyrics, embrace the soul. (MCA-399 SC)

A Joyful Noise (1966 / 12p) ★ ★ M/L: Oscar Brand and Paul Nassau. A joyful beginning—show songs enriched with folk influences—before losing luster in literal pursuit of real Nashville sounds. (Blue Pear BP1018/bootleg live audio from theatre sound system OC)

Jumbo (1935 / 233p) (5 songs heard) M: Richard Rodgers. L: Lorenz Hart. Top drawer Rodgers and Hart.

Juno (1959 / 16p) ★ M/L: Marc Blitzstein. Rarely do the numbers transcend a slavish unmelodic devotion to simple Irish folk tunes. (Columbia OS2013 OC)

Kean (1961 / 92p) ★ ★ M/L: Robert Wright and George Forrest. Morosely heavy-handed retro operetta frames some lovely melodies and rousing choruses in a claustrophobic context. (Columbia KOL5720 OC)

The King and I (1951 / 1,246p) ★ ★ ★ ★ ★ M: Richard Rodgers. L: Oscar Hammerstein II. Tightly integrated songs of quiet, painful enchantment adhere brilliantly to overriding theme of love forbidden or unexpressed. (Decca DL9008 OC)

Kismet (1953 / 583p) ★ ★ ★ ★ M: Alexander Borodin. L: (adapting) Robert Wright and George Forrest. Exotic tale set in Baghdad, gloriously evoked through fine lyric adaptations of the Borodin melodies. (Columbia ML4850 OC)

Kiss Me Kate (1948 / 1,077p) ★ ★ ★ ★ M/L: Cole Porter. Top drawer Porter only lacks his clever comedic hand. Columbia WS32609 OC)

Kiss of the Spider Woman (1993 / 906p) ★ ★ M: John Kander. L: Fred Ebb. Downbeat premise of limited dramatic scope reaps plodding, undisciplined work more sullen than seductive. (RCA 09026 61579-4 OC)

Knickerbocker Holiday (1938 / 168p) ★ M: Kurt Weill. L: Maxwell Anderson. From the show that gave the world "September Song," a tepid mishmash of operetta and pre–'40s romanticism set to vacuous verse—on an album consisting largely of plodding dialogue scenes. (AEI 1148 OC)

Kwamina (1961 / 32p) ★ M/L: Richard Adler. Adler, without Ross, stumbles onto a few decent tunes down the final stretch for which he can't, unfortunately, find the words. (Capitol W1645 OC)

La Cage aux Folles (1983 / 1,761p) ★★★★★ M/L: Jerry Herman. Courageous, life-affirming story inspires Herman's finest score. (RCA HBC-1-4824 OC)

Lady Be Good (1924 / 330p) ★★★ M: George Gershwin. L: Ira Gershwin and others. A modest handful of Gershwin & Gershwin delights. (Smithsonian P 14271 AC)

Lady in the Dark (1941 / 467p) ★★ M: Kurt Weill. L: Ira Gershwin. Variable music and passable lyrics only skim the intriguing premise. (Columbia COS2390 SC)

Last Sweet Days of Isaac (1970 / OB) ★★ M: Nancy Ford. L: Gretchen Cryer. Some pleasant '60s rock songs, now and then enlivened by inventive ideas and affecting music. (RCA LSO-1169 OC)

Leader of the Pack (1985) ★★ M/L: Ellie Greenwich "and friends." Likably fun numbers of pre-hippie innocence form a limited one-note revue. (Elektra 9 60420-1 OC)

Leave It to Jane (1917 / 167p) ★★★★ M: Jerome Kern. L: P.G. Wodehouse. Wonderfully upbeat; the zesty melodies are superior, the amusing lyrics distinguished. (Stet dS15002 LC)

Leave It to Me! (1938 / 291p) (6 songs heard) M/L: Cole Porter. Sounds like a top drawer Porter party. (Smithsonian P14944 AC; Bagley Revisited, Crewe CR 1340 SC; and Columbia OS 2810 SC)

Les Misérables (1987, still running) ★★ M: Claude-Michel Schonberg. L: Herbert Kretzmer (from original French text by Alain Boublil and Jean-Marc Natel). Deceptively simple numbers carved from primary colors, old operetta style, effectively convey revolutionary struggles of French underclass. (Geffen[cas] M5624151 OC)

Let 'Em Eat Cake (1933 / 90p) ★★ M: George Gershwin. L: Ira Gershwin. Some glorious show tunes soar over and around proficiently wordy lyrics and silly satire in a vastly meandering opus. (CBS SM42639 LC)

Let It Ride! (1961 / 68p) ★ M/L: Jay Livingston and Ray Evans. Lots of spirit, lots of comedy, little music. (RCA LSO-1064 OC)

Let's Face It (1941 / 547p) (7 songs heard) M/L: Cole Porter. Sporadic Porter brilliance in pleasing context. (Smithsonian P14944 AC)

The Life (1997 / 465p) ★★★ M: Cy Coleman. L: Ira Gasman. Clever, candid refrains daringly mine the grizzly underside of old Times Square prostitution, pre–Disney. (Sony tape ST 63312 OC)

Li'l Abner (1956 / 693p) ★★★ M: Gene De Paul. L: Johnny Mercer. Dandy little package combines sentiment and satire. (Columbia OL5150 OC)

The Lion King (1997, still running) ★★ M: Elton John. L: Tim Rice; additional songs by Lebo M, Mark Mancina, Jay Rifkin, Julie Taymor, Hans Zimmer. Fairly humdrum hodgepodge stays synthetically fresh with ersatz African chants, jungle drums, exotic laments and, best of all, retro '60s rock. (Walt Disney tape 60802-0 OC)

Little Mary Sunshine (1959, OB 1,143p) ★★ M/L: Rick Besoyan. The better numbers in this harmless little intermittently amusing parody recall the early Jerome Kern bounce. (Capitol WAO1240 OC)

Little Me (1962 / 275p) ★★★ M: Cy Coleman. L: Carolyn Lee. Engaging parade of songs both intimate and theatrical. (RCA LOC-1078 OC)

A Little Night Music (1973 / 600p) ★★★★ M/L: Stephen Sondheim. Richly relevant score, all in 4/4 time, captures jaded European upper class romanticism. (Columbia KS32265 OC)

Little Shop of Horrors (1982 / 2,209p) ★★★ M: Alan Menken. L: Howard Ashman. Brilliant, witty lyrics wryly served by funky '50s-'60s light rock tunes. (Geffen GHSP2020 OC)

The Littlest Revue (1956 / 32p) ★★ M/L: "mostly by" Vernon Duke and Ogden Nash; also by John Latouche, Sheldon Harnick, Lee Adams, Charles Strouse, John Strauss, Sidney Shaw, Sammy Cahn and Michael Brown. Thank mostly to Duke and Nash for the major moments in a minor offering. (Epic LN3275 OC)

Look Ma, I'm Dancin'! (1948 / 188p) ★★ M/L: Hugh Martin. A pair of gems from the gifted Martin, the rest routine. (Columbia reissue of Decca X 14879 OC)

Lost in the Stars (1949 / 273p) ★★ M: Kurt Weill. L: Maxwell Anderson. Stridently religious argument in simplistic free-form verse and ponderous music. (Decca DL79120 OC)

Louisiana Purchase (1940 / 444p) ★★ M/L: Irving Berlin. Moderately appealing, lyrically forgettable sellout to pop trends of the day. (Box Office JJA19746 AC)

Love Life (1948 / 252p) (5 songs heard) M: Kurt Weill. M: Alan Jay Lerner. First draft forgettable. (Bagley Revisited PS1337 SC)

Mack and Mabel (1974 / 65p) ★★★ M/L: Jerry Herman. Rousing, rollicking Herman songfest short on lyrical relief. (ABC ABCH830 OC)

Make a Wish (1951 / 102p) ★★★ M/L: Hugh Martin. Glorious catalog of uptempo delights borders on excess. (RCA LOC1002 OC)

Mame (1966 / 1,508p) ★★★ M/L: Jerry Herman. More stirring feel-good numbers and a pair of nice ballads from the master of rouse. (Columbia KOL6600 OC)

Man of La Mancha (1965 / 2,328p) ★★★ M: Mitch Leigh. L: Joe Darion. Sufficient soaring melody and idealism carry the spotty ingredients. (Kapp KRS-5505 OC)

March of the Falsettos (1981, OB 128p) ★★ M/L: William Finn. The notes don't sing as well as the words in a sporadically interesting, overly cerebral work. (DRG SBL12581 OC)

Marie Christine (1999 / 44p) ★ M/L: Michael John LaChuisa. Straining for operatic lyricism, this rarely melodic exercise flounders in narrative minutiae before bringing down a sad, embarrassing curtain on the last musical to open on Broadway during the twentieth century. (RCA CD 09026-63593-2 OC)

Me and Juliet (1953 / 358p) ★★★ M: Richard Rodgers. L: Oscar Hammerstein II. Five excellent numbers give this pleasantly underdeveloped work a certain definite pleasure. (RCA LSO-1098(e) OC)

Me and My Girl (1986 / 1,412p) ★★★★ M: Noel Gay. L: Noel Gay, L. Arthur Rose and Douglas Furber. Utterly delightful revised version of 1936 British musical, with additional Gay tunes from the era, bubbles with melodious charm, its interpolated "Leaning on a Lamppost" nearly as enchanting as Gene Kelly's classic movie-musical number, "Singing in the Rain." (MCA-6196 OC)

The Me Nobody Knows (1970 / 385p) ★★★ M: Gary William Friedman. L: Will Holt. Fresh, thoughtful songs in tender, melodically affecting early '70s rock vein. (Atlantic SD1566 OC)

Merrily We Roll Along (1981 / 16p) ★★★ M/L: Stephen Sondheim. As exciting and alienated as the stereotypical Hollywood it ridicules. (RCA CBL1-4197)

Merry Widow (1907 / 416p) ★★★ M: Franz Lehar. L(English): Adrian Ross. Grand, sweeping, floridly eclectic and long-winded at times. (Capitol CL838 SC)

Mexican Hayride (1944 / 481p) ★★★ M/L: Cole Porter. From major to modest Porter, a spirited, fun-filled diversion. (CBS release of Decca DL5232 OC)

Milk and Honey (1961 / 543p) ★★★★ M/L: Jerry Herman. Exhilarating, deeply wrought work. (RCA LSO-1065 OC)

Minnie's Boys (1970 / 76p) ★★★★ M: Larry Grossman. L: Hal Hackady. Fine, fine opus includes fabulous comedy numbers and stirring anthems. (Project 3 TS6002SD OC)

Miss Liberty (1949 / 308p) ★★★ M/L: Irving Berlin. A frustratingly uneven listen—the good songs are so good. (Columbia AOL4220 OC)

Miss Saigon (1991 / 4,078p) ★★★★ M: Claude-Michel Schonberg. L: Alain Boublil, adapted by Richard Maltby, Jr. Impressive, powerfully wrought refrains, sensitive every step of the way to the unfolding drama, comprise the most dramatically compelling work since *West Side Story*. (Geffen GHS24271 OC-London)

Mr. President (1962 / 265p) ⋆ M/L: Irving Berlin. Nearly dead on arrival, though a few good chords animate the corpse. (Columbia KOL 5870 OC)

Mr. Wonderful (1956 / 383p) ⋆⋆ M/L: Jerry Bock, Larry Holofcener and George Weiss. Pleasant mediocre hodgepodge offers hit and miss fun, some laughs, a beat, possibly the first real rock and roll ditty in a Broadway show, likable voices and three decent hit parade contenders. (Decca DL9032 OC)

Most Happy Fella (1956 / 676p) ⋆⋆⋆⋆ M/L: Frank Loesser. Plethora of lovely atmospheric numbers create haunting tone-poem operetta, sans musical comedy. (Columbia OL5118 OC)

The Music Man (1957 / 1,375p) ⋆⋆⋆ M/L: Meredith Willson. Affectionate, tuneful postcard from small-town America at turn of the century charmed by a traveling salesman. (Capitol WA/0990 OC)

My Fair Lady (1956 / 2,717p) ⋆⋆⋆⋆⋆ M: Frederick Loewe. L: Alan Jay Lerner. Brilliantly integrated score whose witty verse and elegant tunes serve the story with impeccable taste and integrity. (Columbia AOL5090 OC)

The Mystery of Edwin Drood (1985 / 608p) ⋆⋆ M/L: Rupert Holmes. Crowded, cumbersome score too wordy for its own good sails downhill after boffo beginning. (Polydor 827 969-1 Y-1 OC)

Naughty Marietta (1910 / 136p) ⋆⋆ M: Victor Herbert. L: Rida Johnson Young. Lushly sentimental, the pleasant sum is less than its parts. (Capitol T551 SC)

New Faces of '52 (1952 / 365p) ⋆⋆⋆⋆⋆ M/L: Ronny Graham, Sheldon Harnick, Arthur Siegel, June Carroll, Michael Brown. Murray Grand, E. Boyd, P. De Vries, H. Farjeon, F. Lemarque. Fresh wonderful numbers wisely cover the many twists and turns of love with wry forgiving innocence. (RCA LOC-1008 OC)

New Faces of '56 (1956 / 220p) ⋆⋆⋆ M/L: "mostly by" Ronny Graham, Marshall Barer, June Carroll, Arthur Siegel, Dean Fuller, Murray Grand, Matt Dubey, Harold Karr, Irvin Graham, Paul Nassau, John Rox and Michael Brown. Another suave blend of romance, sophistication and hilarity (including five knock-out comedy numbers) from producer Leonard Sillman. (RCA LOC-1025 OC)

New Faces of '68 (1968 / 52p) ⋆⋆⋆ M/L: Ronny Graham, June Carroll, Arthur Siegel, Clark Gesner, Sam Pottle, David Axelrod, Jerry Powell, David Shire, Richard Maltby, Jr., Murray Grand, Paul Nassau, Hal Hackady, Alonzo Levister, Kenny Solms, Gail Parent, Gene P. Bissell, Carl Friberg, Fred Hellerman, Fran Minkoff, Michael McWhinney, Michael Cohen, Tony Geiss, Sidney Shaw.

Marvelous potpourri of comedy gems, possibly the most ever contained in a single show, spoof the subversive do-your-own-thing '60s. (Warner BS255/OC)

New Girl in Town (1957 / 431p) ★★★ M/L: Bob Merrill. Quietly winsome numbers underscore the sad, quirky tale of a prostitute finding true love outside the brothel. (RCA LOC-1027 OC)

New Moon (1928 / 509p) ★★★ M: Sigmund Romberg. L: Oscar Hammerstein II. A durable workhorse in the older, stiffer tradition, top-heavy with brooding ballads. (Monmouth-Evergreen MES/7051 AC)

Nine (1982 / 739p) ★★ M/L: Maury Yeston. Dreadful lyrics sabotage some excellent music. (CBS JS38325 OC)

No, No, Nanette (1925 / 321p) ★★★★ M: Vincent Youmans. L: Frank Mandel, Otto Harbach, Irving Caesar. Old Broadway charmer overflows with fundamental melodies and emotions. (Stanyan SR16035 OC-London and Columbia S30563 LC-1971)

No Strings (1962 / 580p) ★★★ M/L: Richard Rodgers. Slick package features nice Richard Rodgers melodies skimpily attired in the composer's own simpleminded words. (Capitol SO1695 OC)

Of Thee I Sing (1931 / 441p) ★★★ M: George Gershwin. L: Ira Gershwin. George's music bolts undeniably ahead despite so-so verse and inflated satire from brother Ira. (Capitol T-11651 LC-1952)

Oh, Calcutta! (1969 / 1,314) ★★★ M/L: The Open Window's Peter Schickele, Stanley Walden, and Robert Dennis. Surprisingly diversified work, expertly fashioned, supplies every sort of pleasure from old Broadway to Richard Rodgers to the Doors and Santana. (Aidart AID 9903 OC)

Oh, Captain! (1958 / 192p) ★ M:/L: Jay Livingston and Ray Evans. A few friendly choruses and a few funny lyrics can't overcome tired patchwork mediocrity. (Columbia OL5280 OC)

Oh, Kay! (1926 / 256p) ★★★★★ M: George Gershwin. L: Ira Gershwin and Howard Dietz. Finger-snapping, ballad-soaring George Gershwin at his popular Broadway best. (Columbia CL1050 SC)

Oklahoma! (1943 / 2,248p) ★★★★★ M: Richard Rodgers. L: Oscar Hammerstein II. Astonishing use of music and poetry to convey setting, character and conflict. (MCA-2030 OC)

Oliver! (1963 / 774p) ★★★★ M/L: Lionel Bart. Hard-working integrated score embraces subject matter with admirable fidelity and inspiration. (RCA LOCD-2004)

On a Clear Day You Can See Forever (1965 / 280p) ★★★★★ M: Burton Lane. L:

012

3

Alan Jay Lerner. Blockbuster collaboration mines reincarnation theme for outstanding results. (RCA LOCD-2006 OC)

On the Town (1944 / 463p) ★★★★★ M: Leonard Bernstein. L: Betty Comden and Adolph Green. Inspired collaboration merges humor and lyricism to capture quirky New York City night life during the war years. (Columbia OL5540 OC)

On the Twentieth Century (1978 / 449p) ★ M: Cy Coleman. L: Betty Comden and Adolph Green. Amazingly awful. (Columbia 35330 OC)

On Your Toes (1936 / 315p) ★★★★ M: Richard Rodgers. L: Lorenz Hart. Second-drawer Rodgers and Hart is plenty fine at that, just a bit quieter. (Columbia COS2590 SC)

Once on This Island (1990 / 469p) ★ M: Stephen Flaherty. L: Lynn Ahrens. Among the earnest offerings, a few take passionate flight. (RCA CD 60595-2-RC OC)

Once Upon a Mattress (1959 / 460p) ★ M: Mary Rodgers. L: Marshall Barer. Composer Mary Rodgers, daughter of famed Richard, shows fleeting moments of promise in a pervasively undistinguished effort stood up by vacant by-the-number lyrics. The best tune, "Spanish Panic," goes it instrumentally alone. (Kapp KDL-7004 OC)

110 in the Shade (1963 / 330p) ★★★★ M: Harvey Schmidt. L: Tom Jones. Strong, straightforward songs, lyrically unified, vividly convey taut dramatic premise of spinster aching for love. (RCA LSO-1085 OC)

One Touch of Venus (1943 / 567p) ★★★ M: Kurt Weill. L: Ogden Nash. Its most remarkable numbers crown a fascinating tale with enchantment and wit. (Decca DL9122 SC-Mary Martin; and bootleg of five additional unrecorded songs.)

Out of This World (1950 / 157p) ★★★★ M/L: Cole Porter. Racy, brassy romp loaded with Porter's fascinating gifts. (Columbia CML4390 OC)

Pacific Overtures (1976 / 193p) ★★★★ M/L: Stephen Sondheim. A brilliant sung essay, devoid of empathetic characters or community, about Westernization of Japan. (RCA ARL1-1367 OC)

Paint Your Wagon (1951 / 289p) ★★★★ M: Frederick Loewe. L: Alan Jay Lerner. Stirringly good recreation of the old west during gold rush days, laden with the romance and lore of those turbulent times. (RCA LOC-1006 OC)

Pajama Game (1954 / 1,063p) ★★★★ M/L: Richard Adler and Jerry Ross. Refreshing blend of theatre and pop songwriting paces the story with rare energy and humor. (Columbia OL4840 OC)

Pal Joey (1940 / 374p) ★★★★★ M: Richard Rodgers. L: Lorenz Hart. In a class all its own: a rueful witty portrait about a gigolo's nightclub dreams and affairs, told by two musical theatre giants in top form. (Columbia ML54364 SC)

Parade (1998 / 84p) ★★ M/L: Jason Robert Brown. Plenty of sensitive numbers, full of promising talent, spiral off into somber overkill, calling more attention to themselves than to the grim tale they were meant to serve. (RCA CD 09026-63378-2 OC)

Passion (1994 / 280p) ★★ M/L: Stephen Sondheim. Achingly romantic yarn, stretched thin by maudlin, repetitiously philosophical treatment. (Angel tape 4dQ 7243555251 OC)

Peter Pan (1954 / 149p) ★★ M: Mark Charlap and Jule Styne. L: Carolyn Leigh, Betty Comden and Adolph Green. More manufactured than inspired, the serviceable ditties seem stunted by the questionable premise that children do not want to grow up. (RCA LSO-1019(e) OC)

The Phantom of the Opera (1988, still running) ★★★★★ M: Andrew Lloyd Webber. L: Charles Hart; additional lyrics, Richard Stilgoe. Undeniably thrilling music destined to last the ages, combined with deft lyrics, lifts sad, bizarre tale to light-opera rapture. (Polygram 831273-1 Y-2 OC-London)

Pins and Needles (1937 / 1,108p) ★★★ M/L: Harold Rome. Reliably cheerful opus intimately in tune with the story of striking garment workers. (Columbia OL5810 SC)

Pipe Dream (1955 / 246p) ★★★★ M: Richard Rodgers. L: Oscar Hammerstein II. Fascinating music and colorful lyrics create a vivid sense of place, while failing to flesh out brothel activities at the heart of implicitly daring across-the-tracks tale. (RCA LOC-1023 OC)

Pippin (1972 / 1,944p) ★★ M/L: Stephen Schwartz. Pleasant light-rock originals, more thoughtful than forceful. (Motown 5243ML OC)

Plain and Fancy (1955 / 461p) ★★★ M: Albert Hague. L: Arnold Horwitt. A warm romantic spirit and gracefully amusing verse merge in satisfying balance. (Capitol S603 OC)

Porgy and Bess (1935 / 124p) ★★★★ M: George Gershwin. L: Ira Gershwin and Dubose Heyward. Sad, dreary tale transformed by the power of Gershwin's finest arias. (Columbia OL5410 ST)

Promenade (1969, OB) ★★ M: Al Carmines. L: Maria Irene Fornes. More Brecht on Broadway, wickedly satiric numbers sing themselves into predictable social protest and dumb self-pity. (RCA LSO-1161 OC)

Promises, Promises (1968 / 1,281p) ★★★★ M: Burt Bacharach. L: Hal David. Exciting set of hard-edged originals from pop masters of the day address amoral tale of extramarital affairs with sizzling sophistication. (United Artists UAS 9902 OC)

Pump Boys and Dinettes (1982) ★ M/L: John Schimmel, Cass Morgan, Jim Wann,

Debra Monk, John Foley and Mark Hardwick. Fine fresh lyrics get little lift from yawningly undramatic C&W tunes. (CBS 37790 OC)

Purlie (1970 / 688p) ★ M: Gary Geld. L: Peter Udell. Naggingly unoriginal work recycles blues and gospel idioms to tiresome degree. (Ampex A40101 OC)

Ragtime (1998, 861p) ★★ M: Stephen Flaherty. L: Lynn Ahrens. Synthetic refrains dance high on ragtime appropriations, stumble simple-mindedly over preachy red-white-and-blue anthems. (RCA CD 09026-68629-2. pre-Broadway cast)

Raisin (1973 / 847p) ★ M: Judd Woldin. L: Robert Brittan. Oppressive dabbling in African and blues rhythms up a long slow road to one big number. (Columbia KS32754 OC)

Red, Hot and Blue (1936 / 183p) (6 songs heard) M/L: Cole Porter. Mostly top drawer Porter to cheer about. (Smithsonian R016 AC and Bagley CR1340 SC)

Red Mill (1906 / 274p) ★★★ M: Victor Herbert. L: Henry Blossom. Stolidly crafted old songs, tangy and agreeable. (Capitol T551 SC)

Redhead (1959 / 455p) ★★ M: Albert Hague. L: Dorothy Fields. Irritatingly inconsistent, yet its best offerings cannot be denied. (RCA LOC-1048 OC)

Rent (1996 / still running) ★★ M/L: Jonathan Larson. Erratically fine but overloaded rock concert about struggling young East Village artists on the cusp of adulthood who specialize in good looks, free love and free rent. (CD Dreamworks DRMD2-50003 OC)

Rex (1976 / 48p) ★ M: Richard Rodgers. L: Sheldon Harnick. Remarkable how Rodgers gave lovely singing voice to a few bankrupt lyrics. (RCA ABL1-1683 OC)

The Rink (1984 / 204p) ★★★ M: John Kander. L: Fred Ebb. Character and place come vividly alive through variable entries, some nicely inventive. (Polydor 823 125-1 Y-1 OC)

Roar of the Greasepaint, Smell of the Crowd (1965 / 232p) ★★★★ M/L: Leslie Bricusse and Anthony Newley. Bundle of theatrical charmers high on melody, pizazz and life-affirming rhetoric. (RCA LSO-1109 OC)

Roberta (1933 / 295p) ★★ M: Jerome Kern. L: Otto Harbach. A monotonous rueful loveliness soon sets in, not offset by uneventful verse or the momentarily epic "Yesterdays." (Columbia COS2530 SC)

Rose Marie (1924 / 557p) ★★ M: Rudolf Friml and Herbert Stothart. L: Otto Harbach and Oscar Hammerstein II. Excessive prettiness wears thin. (RCA Lop-1001 SC)

The Rothschilds (1970 / 505p) ★ M: Jerry Bock. L: Sheldon Harnick. Bock and Harnick end a wildly inconsistent 12-year collaboration on a somewhat barren note. (Columbia S30337 OC)

Sail Away (1961 / 167p) ★★★ M/L: Noel Coward. Glib, bright, ruefully sentimental work worthy of solid respect. (Stanyan SR10027 OC-London)

St. Louis Woman (1946 / 113p) ★★★★ M: Harold Arlen. M: Johnny Mercer. Ambitiously sensual work contains a handful of jewels. (Capitol DW2742 OC)

Sally (1920 / 570p) ★★★★ M: Jerome Kern. L: P.G. Wodehouse, B.G. DeSylva, Clifford Grey, Anne Caldwell. Ingratiating chords aplenty weave an enchanting spell. (Monmouth-Evergreen MES7053 OC-London)

Salvation (1969 / OB) ★★★ M/L: Peter Link and C.C. Courtney. Full of youthful passion, a well-realized rock score noteworthy for its atypically positive attitudes. (Capitol SO-337 OC)

Saratoga (1959 / 80p) ★★★ M: Harold Arlen. L: Johnny Mercer. Captivating uptempo charmers make for a fine listen. (RCA LSO-1051)

Say Darling (1958 / 332p) ★ M/L: Jule Styne, Betty Comden and Adolph Green. Say "no" to humdrum verse set to bland melodies rooted in square dance, big band swing, church hymns and a Patty Page waltz, all adding down to generic light. (RCA LOC-1045 OC)

Scarlet Pimpernel (1997 / 772p) ★★★ M: Frank Wildhorn. L: Nan Knighton. Memorable if redundantly romantic work thrills with swashbuckling choruses and haunting ballads. (Broadway Angel CD CDC7543972; highlights, pre–Broadway)

Secret Garden (1991 / 706p) ★ M: Lucy Simon. L: Marsha Norman. Bundle of marginally appealing folk tunes fall short of scoredom. (Columbia tape CT48817 OC)

Seesaw (1973 / 296p) ★★★ M: Cy Coleman. L: Dorothy Fields. High-voltage, dazzlingly orchestrated music rich in syncopation, weak on unity and lyrical support. (CSPI/CBS X15563 OC)

1776 (1969 / 1,217p) ★★ M/L: Sherman Edwards. Authentic, serviceably engaging numbers more introspective than theatrical. (Columbia BOS3310 OC)

Seventh Heaven (1955 / 44p) ★★★ M: Victor Young. L: Stella Unger. Dogged by first-side weaknesses, otherwise ultra uplifting outing delivers pure '50s Broadway magic. (Decca OC)

70 Girls 70 (1971 / 35p) ★★★ M: John Kander. L: Fred Ebb. The big toe-tapping charmers at the head of the parade carry a spotty enterprise successfully forward. (Columbia S30589 OC)

She Loves Me (1963 / 320p) ★★★★ M: Jerry Bock. L: Sheldon Harnick. Exquisitely detailed songs etch out a lovely little romantic tale with unforgettable enchantment. (MGM E41180C-2 OC)

Shenandoah (1975 / 1,050p) ★★ M: Gary Geld. L: Peter Udell. Quietly enchanting work portrays Southern resistance to impending Civil War with more poetry than drama. (RCA ARL1-1019 OC)

Show Boat (1927 / 575p) ★★★★★ M: Jerome Kern. L: Oscar Hammerstein II. A feast of melodic riches rooted in America's two greatest themes—race and show business. (RCA AUM1-1741 AC)

Shuffle Along (1921 / 484p) ★★★ M: Eubie Blake. L: Noble Sissle and others. Loaded with gutsy, foot-tapping gems. (Heard from *Eubie!*, Warner HS 3267 LC-revue, 1978)

Sideshow (1997 / approx. 91p) ★★ M: Henry Krieger. L: Bill Russell. Sensitive on-target lyrics compel interest, although the variable music veers between stock show tunes and floridly overwrought ballads. (Sony tape ST60258 OC)

Silk Stockings (1955 / 478p) ★★★★ M/L: Cole Porter. Amply Porter, amply wonderful. (RCA CBM1-2208 OC)

Skyscraper (1965 / 241p) ★ M: James Van Heusen. L: Sammy Cahn. Two good songs, the rest not. (Capitol SVAS2422 OC)

Something for the Boys (1943 / 422p) ★★★ M/L: Cole Porter. Atypically schmaltzy offering from bon vivant composer warms the heart. (AEI 1157 AC)

Song of Norway (1944 / 860p) ★★ M: Edvard Grieg. L: Robert Wright and George Forrest. Evidently the late Grieg, whose music was here adapted, was good for but half an album. (Decca DL9019 OC)

Sophie (1963 / 8p) ★ M/L: Steve Allen. Slick superficial contrivance, not without a few shining refrains though oddly devoid of the composer's expected humor, at least proves that he was, indeed, something more than a one-song songwriter. (AEI 1130 OC)

The Sound of Music (1959 / 1,433) ★★★★ M: Richard Rodgers. L: Oscar Hammerstein II. Another high-flying collaboration from the masters, however biased in the affirmative, affirms their gut-grabbing showmanship to the very end. (Columbia KOL5450 OC)

South Pacific (1949 / 1,925p) ★★★★★ M: Richard Rodgers. L: Oscar Hammerstein II. Breathtaking craftsmanship and magic from a collaboration made in heaven. (Columbia OL4180 OC)

Starlight Express (1987 / 761p) ★★★ M: Andrew Lloyd Webber. L: Richard Stilgoe. Flamboyant parade of funky tunes cleverly references touching little steam-engine versus diesel locomotive saga. (MCA-5972 SC-1987)

Starting Here, Starting Now (1977 / OB) ★★ M: David Shire. L: Richard Maltby, Jr. When they rip loose from the yoke of Sondheim, especially through the elevating final tracks, Maltby and Shire demonstrate first-rate gifts. (RCA ABL1-2360 OC)

Steel Pier (1997 / 76p) ★★★ M/L: John Kander and Fred Ebb. Irresistibly romantic opus full of the dreams of a Depression-era dance floor between two lonely strangers. (RCA tape 90926 68878-4 OC)

Stop the World, I Want to Get Off (1962 / 556p) ★★ M/L: Leslie Bricusse and Anthony Newley. Abundant if redundant energy and comedy drive the mostly average numbers. (London AMS88001 OC)

Street Scene (1947 / 148p) ★★ M: Kurt Weill. L: Langston Hughes. Tragic uncompromising tale of adultery in a black ghetto, honestly evoked in brooding arias. (Columbia OL4139 OC)

Strike Up the Band (1930 / 191p) ★★★ M: George Gershwin. L: Ira Gershwin. Gershwin goes gloriously Kern and Ira tags along for the ride, creating here warmer, more romantic melodies in the likely shadow of *Show Boat*, while leaving behind four blockbuster numbers from the musically superior 1927 version of the show which folded out of town. (Elektra CD 9 79273-2)

Student Prince (1924 / 608p) ★★★ M: Sigmund Romberg. L: Dorothy Donnelly. Young love irretrievably lost, told stirringly in rich, comforting old-world refrains. (Columbia ML4592 SC)

Subways Are for Sleeping (1961 / 205p) ★★ M: Jule Styne. L: Betty Comden and Adolph Green. Half-baked, carelessly conceived grab bag offers a trio of big redeeming moments. (Columbia AKOS2130 OC)

Sugar (1972 / 505p) ★★ M: Jule Styne. L: Robert Merrill. A few knockout entries enliven booringly serviceable effort. (United Artists UAS-9905 OC)

Sunday in the Park with George (1984 / 604p) ★ M/L: Stephen Sondheim. Cerebrally inclined listeners will find stimulating moments strewn through a repetitively abstract, grand Sondheim drought. (RCA HBC1-5042 OC)

Sunny (1925 / 517p) (5 songs heard) M: Jerome Kern. L: Otto Harbach and Oscar Hammerstein II. Syncopated Kern at his best produces a razzmatazz delight. (Stanyon 10035 OC)

Sunset Boulevard (1995 / 977p) ★★ M: Andrew Lloyd Webber. L: Don Black and Christopher Hampton. Undeveloped patchwork offers ersatz American jazz, old operetta flourishes and soaring modern ballads to keep the listener effectively awake. (Polydor tape 314.52 3507-4 OC)

Superman (1966 / 129p) ★★★ M: Charles Strouse. L: Lee Adams. Grossly uneven work is half loaded with captivating quirky numbers well suited to comic strip culture. (Columbia AKOS2970)

Sweeney Todd (1979 / 558p) ★ ★ ★ M/L: Stephen Sondheim. Powerful sung-through tale offers workable recitative and intermittent Sondheim brilliance. (RCA CBL2-3379)

Sweet Charity (1966 / 608p) ★ ★ ★ M: Cy Coleman. L: Dorothy Fields. Audience-pandering materials rarely capture the tale's deeper pathos. (Columbia PS2900 OC)

Take Me Along (1959 / 448p) ★ ★ M/L: Robert Merrill. Modestly appealing tuner conveys warm small-town sentiments. (RCA LOC-1050 OC)

Tap Dance Kid (1983 / 669p) ★ ★ M: Henry Krieger. L: Robert Lorick. Numbing, Motown-heavy succession of interchangeable dream-and-make-it-better! anthems. (Polydor 820210-1Y-1 OC)

Tell Me on a Sunday (1985 / 474p) ★ ★ ★ ★ M: Andrew Lloyd Webber. L: Don Black. Intelligent lyrics combine with fresh, pop-powered music to create memorable modern-day tale about U.S. singles scene from Brit point of view. (Polydor PODVA OC-London, 1982)

Tenderloin (1960 / 216p) ★ ★ M: Jerry Bock. L: Sheldon Harnick. Naggingly half-baked venture redeems itself with several bravura highlights. (Capitol WAO1492 OC0)

Texas Lil Darlin' (1949 / 300p) ★ ★ ★ ★ M: Robert Emmett Dolan. L: Johnny Mercer. Unsung golden-age treasure evokes the wide-open spaces of the state in which it is set with radiant humor and charm. (CBS reissue of Decca DL5188 OC)

They're Playing Our Song (1979 / 1,082p) ★ ★ ★ M: Marvin Hamlisch. L: Carole Bayer Sager. Fresh, attractive score favors pop market in winning fashion. (Casablanca NBLP 7141BS OC)

This Is the Army (1942 / 113p) ★ ★ ★ M/L: Irving Berlin. Routinely uplifting patriot ditties. (MCA X14877 release of Decca DL 5108 OC)

Threepenny Opera (1933 / 12p) ★ ★ M: Kurt Weill. L: Bertold Brecht (trans. by Marc Blitzstein). Gritty trailblazing work is more theatre than musical theatre. (MGM ES3121 LC-1954)

Three Wishes for Jamie (1952 / 94p) ★ M/L: Ralph Blane. Strange split-personality score of buoyant showtunes and deadly pious ballads. (Capitol STET DS 15012 OC)

Titanic (1997 / 804p) ★ M/L: Maury Yeston. Ponderously self-important numbers are best when imitating Sondheim, worst when patterned after folk music, *1776* chatter, Elgar and Romberg. (RCA 09026 6834-4)

Too Many Girls (1939 / 249p) ★ ★ ★ ★ M: Richard Rodgers. L: Lorenz Hart. Top drawer Rodgers & Hart creations surprisingly mine swing and Latin rhythms. (Bagley Revisited PS1368 SC)

A Tree Grows in Brooklyn (1951 / 267p) ★★★★ M: Arthur Schwartz. L: Dorothy Fields. Wonderful music well served by sensitive words. (Columbia AML4405 OC)

Two by Two (1970 / 343p) ★ M: Richard Rodgers. L: Martin Charnin. Strained, claustrophobic collaboration suffers from tortured lyrics, though the music is adequate. (Columbia S30338 OC)

Two Gentlemen of Verona (1971 / 627p) ★ M: Galt MacDermot. L: John Guare. Lyrically limp onslaught of laid-back '60s funk, the exceptions being exceptions. (ABC BCSY-1001 OC)

Two on the Aisle (1951 / 276p) ★★ M: Jule Styne. L: Betty Comden and Adolph Green. Mildly engaging (and quite funny) to mildly mediocre. (Decca DL 8040 OC)

Two's Company (1952 / 90p) ★★★ M: Vernon Duke. L: Ogden Nash. (Additional song by Sheldon Harnick; additional lyrics by Sammy Cahn.) Even with Bette Davis singing like Bette Davis, featured here—sometimes charmingly—in the only Broadway song and dancer in which she would ever appear, there can be no denying the memorable highlights of a score built on smart verse and beguiling melody. (RCA CBM1-2757 OC)

Unsinkable Molly Brown (1960 / 532p) ★★ M/L: Meredith Willson. Sub-mediocre effort winningly high on spirit. (Capitol WAO1509 OC)

Very Good Eddie (1915 / 341p) ★★★★ M: Jerome Kern. L: Schuyler Greene and others. Snazzy, snappy, and infinitely melodious—as charming as a precocious child in tap shoes. (DRG 6100 LC-Goodspeed)

Very Warm for May (1939 / 59p) (5 songs heard) M: Jerome Kern. L: Oscar Hammerstein II. Very warm off the piano, these numbers fail to deliver much drama or comedy. (AEI 1156 OC)

Walking Happy (1966 / 161p) ★ M: James Van Heusen. L: Sammy Cahn. Memorable refrains are the extreme exception in cliché-heavy work. (Capitol VAS2631 OC)

West Side Story (1957 / 734p) ★★★★★ M: Leonard Bernstein. L: Stephen Sondheim. Breathtaking musical masterpiece, as powerful, scary, sensually compelling and sadly doomed as the racially divided world it wraps its dancing feet around. (Columbia OL5230 OC)

What Makes Sammy Run? (1964 / 540p) ★ M/L: Ervin Drake. Not much, judging by a surfeit of pedestrian numbers. (Columbia KOS-2440 OC)

Where's Charley? (1948 / 792p) ★★ M/L: Frank Loesser. Pleasant rag bag collection reveals scarce traces of the Loesser genius to follow. (Monmouth-Evergreen MES/7029 LC-1958, London)

Whoop Up (1958 / 56p) ★ M: Moose Charlap. L: Norman Gimbel. A few funny numbers keep this turkey barely off the table. (MGM E3745 OC)

Whoopee (1928 / 379p) ★★★★ M/L: Gush Kahn, Walter Donaldson and others. Chock full of keen humor and crackling '20s syncopation. (Smithsonian/RCA AC)

Wildcat (1960 / 171p) ★★★ M: Cy Coleman. L: Carolyn Leigh. Buoyantly ingratiating work rides obliviously high over rough and tumble subject matter. (RCA LOC1060 OC)

Will Rogers Follies (1991 / 983p) ★★★ M: Cy Coleman. L: Betty Comden and Adolph Green. Welcome parade of stirring show tunes and thoughtful ballads, lushly presented in old movie musical style. (Columbia CD CK 48606)

Wish You Were Here (1952 / 598p) ★ M/L: Harold Rome. Four fine end numbers arrive too late to rescue lyric-deficient dog. (RCA LSO-1108(e) OC)

The Wiz (1975 / 1,672p) ★★★ M/L: Charles Smalls. Generally amusing adaptation of classic movie dances on black humor to a funky Motown beat. (Atlantic SD18137 OC)

Woman of the Year (1981 / 770p) ★★★ M: John Kander. L: Fred Ebb. Carelessly mixed bag contains ample delights. (Arista AL8303 OC)

Wonderful Town (1953 / 559p) ★★★★ M: Leonard Bernstein. L: Betty Comden and Adolph Green. Hot jazzy choruses and hilarious verse conjure one whale of a party, if not exactly a well made singing play. (MCA-2050 reissue of Decca 9-391 OC)

Working (1978 / 25p) ★★ M/L: Craig Carnelia, Micki Grant, Mary Rodgers, Susan Birkenhead, Stephen Schwartz, James Taylor. Great revue premise haphazardly realized through disparate contributions stressing beat over content, the outstanding exceptions virtually all composed by dark horse contributor to-the-rescue, Craig Carnelia. (Columbia 35411 OC)

Your Arms Too Short to Box with God (1976, OB) ★★ M: Alex Bradford. L: Bradford and Micki Grant. Gospel version of the Jesus story no better or more original than a Sunday morning revival service. (ABC AB1004 OC)

Your Own Thing (1968 / 933p) ★ M/L: Hal Hester and Danny Apolinar. Pleasantly marginal effort in the early key of rock. (RCA LSO-1148)

You're a Good Man, Charlie Brown (1967 / 1,597p) ★★ M/L: Clark Gesner. Half delightful, half humdrum. (MGM 1E/S1E-90C OC)

Ziegfeld Follies of 1919 (1919 / 171p) ★★★ M: Irving Berlin and others. L: Irving Berlin and others. Full of tasteful, topical humor, surprisingly short on big chorus numbers. (Smithsonian P 14272 AC)

Zorba (1968 / 305p) ★★★ M: John Kander. L: Fred Ebb. Beguiling musicalization of the exotic folk culture at its center. (Capitol SO118 OC)

Notes

Abbreviations for frequently cited sources:

KM   Ken Mandelbaum, *Not Since Carrie*

LAT   *Los Angeles Times*

NYT   *New York Times*

SSM   Steven Suskin, *More Opening Nights on Broadway*

SSO   Steven Suskin, *Opening Nights on Broadway*

SSS   Steven Suskin, *Show Tunes*

TT   *Rodgers and Hammerstein Interviews with Tony Thomas*, broadcast over the radio network of the Canadian Broadcasting Corporation, February 1960. F/CD 8108; Facet.

Chapter 1

1. McCabe, *George M. Cohan*, p. 51.
2. Cohan, *Twenty Years on Broadway*, p. 211. Cohan recounted how he took some incidental music from his first flop play, *Popularity*, and "blended two of the strains into a march," which was published as "The Popularity March" and became "one of the first rag marches to score a popular hit." As a child, one of his ambitions had been to be "a black faced comedian in a musical comedy act" (p. 9). He had plenty of influences to draw upon, including African American musicians already composing generally in a ragtime march style, as well as vaudevillians, in particular Edward Harrigan of Harrigan and Hart, whose personal characteristics and comedy talents Cohan much admired (p. 50).
3. McCabe, *George M. Cohan*, p. 51.
4. Bordman, *American Operetta*, p. 67.
5. Freedland, *Jerome Kern*, p. 19.
6. NYT, January 19, 1919.
7. *Ibid.*, December 2, 1924.
8. *Ibid.*

9. Nolan, *Lorenz Hart*, p. 55. Nolan's account—which quotes Dreyfus telling Rodgers, "There's nothing of value here. I don't hear any music and I think you'd be making a great mistake"—runs contrary to the one offered by Max Wilk (*OK!*, p 43), relating how Dreyfus saw potential talent but felt that Rodgers and Hart were "too young for the business" and encouraged them to seek more study.

10. Mordden, *Broadway Babies*, p. 12.

11. *Ibid.*, p. 7.

12. *Variety*, December 1, 1926.

Chapter 2

Oscar Hammerstein's personality has been consistently documented in theatre books. Hugh Fordin, who offers the more nuanced account, supplies details of Hammerstein's tougher literary nature as well as his rather rigid relationship to his sons.

1. TT.

2. Lerner, *The Musical Theatre*, pp. 61–63.

3. Hammerstein, *Lyrics*, pp. 41–43.

4. Fordin, *Getting to Know Him*, p. 70.

5. *Ibid.*, p.79.

6. *Variety*, January 4, 1928.

7. Bordman, *American Operetta*, p. 136.

8. Mordden, *Broadway Babies*, p. 77.

9. Hammerstein, *Lyrics*, p. 19.

10. Green, *Broadway Musicals*, p. 101.

11. *Variety*, October 3, 1933.

12. *Ibid.*, June 9, 1931.

13. Specific details of Cole Porter's personal life are exhaustively chronicled in *Cole Porter* by Schwartz.

14. Schwartz, *Cole Porter*, p. 137.

15. *Variety*, November 27, 1934.

16. TT. These revealing interviews, inexplicably ignored by virtually all books on the subject, are recommended to all Rodgers and Hammerstein fans, and to scholars and historians in general.

17. Nolan, *Lorenz Hart*, p. 262.

18. TT.

19. Nolan, *Lorenz Hart*, p 245.

20. Rodgers, *Musical Stages*, p. 198.

Chapter 3

1. Rodgers, *Musical Stages*, p. 200.

2. *Variety*, January 1, 1941.

3. Green, *Rodgers & Hammerstein Fact Book*, p. 245.

4. From jacket liner notes, by Richard Rodgers, for Columbia Records (COL 4364) studio recording of *Pal Joey*.

5. SSO, p. 537.

6. Hammerstein, *Lyrics*, p. 8.

7. Nolan, *The Sound of Their Music*, pp. 25–26. The remark is attributed to producer Mike Todd. However, according to Max Wilk in his informative account of the making of this legendary work (*OK!*, p 17), Walter Winchell's secretary, Rose, dispatched to New

Haven to review the show, walked out at intermission and wired back to the boss the tart critique he ran in his next day's column, "NO LEGS NO JOKES NO CHANCE." In any event, the doubters overlooked, as reported by author Nolan, the "encouraging reaction of the New Haven audience."

    8. Fordin, *Getting to Know Him*, p. 201.
    9. Atkinson, *Broadway*, p. 338.
    10. Anderson, Mantle, and Waldorf quotes all from SSO, p. 499.
    11. *Variety*, April 7, 1943.
    12. SSO, p. 144.
    13. *Variety*, October 13, 1943.
    14. SSO, p. 525.
    15. *Ibid.*, p. 120.
    16. Tharin, *Chart Champions*. Tharin's work offers a careful listing, year by year and week by week, of top 100 singles on the popular charts. The songs from *Annie Get Your Gun* became so well known to the public that it is, indeed, tempting to think of them each as a chart champion. Such was simply not the case.
    17. SSO, p. 445.
    18. Atkinson, *Broadway*, p. 344.
    19. *Variety*, January 15, 1947.
    20. *Ibid.*, November 2, 1949.
    21. *Ibid.*, April 3, 1946.
    22. SSO, p. 587.
    23. *Ibid.*, p. 589.
    24. Wilk, *They're Playing Our Song*, p. 218.
    25. SSO, p. 212.
    26. *Ibid.*, p. 369.

Chapter 4

    1. Freedland, *Jerome Kern*, p. 81.
    2. Liner notes by Ben Bagley, *Vernon Duke Revisited* album, on Painted Smiles Records, PS 1342.
    3. *Variety*, November 30, 1949.
    4. KM, p. 230.
    5. Wilk, *They're Playing Our Song*, p. 147.
    6. Lerner, *The Musical Theatre*, p. 104.
    7. SSO, p. 288.
    8. *Ibid.*
    9. *Ibid.*, p. 222.
    10. *Ibid.*, p. 236.

Chapter 5

    1. TT.
    2. Frommer, *It Happened on Broadway*, p. 117.
    3. Rodgers, *Musical Stages*, p. 306.
    4. Wilk, *They're Playing Our Song*, p. 53.
    5. Fordin, *Getting to Know Him*, p. 343.
    6. *Ibid.*
    7. Jablonski, *Alan Jay Lerner*, p. 50.

8. TT. Rodgers' preposterous claim that he had no knowledge of salaries, etc.—probably advanced to sustain the image of creative artist rather than corporate head—is clearly at odds with well-known details about his active involvement in every aspect of the operation. See Hyland, *Richard Rodgers*, p. 188.

9. Nolan, *The Sound of Their Music*, p. 149.

10. Hyland, *Richard Rodgers*, p. 224.

11. TT.

12. *Ibid.*

13. Jablonski, *Alan Jay Lerner*, p. 204.

14. Tynan, *Curtains*, p. 245.

15. SSO, p. 360.

16. *Variety*, October 15, 1947.

17. Green, *Rodgers and Hammerstein Fact Book*, p. 556.

18. SSO, p. 43.

19. Rodgers, *Musical Stages*, p. 253.

20. SSO, p. 426.

21. Fordin, *Getting to Know Him*, p. 326.

22. *Ibid.*

23. SSO, p. 554.

24. Rodgers, *Musical Stages*, p. 287.

25. SSO, p. 226.

26. *Variety*, December 3, 1958.

27. Tynan, *Curtains*, p. 289.

28. TT.

29. *Variety*, October 7, 1959.

30. SSO, p. 637. The lingering assertion of "mixed reviews" ignores the notices issued by the seven major New York newspaper drama critics, their collective reception to any new work then deemed to represent the highest forum of theatrical adjudication.

31. Tynan, *Curtains*, p. 330.

Chapter 6

1. *Variety*, May 21, 1952.

2. SSO, p. 602.

3. Tynan, *Curtains*, p. 282.

4. SSO, p. 205.

5. *Ibid.*, p. 453.

6. *Ibid.*, p. 608.

7. *Ibid.*, p. 656.

8. *Ibid.*, p. 674.

9. *Ibid.*, p. 350.

10. KM, p. 53.

11. SSO, p. 271.

12. Tynan, *Curtains*, p. 345.

13. KM, p. 108.

14. SSO, p 302.

15. SSM, p. 157.

16. SSO, p. 637.

17. *Variety*, December 7, 1960.

18. SSO, p. 125.

19. Rodgers, *Musical Stages*, p. 315.
20. SSM, p. 669.
21. Jablonski, *Alan Jay Lerner*, p. 257.
22. *Ibid.*, p. 298.
23. SSM, p. 227.
24. *Ibid.*, p. 410.
25. *Ibid.*, p. 151.
26. *Ibid.*, p. 464.

Chapter 7

1. Secrest, *Stephen Sondheim*, p. 126.
2. SSO, p. 695.
3. Tynan, *Curtains*, p. 280.
4. Secrest, *Stephen Sondheim*, p. 150.
5. Mordden, *Broadway Babies*, p. 166.
6. Bergreen, *As Thousands Cheer*, p. 502.
7. SSO, p. 535.
8. *Ibid.*, p. 171.
9. *Ibid.*, p. 215.
10. *Ibid.*, p. 305.
11. *Ibid.*, p. 704.
12. *Ibid.*, p. 706.
13. *Ibid.*, p. 397.
14. The music of Mary Rodgers fell short of the promise that at least one critic saw. Brooks Atkinson was utterly charmed, writing, "She has a style of her own, an inventive mind, and a fund of cheerful melodies ... be comforted by the fact that the musical theatre has acquired a genuine new composer" (SSO, p. 519). When Rodgers returned to Broadway three years later, in collaboration with another hack lyric writer, Martin Charnin, on the 43-performance disaster *Hot Spot*, the experts were no longer genuflecting. In 1978, Rodgers contributed a single unmemorable tune to *Working*. Rarely will a composer achieve distinction without distinguished lyrics.
15. *Ibid.*, p. 200.
16. *Variety*, April 25, 1951.
17. SSO, p. 676.
18. KM, p. 267.
19. SSM, p. 265.
20. SSO, p. 241.

Chapter 8

1. SSO, 450. Identifying the first rock song ever sung in a stage musical would probably be as difficult as pinpointing the first rock and roll number itself. "Jacques D'Iraque" is the most striking candidate. According to Steve Suskin (SSS, p. 418), producer Jule Styne (yes, the composer), too busy with work on screen and television projects to write a score for the Sammy Davis, Jr., vehicle, scouted for songwriters and took something of a chance on Bock and Holofcener, and then added pop tunesmith George Weiss to the mix.
2. Wilk, *They're Playing Our Song*, p. 66.

3. SSM, p. 657.

4. *Ibid.*, p. 599.

5. *Ibid.*, p. 951.

6. Richard, *Great Rock Musicals*, p. x.

7. SSM, p. 729.

8. *Ibid.*, p. 387.

9. *Ibid.*, p. 91.

Chapter 9

1. Peyser, *Bernstein*, p. 262. Bernstein, who was originally granted co-lyricist credit by contract, had begun sketching out words before Sondheim came on board; he had given Sondheim a number of his own lines as starting points, and he had fostered an intense and prolific communication between the two during the creation of the score. For these reasons, it seems clear that Bernstein was a de facto contributor to the lyrics. More importantly, he may well have provided Sondheim the critical runway into the terse stylistic approach the neophyte collaborator employed, by handing over to him such lines as "Boy, boy, crazy boy/Get cool, boy!"

2. Secrest, *Stephen Sondheim*, p. 31.

3. *Ibid.*, p. 270.

4. *Ibid.*, p. 37.

5. *Ibid.*, p. 56.

6. *Ibid.*, p. 91.

7. *Variety*, October 2, 1957.

8. Secrest, *Stephen Sondheim*, p. 117.

9. *Ibid.*, pp. 126–127.

10. Fordin, *Getting to Know Him*, p. xiii.

11. SSO, p. 58.

12. Rodgers, *Musical Stages*, p. 318.

13. Secrest, *Stephen Sondheim*, p. 178.

14. Rogers, *Musical Stages*, p. 319.

15. Secrest, *Stephen Sondheim*, p. 179.

16. SSM, p. 237.

17. *Ibid.*, p. 193.

18. *New Yorker*, May 2, 1970.

19. SSM, p. 299.

20. Secrest, *Stephen Sondheim*, p. 216.

21. SSM, p. 692.

22. Zadan, *Sondheim & Company*, p. 221.

23. SSM, p. 690.

24. *Variety*, May 9, 1984.

25. Zadan, *Sondheim & Company*, p. 363.

26. *Ibid.*, p. 287.

27. *Ibid.*, p. 364.

28. NYT, January 4, 1976.

29. Secrest, *Stephen Sondheim*, p. 179.

30. SSM, p. 889.

31. *Ibid.*, p. 603.

32. Secrest, *Stephen Sondheim*, p. 324.

33. Zadan, *Sondheim & Company*, p. 361.

Chapter 10

1. SSM, p. 645.
2. *Ibid.*, p. 895.
3. *Ibid.*, p. 806.
4. *Ibid.*, p. 823.
5. KM, p. 271.
6. SSM, p. 164.
7. SSS, p. 514.
8. As quoted in the jacket liner notes of the original cast album, RCA Victor LSO-1161.
9. SSM, p. 253.
10. Kelly, *One Singular Sensation*, p. 255.

Chapter 11

1. SSS, p. 567.
2. *Variety*, December 11, 1985.
3. KM, pp. 277–278.
4. SSM, p. 106.
5. KM, p. 280.
6. Mordden, *Broadway Babies*, p. 220.
7. SSO, p. 288.
8. Lerner, *The Musical Theatre*, p. 216. Lerner recounts that the only person who did not enjoy the show was Bacharach, who suffered from his inability to control the quality of singing as he could in a recording studio, and thereafter resisted encouragement—including from Lerner himself with offers to collaborate—to embark on more stage musical projects. Lerner lamented, as would many, the theatre's loss of "that amazingly talented man."
9. Gottfried, *Broadway Musicals*, p. 339.
10. As quoted in the jacket liner notes of the original cast album, CBS Records, 37790.
11. *Variety*, May 12, 1982.
12. *Ibid.*, December 7, 1983.
13. *Ibid.*, September 25, 1995.
14. *Ibid.*, May 9, 1984.
15. *Ibid.*, November 11, 1987.

Chapter 12

1. McKnight, *Andrew Lloyd Webber*, p. 38.
2. *Ibid.*, p. 244.
3. *Ibid.*, p. 68.
4. *Ibid.*, p. 72.
5. SSM, p. 490.
6. *Ibid.*, p. 498.
7. *Ibid.*, p. 271.
8. McKnight, *Andrew Lloyd Webber*, p. 125.
9. *Ibid.*, p. 223.
10. One is likely to encounter throughout U.S. theatrical circles a pervasive disdain for Webber's work. And often in expressing their contempt, Webber haters reveal themselves to be ardent Sondheim fans, suggesting that the theatre world offers only two creative

options. San Francisco's 42nd Moon, which presents staged readings of old American musicals, for a few seasons featured prominently on its annual promotional fliers the quip of a local critic praising its fare for offering "the perfect antidote to Andrew Lloyd Webber." During one of the company's special fund raising activities, Webber was dismissed in derisive terms and audiences laughed approvingly.

11. Lerner, *The Musical Theatre*, p. 225.
12. *Ibid.*, p. 232.
13. *Ibid.*, p. 234.

Chapter 13

1. "At The Revolution's Fore," LAT, December 12, 1999.
2. NYT, January 21, 1903.
3. Rodgers, *Musical Stages*, p. 323.
4. McKnight, *Andrew Lloyd Webber*, p. 248.
5. NYT, October 17, 1982.
6. *Ibid.*, October 8, 1982.
7. *Ibid.*, March 16, 1987.
8. *Ibid.*, January 27, 1988.
9. *Ibid.*, February 14, 1988.
10. *Boston Globe*, April 27, 1990.
11. *Ibid.*
12. *The Times*, May 25, 1990.
13. McKnight, *Andrew Lloyd Webber*, p. 191.
14. Recapped in LAT, March 14, 1987.
15. NYT, March 13, 1987.
16. *Variety*, March 18, 1987.
17. LAT, April 12, 1991.
18. *Variety*, August 8, 1994.
19. LAT, April 12, 1991.
20. As reported in NYT, July 18, 1996.
21. NYT, November 12, 1996.
22. *Variety*, July 22, 1996.
23. *Ibid.*, July 13, 1998.
24. *Ibid.*, January 11, 1999.
25. From an AP story printed in the *Cleveland Plain Dealer*, April 26, 1998.
26. AP story printed in *The Columbian*, March 8, 1998.

Chapter 14

1. NYT, July 12, 1992.
2. From review excerpts printed in ad for the show.
3. *Variety*, April 27, 1997.
4. NYT, April 24, 1997.
5. LAT, January 24, 1999.
6. *Wall Street Journal*, April 25, 1997.
7. NYT, October 16, 1997.
8. *Variety*, October 20, 1997.
9. *Ibid.*, April 29, 1996.
10. Lerner, *The Musical Theatre*, p. 192.

11. LAT, September 5, 1999.

12. *Ibid.*, January 3, 1999.

13. NYT, October 5, 1997.

14. NYT, April 29, 1997.

15. LAT, May 5, 2000.

Chapter 15

1. *Variety*, November 21, 1962.

2. SSM, P. 139.

3. NYT, January 4, 1976.

4. SSM, p. 643.

5. Rodgers, *Musical Stages*, p. 318.

6. Tynan, *Curtains*, p. 322.

7. *Playbill*, Orpheum Theatre, San Francisco, May, 1998, p. 18.

8. Kreuger, *Show Boat*, p. 43.

9. NYT, September 25, 1988.

10. *The Daily Telegraph*, January 31, 1998.

11. AP story printed in *The Ottawa Citizen*, March 9, 1998.

12. *Back Stage*, March 27, 1998.

13. TT.

14. Hyland, *Richard Rodgers*, p. 320. In addition to the clause prohibiting the addition of new lyrics to his work, in his 1975 will Richard Rodgers included remarks to wife Dorothy and daughter Mary (his executors and trustees) that "The artistic integrity and reputation of the musical compositions and lyrics written by me and the manner in which my works will be performed or otherwise presented after my death is of great importance to me" (Hyland, p. 299).

15. *Variety*, October 9, 1995.

16. NYT, October 15, 1995.

17. *Ibid.*, November 20, 1995.

18. *Ibid.*

Chapter 16

1. *Variety*, November 17, 1997.

2. LAT, June 7, 1998.

3. *Ibid.*, October 8, 2000.

4. NYT, April 23, 1994.

5. *Ibid.*

6. LAT, June 7, 1998.

7. NYT, January 25, 1998.

8. Before his financial fall, Drabinsky's high expectations for future success were well cataloged in two feature stories about him: "He Just Keeping Rolling Along," LAT, November 10, 1996, and "Gambling from *Ragtime* to Riches," NYT, February 19, 1998.

9. LAT, December 5, 1999.

10. *Wall Street Journal*, March 20, 2000.

11. *Variety*, December 21, 1998.

12. NYT, December 28, 1998.

13. *Wall Street Journal*, April 14, 1998. Offers fascinating inside information, including ill-advised cost-consuming practices in the marketing and logistics aspects of the operation.

For example, sets for *three* separate touring companies of *Show Boat*, which lost massive amounts of money—"a big mistake," according to Drabinsky himself—were not compactly designed, making them difficult to move in and out of theatres on the road. This oversight caused the producer to incur an additional $300,000 in transpiration charges for each move from city to city. See also "Shaky *Ragtime* Producer Is Said to Find Lenders," NYT, November 30, 1998.

Chapter 17

1. Author's tape recording of rebroadcast, circa 1988, by Bob Lyons on his "Old Time Radio Show," KCRW-FM, Los Angeles, of "A Musical Tribute to Jerome Kern," originally aired December 9, 1945 (radio network unknown).
2. SSO, p 612.
3. *Ibid.*
4. SSM, p. 662.
5. From *New York Times* story printed in *The Arizona Republic*, March 22, 1998.
6. *Time*, December 13, 1999.
7. *Ibid.*
8. NYT, December 19, 1999.
9. *Variety*, December 6, 1999.

Bibliography

Atkinson, Brooks. *Broadway* (New York: Macmillan, 1970).

Bergreen, Laurence. *As Thousands Cheer: The Life of Irving Berlin* (New York: Viking, 1990).

Bordman, Gerald. *American Musical Comedy: From Adonis to Dreamgirls* (New York: Oxford University Press, 1982).

_____. *American Operetta from H.M.S. Pinafore to Sweeney Todd* (New York: Oxford University Press, 1981).

Cohan, George M. *Twenty Years on Broadway* (New York: Harper & Brothers, 1924).

Fordin, Hugh. *Getting to Know Him: A Biography of Oscar Hammerstein* (New York: Random House, 1977).

Freedland, Michael. *Jerome Kern* (New York: Stein and Day, 1978).

Frommer, Myrna Katz, and Frommer, Harvey. *It Happened on Broadway: An Oral History of the Great White Way* (New York: Harcourt Brace, 1998).

Gottfried, Martin. *Broadway Musicals* (New York: Abradale/Harry N. Abrams, 1979).

Green, Stanley. *Broadway Musicals: Show by Show.* 4th ed. (Milwaukee: Hal Leonard, 1994).

_____, editor. *Rodgers and Hammerstein Fact Book: A Record of Their Works Together and with Other Collaborators* (New York: Drama Book Specialists, 1980).

Guernsey, Otis L., Jr. *Playwrights, Lyricists, Composers on Theatre* (New York: Dodd, Mead, 1974).

Hammerstein, Oscar, II. *Lyrics* (New York: Simon and Schuster, 1949).

Hyland, William G. *Richard Rodgers* (New Haven: Yale University Press, 1998).

Jablonski, Edward. *Alan Jay Lerner: A Biography* (New York: Henry Holt, 1996).

Kelly, Kevin. *One Singular Sensation: The Michael Bennett Story* (New York: Doubleday, 1990).

Kreuger, Miles. *Show Boat: The Story of a Classic American Musical* (New York: Oxford University Press, 1977).

Lerner, Alan Jay. *The Musical Theatre: A Celebration* (New York: McGraw-Hill, 1986).

_____. *The Street Where I Live* (New York: W. W. Norton, 1978).

Mandelbaum, Ken. *Not Since Carrie: Forty Years of Broadway Musical Flops* (New York: St. Martin's, 1991).

McCabe, John. *George M. Cohan: The Man Who Owned Broadway* (New York: Doubleday, 1973).

McKnight, Gerald. *Andrew Lloyd Webber: A Biography* (New York: St. Martin's, 1984).

Mordden, Ethan. *Broadway Babies: The People Who Made the American Musical* (New York: Oxford University Press, 1983).

New York Times Theatre Reviews. Volumes: 1896–1903, 1912–1919, and 1920–1926 (New York: New York Times and Arno Press, 1971 and 1975).

Nolan, Frederick. *Lorenz Hart: A Poet on Broadway* (New York: Oxford University Press, 1994).

_____. *The Sound of Their Music: The Story of Rodgers and Hammerstein* (New York: Walker, 1978).

Peyser, Joan. *Bernstein: A Biography*. (New York: Beech Tree Books/William Morrow, 1987).

Richards, Stanley. *Great Rock Musicals* (New York: Stein and Day, 1979).

Rodgers, Richard. *Musical Stages: An Autobiography* (New York: Random House, 1975).

Schwartz, Charles. *Cole Porter: A Biography* (New York: Dial, 1977).

Secrest, Meryle. *Stephen Sondheim: A Life* (New York: Alfred A. Knopf, 1998).

Suskin, Steven. *More Opening Nights on Broadway* (New York: Schirmer, 1997).

_____. *Opening Nights on Broadway* (New York: Schirmer, 1990).

_____. *Show Tunes 1905–1985* (New York: Dodd, Mead, 1986).

Tharin, Frank C. *Chart Champions* (San Francisco: Chart Champions, 1980).

Tynan, Kenneth. *Curtains* (New York: Atheneum, 1961).

Wilk, Max. *OK!: The Story of Oklahoma* (New York: Grove, 1993)

_____. *They're Playing Our Song* (New York: Atheneum, 1973).

Zadan, Craig. *Sondheim & Company*. 2d ed. (New York: Da Capo, 1994).

Index